Duet and Dialogue in the Age of Monteverdi

Studies in British Musicology, No. 7

Nigel Fortune, Series Editor

Reader in Music
The University of Birmingham

Other Titles in This Series

Duet and Dialogue
in the Age of
Monteverdi
Volume 1

by
John Whenham

UMI RESEARCH PRESS
Ann Arbor, Michigan

Produced and distributed by
UMI Research Press
an imprint of
University Microfilms International
Ann Arbor, Michigan 48106

Library of Congress Cataloging in Publication Data

Whenham, John.
  Duet and dialogue in the age of Monteverdi.

  (Studies in British musicology ; no. 7)
  Revision of the author's thesis (doctoral–Oxford,
1978)
  Bibliography: p.
  Includes index.
  1. Vocal duets–History and criticism. 2. Vocal music–
Italy–History and criticism.   I. Title. II. Series.

ML1633.W5 1982   784.3'00945   82-1837
ISBN 0-8357-1313-X (set)   AACR2
ISBN 0-8357-1355-5 (v.1)

For my Parents

Contents

Abbreviations

A	Alto
Acta	*Acta Musicologica*
AfMw	*Archiv für Musikwissenschaft*
An Mus	*Analecta Musicologica*
B	Bass
C	Canto
DTB	*Denkmäler der Tonkunst in Bayern*
ed.	edited
edn	edition
JAMS	*Journal of the American Musicological Society*
JMP	*Jahrbuch der Musikbibliothek Peters*
MezzoSop	Mezzo Soprano
MD	*Musica disciplina*
Mf	*Die Musikforschung*
ML	*Music and Letters*
MMg	*Monatshefte für Musikgeschichte*
MQ	*The Musical Quarterly*
MR	*The Music Review*
MT	*The Musical Times*
NA	*Note d'archivio per la storia musicale*
NOHM	*The New Oxford History of Music*
NRMI	*Nuova rivista musicale italiana*
PRMA	*Proceedings of the Royal Musical Association*
rev.	revised
RIM	*Rivista italiana di musicologia*
RISM	*Répertoire international des sources musicales*
RMI	*Rivista musicale italiana*
S	Soprano
SIMG	*Sammelbände der internationalen Musikgesellschaft*
SMw	*Studien zur Musikwissenschaft*
T	Tenor
trans.	translated
ZMw	*Zeitschrift für Musikwissenschaft*

Published volumes of music referred to by date only may be found listed in the appendix, volume 2. The *RISM* library sigla used in the text are listed in the introduction to the appendix.

Acknowledgments

The preparation of a study of this kind necessarily incurs many debts of gratitude which can never be fully repaid. Among the many who have aided my work, I have first to thank the librarians of various institutions in Europe and America who answered my requests for information and microfilms speedily and courteously. In particular, I should like to thank Mr. J. Wing of Christ Church, Oxford, and Signor Sergio Paganelli of the Civico Museo Bibliografico Musicale, Bologna, both of whom went out of their way to be helpful when I was working in their libraries. Others whose assistance has been particularly valuable are thanked at appropriate points in the text. For financial assistance, without which this study could not have been completed, I have to thank the trustees of the Longwill Trust, the Committee for Advanced Studies of the University of Oxford, the Italian Government and the Arts Faculty Research Board of the University of Birmingham. For allowing me the privilege of hearing performances of some of the music transcribed for this study, I have to thank Anthony Rooley and The Consort of Musicke, and Mr. Pieter Andriessen of the Belgian Radio and Television Service.

I owe a particular debt to individual members of the staff of Oxford University who offered expert help and advice: to my supervisor, Dr. F.W. Sternfeld, for his friendly, patient, and perceptive counseling; to Professor Cecil Grayson, for the insights that he offered a novice in the field of Italian poetry; and to Professor Denis Arnold, who saw the study through its final stages. At Birmingham, I must thank my colleague Dr. Nigel Fortune for allowing me access to his research notes on Florentine monody and for the almost indefinite loan of microfilms and books.

Last, and most certainly not least, my gratitude goes to my wife for her unfailing moral support during the long gestation of this work and for undertaking the task of typing my manuscript.

The spelling of composers' names in this study conforms with the usage in *The New Grove Dictionary of Music and Musicians,* 20 vols., London, 1980. I have used articles in *The New Grove* to correct some of the biographical information given for individual composers. Since it has not always been possible to acknowledge this in the text, I do so now.

Chapter 5, exx. 6c, 11, 12, 13, and 14; chapter 6, exx. 1 and 2; chapter 7, ex. 19; and chapter 9, exx. 2 and 3 are reproduced by permission of Universal Edition (Alfred A. Kalmus Ltd.).

Chapter 5, exx. 4 and 5: the polyphonic models are quoted from Jacob Arcadelt, *Opera Omnia,* ed. A. Seay (*Corpus Mensurabilis Musicae,* xxxi), [Rome]: American Institute of Musicology, 1965-; ex. 6: the polyphonic model is quoted from Adrian Willaert, *Opera Omnia,* ed. H. Zenck, W. Gerstenberg, B. & H. Maier (*Corpus Mensurabilis Musicae,* ii), [Rome]: American Institute of Musicology, 1950-.

1

Introduction

In Italy, the early years of the seventeenth century saw a resurgence of interest in music for small vocal ensembles, and one which paralleled the new vogue for accompanied solo song. During the early decades of the century, duets, trios, and quartets with *basso continuo* accompaniment grew rapidly in popularity until, by the middle of the century, they had become established with solo song as the normal vehicles for secular vocal composition, ousting the five-part madrigal from the dominant position that it had once occupied.

The present study deals with some aspects of the emergence and growth in importance of this new *concertato*[1] ensemble music, concentrating in particular on the secular duet and a related, though distinct genre, the recitative-dialogue.[2] It represents an attempt to trace the relationship of these two apparently new types of composition to their forerunners in the music of the sixteenth century and to survey their development from around 1600 to the death, in 1643, of Claudio Monteverdi, a composer who played a vital role in fostering the *concertato* duet and who wrote some of the finest works in its early literature.

In quantitative terms, the corpus of secular duets and dialogues surviving from the years c. 1600 to c. 1643 is only about half as large as that of solo songs. Nevertheless, well over a thousand works are found in the sources catalogued in the appendix to this study, volume 2. The vitality of the Italian, and particularly the Venetian music publishing trade during the first four decades of the seventeenth century ensured that the majority of these duets and dialogues survive in printed sources. Toward the end of the period, however, there is evidence of a decline in the output of secular music from the Italian presses. The reasons for this have never been fully explained. As far as Venice is concerned, however, two factors—the economic and social conditions following the disastrous outbreak of plague in 1630, and the establishment of commercial opera in 1637—may have contributed to the situation. Following a peak of production in the mid 1620s, the output of the Venetian presses was already declining towards 1630. In 1631, the year following that of the plague, neither Alessandro Vincenti, nor his rival Bartolomeo Magni issued any volumes of secular music. Production recovered after 1632 to reach another peak in 1636, but it dipped again in 1637-38 and declined, if fitfully, during the 1640s.

The presses of Rome, the other main center of Italian music publishing during the early seventeenth century, produced scarcely any volumes of secular music during the 1630s and 1640s. There is no obvious reason for this, though it may reflect a general awareness on the part of printers and composers that there was a better market in Rome for publications of sacred music. It is perhaps worth noting, though, that Roman publications of secular music were subject to strict censorship by the ecclesiastical authorities, as Giovanni Francesco Anerio revealed in a note to the reader printed in his *Diporti Musicali* (Rome, 1617):

> If in singing some of these my madrigals you should meet with any breaks [in the texts], know that this is done to comply with the just commands of my Superiors, who will not permit in print any words which, at times, have overtones of sensuality: such as "kiss," "God" applied to worldly love, and so on; these can easily be gathered from the sense of the text.[3]

Given this constraint, it is, perhaps, not surprising that several Roman composers chose to have some, or all of their secular music published outside Rome: Frescobaldi at Florence, for example, Stefano Landi and Loreto Vittori at Venice.

Compared with the number of printed sources, the number of manuscripts listed in the appendix is small. This is partly because the substantial corpus of music written by the Roman school of "cantata" composers, including Luigi Rossi, Giacomo Carissimi, Mario Savioni, and Marco Marazzoli, which survives mainly in manuscript, has been omitted. The problems of dating and attribution associated with these manuscripts are such that the chronological approach employed in this study is inappropriate to dealing with them. This material has not been omitted in the belief that the duets and dialogues contained in Roman manuscripts were necessarily written after 1643, even in those cases where the manuscript itself is known to date from a later year. Still less has it been done from a conviction that the manuscripts contain music written in a new form—the cantata—which emerged around 1640,[4] an idea which is implicit in many earlier writings on seventeenth-century vocal music.

The music of one Roman composer, Orazio Michi, whose work survives in manscript, certainly dates from before 1641, since Michi died on 26 October of that year. His fine duets, however, belong to the realms of spiritual music,[5] a type which is not specifically covered in this study. Our knowledge of the life and career of such composers as Luigi Rossi (c. 1597-1653) and Giacomo Carissimi (1605-74) leads us to believe that they may have been writing their "cantatas" from at least the late 1620s. Rossi, for example, was an almost exact contemporary of the Venetian composer Giovanni Rovetta (1596-1668), whose first book of madrigals was published in 1629, and who had already had a volume of sacred music—*Salmi Concertati a cinque et sei voci*—published in 1626. Rossi entered the service of Marc'Antonio Borghese at Rome in 1621, but the only cantata that he is known to have written for this patron—"Io ero pargoletta" (for solo voice)—is found in a manuscript dating from after c. 1630 (*I-Bc,* MS Q 49). It is only with Bianchi's anthology *Raccolta d'Arie Spirituali* of 1640 and the later anthologies of the energetic Florido de Silvestri that we begin to see the work of the younger Roman school in print, and even then rather in the field of sacred than of secular music. Nevertheless, at least part of the output of all the Roman composers mentioned above may well date from before 1643, so that while the omission of the manuscript "cantatas" of the Roman school provides a convenient way of limiting the musical source material covered by the present study we have to bear in mind that there may not be sound historical reasons for considering the Roman school as active only from c. 1640. Fortunately, a number of recent dissertations on the work of individual Roman composers[6] have made it possible to compare the characteristics of Roman duets and dialogues with those found in printed sources.

The awakening of scholarly interest in the baroque duet dates from the mid-nineteenth century and Chrysander's study of Handel. In tracing the antecedents of Handel's chamber duets, Chrysander turned to the work of Agostino Steffani and looked back from him to Stradella and Carissimi.[7] In the early years of the twentieth century, the appearance of an edition of some of Steffani's duets[8] prompted Eugen Schmitz to publish a survey of the development of the chamber duet from around 1600 to the period of Steffani's work.[9] And although more recent monographs, articles, and dissertations have added considerably to our knowledge of the work of individual composers, Schmitz's article today remains the fullest and most informative general survey of the field. Its coverage of the early seventeenth-century duet is limited, however, by the fact that Schmitz chose to omit from his discussion the large corpus of early duets that appeared in volumes of polyphonic *concertato* madrigals.

The reason for this omission seems to be that Schmitz shared with his contemporaries the view that two groups of early seventeenth-century composers may be identified by the types of publication in which their music was issued: a group of "radicals," followers of Giulio Caccini, whose music was issued in monody books, and a group of "conservatives" who continued to publish madrigal books. One of the purposes of the present study is to suggest that this view, colored as it is by a preoccupation with opera and solo song, is false and limits our understanding of a period remarkable for the richness and diversity of its secular music. And one of the main reasons for choosing the duet as the subject of a specialized study, quite apart from the intrinsic merit of much of the surviving music, is that it allows us a broader perspective of the sources of early seventeenth-century vocal music than is possible in a study of solo song; and I hope to show that the composers who issued their duets in madrigal books were as alive to new developments in style and technique as those composers who issued their duets in monody books.

The recitative-dialogue has fared rather better than the duet in the published scholarly literature of the present century, chiefly because of its associations with opera and Florentine solo song. Leichtentritt viewed dialogue settings as forerunners of the chamber cantata and discussed examples by Melli, Rasi, Grandi, Monteverdi, and Domenico Mazzocchi.[10] Riemann referred to the dialogue both as a type of duet and as an independent genre and cited examples by Marco da Gagliano and Rasi;[11] and Schmitz included discussion of dialogue settings not only in his study of the duet,[12] but also in those which he wrote on monody,[13] the solo cantata,[14] and the *concertato* madrigal.[15] In Racek's more recent monograph on Italian monody, the "dramatic dialogue" is allotted a place in the history both of solo song and of the oratorio.[16] The dialogues of individual composers, too, have received some notice. Domenico Mazzocchi's secular dialogues have been discussed in detail by Witzenmann,[17] and his "Poichè il crudo Alandin" (1638) also formed the basis of an article by Gallico.[18] Dialogues by Tarquinio Merula, Il Fasolo and Francesco Manelli have been discussed in articles by Elena Ferrari Barassi.[19]

The majority of seventeenth-century recitative-dialogues were written for two voices and continuo. This has led to their being regarded as a type of duet, as can be seen from the work of Riemann and Schmitz ("Kammerduetts") cited above, and it is the reason for their inclusion in the present study. Nevertheless, even a glance at the other contexts in which Riemann and Schmitz themselves discussed dialogue settings will suggest that this classification is not altogether satisfactory. For reasons which are given more fully in chapter 8, the recitative-dialogue has been regarded for the purposes of the present study as a distinct genre, though one whose history in the seventeenth century impinges on that of the duet. It will be argued that it is misleading to regard the dialogue as a kind of duet, for dialogues represent a literary genre in musical setting and may call for two, three, or even four voices, depending on the number of characters involved. The considerations which led composers to set dialogue texts using the new recitative styles of the early seventeenth century are quite distinct from the purely musical considerations which led to the creation of the *concertato* duet.

2

The *Concertato* Duet: Sources and Forms

And from all these things one comes to understand clearly...that the style and manner of singing changes from time to time according to the taste of the Gentlemen and great Princes who take pleasure in it, just as happens in the manner of dress, which changes constantly according to the fashion that has been introduced in the courts of the great...

Thus the Roman nobleman and musical amateur Vincenzo Giustiniani, writing in or about 1628, and summing up the brief, but invaluable survey of Italian vocal music from c. 1570 to c. 1628 that he included in his *Discorso sopra la musica de' suoi tempi*.[1] As a moderate man of catholic taste, and a comparatively objective observer, Giustiniani was able to bring to his survey a sense of perspective rare among early seventeenth-century commentators. Unlike later, and more partial writers such as Pietro de' Bardi,[2] he does not concentrate on Florentine achievements; and he discusses the merits of both solo song and polyphony. The picture that he paints of the diversity of music making in early seventeenth-century Italy serves as a reminder that we can easily present a distorted view of the period if we show it as one in which the creation of opera and Florentine solo song are the only focal points. In this chapter, then, I shall look briefly at some aspects of change and continuity in the vocal music of the early seventeenth century, as reflected in published volumes of music, before going on to survey the sources in which *concertato* duets are found and to look in general terms at the forms cultivated by the early composers of duets.

Although opera is now regarded as the most important genre to emerge from the years around 1600, it is easy to exaggerate its importance for the early seventeenth century. Prior to the opening of public opera houses at Venice during the fourth and fifth decades of the century, and the establishment of touring opera companies,[3] opera was an occasional rather than an integral part of Italian musical life. The majority of composers continued to work in the smaller-scale genres of chamber music.

The radically new style that Jacopo Peri evolved in his operatic recitative made relatively little impact on early seventeenth-century composers of chamber music, though one essential of the style—the use of dissonance against a sustained harmony—can be found in some early duets and dialogues. It can be seen, for example, in bar 31 of Melli's dialogue setting "E quando cessarai?" (1602),[4] and dialogue settings are, perhaps, the form in which one might expect to find an operatic style of recitative. Nevertheless, the use of accented and unaccented dissonances can also be traced in duet settings as, for example, in bars 3, 13, and 26 of Giovanni Valentini's "Vanne, O carta amorosa" (1622),[5] in bars 16-18 of Monteverdi's "Ardo e scoprir" (1638),[6] and in several of Marco da Gagliano's duets.[7] It is no coincidence, however, that the last two of these composers had themselves written operas.

Giustiniani does not discuss opera, but he does mention Giulio Caccini's solo singing and praises it for its "exquisite passage-work [passaggi]... extraordinary emotive quality [affetto] and particular genius for allowing the words to be heard clearly."[8] Nowhere does he claim, however, that Caccini was the pioneer of accompanied solo song or of the *basso continuo* as a means of accompaniment. Nor does he use the merits of Caccini's new manner of singing as the basis for a denunciation of the polyphonic madrigal. Indeed, having concluded his survey, Giustiniani goes on to offer criteria for judging the qualities of both solo songs and polyphonic compositions.

Giustiniani's measured and dispassionate approach to the changes in musical taste and technique that he observed, his recognition of local musical traditions other than those of Florence, and his delight in the diversity of Italian musical culture are gradually being reflected in modern research. It is now recognized, for example, that the madrigals and strophic variations of Caccini's *Le Nuove Musiche* (1602) as well as the canzonettas, are an essentially Florentine refinement of earlier traditions of solo song,[9] and that Caccini's achievement lay chiefly in the respect that he shows for poetry and the limits that he placed on the use of ornamentation;[10] precisely the qualities that Giustiniani found praiseworthy in his work.

Just as we should see Caccini's achievement in perspective, so we should also take a more measured view of the dissemination of the new fashion for Florentine solo song and the impact that *Le Nuove Musiche* made on the patterns of music making in early seventeenth-century Italy. The evidence of surviving manuscripts suggests a good deal of activity in the field of solo song in Florentine circles during the first decade of the century;[11] but the evidence of printed sources suggests that we can only speak with confidence of the fashion being more widely and generally accepted after about 1609 and, more particularly, during the second decade of the century.[12] This is not altogether surprising. The madrigals and strophic variations of *Le Nuove Musiche* are sophisticated examples of singers' music, entirely appropriate for a professional singer like Caccini and for circles where his new marriage of music and poetry were fully appreciated, but less appropriate for smaller musical centers,

centers with different traditions and among composers writing for amateur performers. Indeed, the very sophistication of the Florentine-style solo madrigal must account, in part, for its relatively short lifespan as an art form as compared with the simpler and more colorful strophic aria.

The publication of music for solo voice and small ensemble with continuo was not, of course, restricted to secular music. Lodovico Viadana, whose *Cento Concerti ecclesiastici* was published at Venice in 1602, has some claim to have been the first composer to employ a genuine *basso continuo*.[13] Viadana's sacred music for one, two, three, and four voices was created as an answer to the practical problems faced by choirmasters of churches with limited choral resources,[14] and unlike Caccini's solo songs it is not innovatory in style.

Because it answered a practical need, the published literature of the sacred *concerto* grew rapidly, and from 1605 onward a steady stream of volumes containing, *inter alia,* duets flowed from the Italian presses. A list of the composers who made important contributions to this literature during the first forty years of the seventeenth century includes men like Grandi, Donati, Crivelli, Monteverdi, and Rovetta, and it serves to remind us that a number of the composers of secular duets were also church musicians. Several of them, in fact, published sacred duets before their secular duets had appeared in print. At Rome in 1609, for example, Antonio Cifra published four volumes of motets for two, three, and four voices, and Giovanni Francesco Anerio his *Motecta* for one, two, and three voices.[15] It is particularly interesting to note that Alessandro Grandi's earliest sacred duets were published in 1610, some five years before the duets of his seminal first book of madrigals; and by 1619 he had no fewer than five volumes of continuo motets in print.

The composers of sacred duets did not limit themselves to the conservative styles found in Viadana's *Cento Concerti*. The newer styles of Florentine solo song also played a part in the development of the genre. From the outset, however, many of the composers involved were concerned to produce music with a simple melodic outline that could be performed by singers of average ability. This becomes clear if we contrast the simple, but powerful arioso of Grandi's motet "Hodie nobis de caelo" (1610)[16] with the ornate and complex style of d'India's *ottava* "Dove potrò mai gir tanto lontano" (1609).[17] The two duets were written for quite different performers: d'India's for court virtuosi, Grandi's for the church singers of Ferrara, and their styles are as much a reflection of these practical circumstances as of the composer's whim. When we examine Grandi's early secular duets, which were also written for Ferrara, and perhaps for the same singers, we should not be surprised to find the same simplicity of approach.

Whatever its importance for the longer-term development of vocal music in Italy, Caccini's *Le Nuove Musiche* did not change the face of Italian music overnight. Many of the traditional features of Renaissance music survived into the seventeenth century in forms and styles that are virtually indistinguishable from those of the late sixteenth. Indeed, the publication of *a cappella* polyphonic madrigals and canzonettas continued unabated during the first fifteen years or so of the century and declined only towards 1620 as the fashion for employing a *basso continuo* became so deeply rooted as to make the composition of secular *a cappella* music a consciously conservative act.

In many respects the cultivation of the *basso continuo* technique and its adoption in genres derived directly from sixteenth-century music proved as significant for the early seventeenth century as the creation of Florentine solo song itself. The publication of *Le Nuove Musiche* certainly seems to have stimulated other composers to issue examples of their *concertato* music, whether or not it owed anything to Florence in terms of style and scoring. The earliest examples of polyphonic *concertato* madrigals appeared in the same year as Caccini's songs in the *Secondo Libro de Madrigali a cinque voci ... con il Basso continuo per sonare in concerto* (Venice, 1602) of the Mantuan composer Salamone Rossi.[18] Rossi's lead was soon followed by other Mantuan composers. A collection of canzonettas for three voices and continuo by Amante Franzoni was published in 1605 under the title *I Nuovi Fioretti musicali,* and in the same year Monteverdi issued his fifth book of five-part madrigals, including six *concertato* madrigals at the end of the volume. Once established, the popularity of *concertato* music for three and more voices grew almost as rapidly as that of solo song, lending the polyphonic madrigal a new lease of life by allowing it to adapt to changes in taste.[19]

Volumes of *a cappella* madrigals, too, were later revived alongside the newer *concertato* pieces and made to conform to the prevailing fashion. In 1621, for example, Pomponio Nenna's *Primo Libro de Madrigali a quattro voci* (first published Naples, 1613) was reissued with a *basso continuo* added by the Venetian composer Carlo Milanuzzi. And outside Italy the enterprising Flemish publishing house of Phalèse reissued Monteverdi's third and fourth madrigal books in 1615 "con il basso continuo per il clavicembalo, citharone od altro simile istromento."[20]

As far as secular music is concerned, then, we can distinguish three main types of musical publication during the early seventeenth century: (a) volumes of *a cappella* polyphonic madrigals, canzonettas, and villanellas, a type of publication that was declining in popularity by about 1620, (b) monody books—that is, books containing a substantial proportion of solo songs as compared with ensemble music—which were usually issued in a fairly large folio format with the music printed in score,[21] and (c) volumes of *concertato* polyphonic madrigals and canzonettas which, like their *a cappella* counterparts, were generally issued in part-books in a smaller quarto format.

Although some composers, judged by their publications, are recognizably "monodists" rather than "madrigalists" (and *vice versa*), the distinction between these two groups is often blurred. In a number of cases the same composers who contributed to the growing literature of accompanied solo song also wrote and published polyphonic madrigals. Among them were Antonio Cifra, Pietro Pace, Francesco Turini, Domenico Visconti, and Filippo Vitali. Some of the finest of the early monodists also contributed to the literature of the polyphonic madrigal. The Florentine composer Marco da Gagliano, for example, published six books of madrigals for five voices between 1602 and 1617;[22] and between 1607 and 1624 Sigismondo d'India published no fewer than eight books of madrigals for five voices, one for four, and two volumes of three-part villanellas. Even Alessandro Grandi, who did so much during his years at Venice to popularize the new *bel canto* aria, published two volumes of *concertato* madrigals, in 1615 and 1622 respectively. Significantly, though, his madrigals were scored for two, three, and four voices, testifying to the growing popularity of music for small vocal ensemble and continuo during the second decade of the seventeenth century.

The distinction between monodists and madrigalists is blurred still further by the fact that many individual publications contain a mixture of solo songs and ensemble music. Comparatively few of the monodists published solo songs only. Caccini was one,[23] but in this respect he was by no means typical. The majority of composers who followed his lead also included music for small ensemble—usually of two and three voices, sometimes four—in their monody books.[24] Conversely, during the second decade of the century, solo songs became an accepted constituent of volumes containing polyphonic *concertato* madrigals and canzonettas.[25] Amante Franzoni, with his *Fioretti Musicali...* *Libro Terzo* (1617), and Biagio Marini, with his *Madrigali et Symfonie a 1.2.3.4.5* (1618), led the way here; and they were followed, in 1619, by Monteverdi, who set his seal on the new type of madrigal book by calling his seventh book of madrigals *Concerto,* only the second time that this term had been used so boldly on the title page of a secular publication.[26]

It was during the second decade of the century, too, that duets were first published in madrigal books. Grandi's first book of *Madrigali concertati* (1615) set the fashion here; and it established not only one of the most popular titles for books of *concertato* madrigals, but also a new type of madrigal book, with music for two, three, and four voices only. Almost a third of the books of *concertato* madrigals published between 1615 and 1643 contain music for these voice groupings.

The vocal chamber music of early seventeenth-century Italy, viewed as a whole, is characterized by the persistence of polyphonic idioms alongside the more radical innovations of Florentine monody. It would seem from this that many composers of the period—and particularly professional musicians—regarded the novelties of monody as an enrichment of, rather than a substitute for, the artistic heritage of the late sixteenth century.

This state of affairs would scarcely have surprised Vincenzo Galilei, the most vehement and outspoken of the Florentine theorists. In a revealing passage from his seminal work, the *Dialogo della musica antica et della moderna,* he asserted his own intellectual position with regard to the use of counterpoint in vocal compositions, but predicted that his words would have little effect:

> There is no one who does not consider these rules of counterpoint excellent and necessary for the mere delight the ear takes in the variety of the harmonies, but for the expression of conceptions they are pestilent, being fit for nothing but to make the concentus varied and full, and this is not always, indeed is never suited to express any conception of the poet or the orator. I repeat, therefore, that if the rules in question had been applied to their original purpose [i.e. instrumental music], those who have amplified them in modern times would deserve no less praise than those who first laid them down . . . But the matter has always been understood in the opposite way by their successors, and this belief has endured so long that I think it will be most difficult, if not impossible to remove and dispel it from men's minds, especially from the minds of those who are mere practitioners of this kind of counterpoint, and therefore esteemed and prized by the vulgar and salaried by various gentlemen . . . [27]

The petulant and dogmatic tone of this passage is typical of Galilei. As an intellectual he was inclined to take a negative view of the role of counterpoint in vocal music, a view, incidentally, that he never fully reconciled with his work as a composer, as such conventional madrigals as "Ippolita gentil" and "Vedi che torni" from his *Secondo Libro de Madrigali a quattro voci* (Venice, 1587)[28] show. Through the work of composers like Peri and Caccini, Galilei's ideas took on a creative aspect for the seventeenth century. It was, however, as he gloomily foresaw, inherently unlikely that the majority of his contemporaries and successors would forsake contrapuntal techniques in vocal music, though for positive reasons as well as the negative ones which he himself advanced. Prior to the evolution of organized tonality and of multi-movement structures in solo song, imitation and textural contrast were fundamental to the writing of cohesive large-scale musical compositions. The positive virtues of counterpoint, overlooked by Galilei in his *Dialogo,* account in large measure for the persistence of polyphonic idioms in both vocal and instrumental music during the early seventeenth century and for the popularity of genres like the duet.

Of the smaller *concertato* ensembles which enjoyed a new vogue in the early seventeenth century, duets appealed equally to the monodists, to those composers like Monteverdi and Rovetta who wrote few solo songs, and to those like Galeazzo Sabbatini who wrote none at all. The composers of the seventeenth century found in the *concertato* duet a novel medium, yet one which transcended the boundaries between the old and the new: a medium in which the imitative techniques and sonority of the polyphonic madrigal and the melodious quality of the canzonetta could be mingled with the rhetorical declamation of Florentine solo song. It was a medium, too, that was equally appropriate for virtuoso music and for simple, tuneful music for amateur singers. It was, in short, a compromise, though one that held considerable potential for future development.

From the historian's point of view, the *concertato* duet is of interest precisely because its early development cuts across the boundaries between the parallel traditions of solo song and the polyphonic *concertato* madrigal. This is reflected, first of all, by the types of publication in which duets appeared during the early seventeenth century. Comparatively few were issued in books containing nothing but duets. Most composers seem to have viewed the genre as an adjunct either to their monodies or to their larger-scale *concertato* madrigals, and monody books and volumes of *concertato* madrigals are thus the two main sources of duets during this period.

Some six books published between 1605 and 1610 are, however, devoted entirely, or almost entirely to duets for high voice (i.e. soprano or tenor) and bass in which the bass part also serves for an instrumental *basso seguente*. These are the first four books of *Canzonette, Madrigali, et Arie alla romana* (1605, 1606, between 1606 and 1610, 1610)[29] of Enrico Radesca di Foggia, the *Passatempi* (1608) of Maffeo Cagnazzi of Lodi, and the *Madrigali, e Pazzarelle* (1610) of the Modenese composer Nicolò Rubini.[30]

Only three further volumes of duets survive from the period before 1643. These contain duets with independent *basso continuo*. They are Sigismondo d'India's *Musiche* (1615), Giovanni Valentini's *Musiche* (1622), and the second part of the *Cantade ... Libro Secondo* (1633) of Giovanni Felice Sances.

During the first decade of the century, too, we find several volumes of unaccompanied villanellas by the two Neapolitan musicians Giovanni Domenico Montella (second and third books of villanellas for four voices, 1604 and 1605 respectively) and Francesco Lambardi (*Villanelle a 3 et a 4 voci,* 1607) which include *arie* for two voices. Although none of Montella's villanella publications survives complete, his *arie* appear to be, like those of Lambardi, duets of the high voice and bass/*basso seguente* type, though he does not mention an instrumental accompaniment.

Independent duet settings first began to appear in monody books from about 1605 with the first printing (now lost) of the *Madrigali di diversi autori posti in musica* by Bartolomeo Barbarino, sometime singer at the chapel of the Holy House of Loreto, musician at Urbino and, from 1602 to 1605, organist of Pesaro cathedral.[31] Barbarino's book, however, contains only one duet, a clumsy and artificial set of strophic variations which are a setting of Sannazzaro's "I tuoi capelli, O Filli" (*Arcadia,* Eclogue XII). More interesting and important is the *Euterpe* of the inventive young Bolognese composer Domenico Brunetti, which was published in 1606. Brunetti's book contains no fewer than eleven duets. Some of them are madrigals and arias of the high voice and bass/*basso seguente* type, but the book also includes the earliest published examples of two-part madrigals with independent *basso continuo*. From the date of Brunetti's *Euterpe,* the list of monody books which are also sources for duets conforms quite closely with Dr. Fortune's "Handlist," with the exception of the work of those composers listed earlier who published solo songs only.[32]

Following the publication of Grandi's *Madrigali concertati* in 1615, madrigal books also became an important source for duets. Grandi's book was followed in 1616 by Ugoni's *Giardinetto di Ricreatione,* and in 1617 by Anerio's *Diporti Musicali,* Franzoni's *Il Terzo Libro delli Fioretti Musicali,* and by the fancifully titled *La Turca Armoniosa: giovenili ardori* of the Roman composer Giuseppe Olivieri, who described his madrigals as being "for the convenience, sometimes, of a few singers."[33] In northern Italy, the madrigal books of Biagio Marini (1618, at Venice), Stefano Bernardi (1619, at Verona), Antonio Marastone (1619, at Peschiera, near Verona), and Monteverdi (1619) make up the total of madrigalian sources before 1620. After 1620, however, the floodgates opened as more and more composers began to include duets in their madrigal books. Between 1620 and 1635 madrigal books rival, and, indeed, outnumber monody books as sources for duets. From 1636 there is a sharp decline in the number of monody books containing duets—eight new sources only between 1636 and 1643. The decline is by no means as sharp, however, in the case of madrigal books, for some twenty new publications were issued during the same years.

This survey of published sources begs a question. Were composers such as Barbarino and Brunetti, who were the first to publish independent continuo duets in their monody books, in fact the creators of the new medium, or was this, like continuo song, a fashion that stemmed from Florence? The earliest published continuo duets are certainly by composers associated with Florence, for they are found in the scores of Cavalieri's *Rappresentatione di Anima e di Corpo* (Rome, 1600) and Caccini's *Euridice* (Florence, 1600).[34] Outside the field of opera, Peri's duet "Intenerite voi, lacrime mie"[35] survives in two manuscripts—*B-Bc,* MS 704 and *I-Fn,* MS Magl. XIX. 66—which may date from the turn of the sixteenth century or the early years of the seventeenth. One further Florentine manuscript—*I-Fc,* Barbera MS—and three others that may be of Florentine origin—*I-Bc,* MS Q. 140, and *I-Fn,* MSS Magl. XIX. 24, XIX. 25—contain duets which may well have been written during the first decade of the century,[36] though some were published later. And Florentines figure prominently among the composers who published duets during the second decade of the century. If we allow for a time-lag between composition and publication, then some at least of their duets may also have been circulating in manuscript before 1610.

The evidence for Florentine involvement in the creation of the chamber duet is suggestive, but inconclusive, as is a reference to duet writing in one of

Marco da Gagliano's letters, addressed to Michelangelo Buonarroti, dated 8 March 1608, and written from Mantua, where Gagliano was currently involved in the staging of his opera Dafne:

> I was just beginning to believe that it would be possible to return to Florence, where I would be able to serve my patrons according to my duty, but then, since these Highnesses [of Mantua] were pleased that I should serve them in these wedding celebrations and since it is not worth presenting any excuse, I did not wish to fail in giving them [his Florentine patrons] an account of everything and how the most Illustrious Lord Cardinal [Ferdinando Gonzaga] has written to Signor Jacopo Peri asking him to rehearse for me my music for one voice, for two and for three . . . [37]

Is the "Musiche per una voce per due e per tre" to which Gagliano refers the same music that he published in 1615 under the title *Musiche a una dua e tre voci?* We may never know for certain, though the music of one of the duets in the 1615 book certainly dates from around 1608. This is the aria "Alma mia, dove ten vai?" which is an adaptation to new words of music first published in the score of Gagliano's *Dafne* (Florence, 1608). [38]

The first major distinction that we should draw between duet and solo song is in the matter of form. Although, broadly speaking, the composers of duets worked in the same forms as the writers of solo songs—madrigal, strophic aria, strophic variations, and variations on stylized arias—they showed a distinct preference for madrigal writing. Taking the period c. 1600 to c. 1643 as a whole there are some one and a half times as many madrigals and madrigalian settings of other verse forms as there are strophic duets. Moreover, in contrast to the monodic madrigal, which was already declining in popularity towards 1620 and was to all intents and purposes a spent force after 1625, [39] the madrigalian duet actually increased in popularity during the second decade of the seventeenth century and enjoyed a heyday during the 1620s and 1630s, apparently declining only as the output from the Venetian presses declined during the 1640s.

This general picture, however, requires immediate qualification. The rise in popularity of the madrigalian duet towards 1620 corresponds with the growing number of madrigal books which include music for two voices, and the number of strophic duets included in madrigal books is not sufficiently large to alter the general picture, even though some of these works are important in pointing to the future development of the chamber duet. [40]

The patterns of composition revealed by the duets published in monody books are, however, strikingly different. There is no corresponding rise in the popularity of the madrigal here during the second decade of the century. And after 1623 scarcely any madrigalian duets were published in monody books. Just as in the case of solo song, strophic duets seem, by this time, to have become more popular than madrigals. The parallel with solo song is not, however, exact, for even before 1620 monody books containing more strophic duets than madrigals outnumbered those containing more madrigals than strophic duets.

As far as the other early sources of seventeenth-century duets are concerned, the villanella books of Montella and Lambardi contain, as one might expect, a preponderance of strophic duets. The collections of duets for high voice and bass/*basso seguente* contain equal numbers of madrigals and arias, with the exception of Radesca's first book of *Canzonette* (1605) and Cagnazzi's *Passatempi* (1608), both of which contain a preponderance of madrigalian duets. The contents of the later volumes devoted to duets with *basso continuo* conform to the general pattern for their monody-book format. That is, they contain more strophic duets than madrigals.

Crude though these statistics may be as a guide to stylistic sources, they do suggest that the lighter strophic forms of the late sixteenth century played an important role in determining the early stylistic and formal development of the *concertato* duet. Moreover, they suggest that the great flowering of the madrigalian duet was closely bound up with what we might call the Indian Summer of the madrigal book; and, as we shall see, the publication of duets in madrigal books was very largely a north Italian phenomenon.

As the *concertato* polyphonic madrigal, and with it the madrigal book, suffered a gradual decline during the 1640s, so the underlying trend towards strophic forms, observable among the duets published in monody books, becomes apparent again; and it is a trend which seems to be confirmed by the duets of Luigi Rossi, most of which are strophic, or employ the repetition patterns of strophic arias. A comment written towards 1650 by the Florentine composer Severo Bonini seems also to confirm the new position of the strophic duet:

> Don't you see that today they expect only to compose little songs [canzonette] for one or two voices concerted with harpsichords or other instruments? Madrigals to be sung at a table without being concerted have been sent off forgotten.[41]

One interesting finding to emerge from our statistical survey is that composers such as Biagio Marini and Filippo Vitali who issued duets in both monody-book and madrigal-book format seem to have conformed, in terms of the relative numbers of madrigalian and strophic duets included, to the general pattern for the format. Thus, when issuing monody books these composers included more strophic than madrigalian duets.

There are two possible explanations for this. The first is bound up with the economics of publication. While it was economically feasible to print short strophic duets in score, larger collections of ensemble music, particularly those that included through-composed settings, were cheaper to print in part-books.

The second possibility is that these economic considerations also created two distinct and recognizable types of publication for *concertato* music. For as monody books became sources for the lighter music of the day, so it became less appropriate to include in them complex madrigalian duets (or, even, more complex arias). These were reserved for the more serious type of publication, the madrigal book. As we shall see, however, even those madrigalists who seem to form a group distinct from the writers of solo song were not necessarily narrow conservatives, and their madrigals were not immune from changing aesthetics in style. Indeed, in some cases they were in the vanguard of new developments.

Before looking more closely at the stylistic development of the early seventeenth-century duet in chapters 6 and 7, however, we must turn aside to discuss some of the poets whose texts were set as *concertato* duets and to identify the musical traditions from which the seventeenth-century duet emerged.

3

The Poets and Their Texts

Musica e Poesia son due sorelle
Ristoratrici delle afflitte genti,
De' rei pensier le torbide procelle
con liete rime a serenar possenti.
(Giambattista Marino, *Adone,* VII. 1)

Although we can build a picture from the musical sources alone of the kinds of poetry that appealed to the composers of duets, a more precise knowlege of the literary sources from which they drew their texts helps to focus the picture more clearly. By identifying as far as possible the poets whose texts were chosen for musical setting we can test the literary tastes both of individual composers and of the period in general.[1] Moreover, identification of the poet and, thus, of the original form of his text, is a necessary adjunct to musical analysis, particularly in the case of a composer like Monteverdi, who was quite capable of rearranging a text to suit his own musical conception.

The musical sources themselves are of little help in this respect, for in the seventeenth century, as in the sixteenth, few composers named the poets whose texts they set to music. Of those that did, five at least—Barbarino, Benedetti, Rasi, Castaldi, and Benedetto Ferrari—had a clear motive for doing so since they were themselves poets. Their verses do not, however, seem to have been set by other composers of duets, and only those of Rasi and Ferrari seem to have been published independently of musical setting.[2]

Two other composers, Fontei and Laurenzi, left fairly complete records of their poets. The dedications of Fontei's 1635 and 1636 books reveal his close relationship with the Venetian poet Giulio Strozzi, while the mixture of contemporary Roman and Venetian poets in Laurenzi's *Concerti* of 1641 reflects the course of the composer's career. Only rarely were whole volumes of music devoted to the work of one poet. Perhaps the most interesting is the volume of madrigals issued in 1624 by Giovanni Battista Anselmi. Anselmi, a Trevisan nobleman, collected, and probably commissioned for this publication, settings of his own poetry by a variety of composers, including Monteverdi and Grandi.

Even those composers who were scrupulous in acknowledging the work of their poets had to admit, on occasion, that a text was of uncertain authorship, for some of the anthologies from which they drew their texts themselves fail to identify the poet. Of the anthologies of poetry by named poets that I have seen, the largest is the *Gareggiamento poetico del Confuso Accademico Ordito,* published at Venice in 1611. The anthology is divided into nine parts, with the texts grouped according to their characteristics—*madrigali amorosi, madrigali morali, madrigali di nozze, madrigali giocose,* and so on—and with some texts appearing under more than one heading.

Some texts, like Marino's *Canzone dei Baci* and sections of the *Adone,* were circulated in manuscript before being published by the poet. Others may have been the work of literary friends of the composer. Camillo Orlandi, for example, acknowledged in his 1616 book the work of two poets from his native city of Verona: Alessandro Becelli and Alberto Fabriani.

Of one thing we can be certain, however, and that is that few composers of the early seventeenth century looked beyond the immediate past for the texts of their duets. In this respect their attitude toward poetry was unlike that of the mid sixteenth-century madrigalists, whose work had coincided with, and was stimulated by a rebirth of interest in, the vernacular lyrics of the fourteenth-century poet Francesco Petrarca. The leading spirit of the Petrarchan renaissance, Cardinal Pietro Bembo (1474-1547), was himself a poet; through his advocacy of Petrarch as the model for vernacular poetry, in the *Prose della volgar lingua,* and his own imitation of Petrarchan lyrics, he influenced two generations of able, sometimes outstanding poets. In the fields of epic verse and the pastoral, too, vernacular poetry received a new impetus at the beginning of the sixteenth century from Ariosto's *Orlando furioso* and Sannazzaro's *Arcadia.*[3]

In marked contrast, the period which saw the emergence of the *concertato* duet has generally been held by literary critics to be one in which poetry declined to a nadir of shallow virtuosity in the hands of Giambattista Marino and his imitators. Even before the end of the seventeenth century the fortunes of Marinist verse had begun to fail, and its fate was sealed by the foundation of the Arcadian academy at Rome in 1690. Few seventeenth-century poets escaped the strictures of the Arcadians—Gabriello Chiabrera was one exception—and their judgments have colored critical opinion down to the present day. During the eighteenth and nineteenth centuries in particular, the term *secentismo* came to symbolize all that was meretricious and decadent in Italian poetry.[4]

To be fair, this judgment seems rather harsh, certainly too sweeping when applied to the musical poetry of the early seventeenth century. In poetry, as in the field of music, it is misleading to postulate a clear break with tradition in the years around 1600, and to suggest, as Professor Einstein did, that at the beginning of the seventeenth century "music demanded of poetry merely that it should be a poetic foundation for its fixed musical form."[5] Marino's poetry, for example, can be seen in some respects as the culmination of three main streams of late Renaissance Italian poetry—the amatory lyric, the pastoral, and the epic—and even at his most shallow he remains a recognizably literary figure and not a mere purveyor of *poesia per musica.*

Nevertheless, a number of changes of emphasis can be detected in the poetry of the late sixteenth century and early seventeenth century. In the amatory lyric, for example, we can see a movement away from the Petrarchan tradition of platonic, unrequited love to a more explicitly physical lovemaking. And changes can be detected, too, in matters of form and technique: in an increasing emphasis on the madrigal and on strophic verse and in the conscious exploitation of varied rhythmic patterns in the work of Marino and, more particularly, of Chiabrera. Before studying the work of individual poets, then, we must set the background to these latter changes by introducing some of the basic concepts of Italian versification and the principal poetic forms chosen for musical setting during the sixteenth and early seventeenth centuries.

Elements of Italian Versification

Unlike the lines of Latin or English poetry, which are classified according to the type and number of metrical feet that they contain (e.g. *iambic pentameter:* a line containing five iambic feet), the lines of Italian poetry *(versi)* are classified primarily in terms of the number of their syllables (e.g. *endecasillabi:* lines of eleven syllables; *settenari:* lines of seven syllables). Rhythm, though of crucial importance to the poetic superstructure, is only of secondary importance in this respect, for two lines of different rhythm are considered equivalent providing that they contain the same number of syllables. The process of reckoning the number of syllables in a line is complicated only by the conventions governing the pronunciation of two consecutive vowels. Since these conventions have a bearing not only on the appreciation of poetic form, but also on the correct underlay of a musical text, they are outlined here for reference.[6]

When two vowels appear consecutively within a single poetic line they are, for the most part, fused into a single syllable: that is, although both are articulated, they are counted as a single metrical unit. The same convention applies whether the two vowels appear consecutively within a single word *(sineresi)* or as the final and initial letters respectively of two different words *(sinalefe).* The first line of this madrigal by Guarini shows an example of each type of fusion in a *settenario: sinalefe* at the third syllable and *sineresi* at the fourth:

Non miri il mio bel Sole
　1　　2 3　4　 5　 6 7

Normally, the two vowels involved in *sinalefe* are also fused for the purpose of musical underlay. In practice, however, composers do occasionally separate them, especially when words are repeated or different phrases given their own individual musical treatment. The latter case is illustrated in bars 49-50 of Radesca's "Ahi, ch'io mi svegl'ohimè" (see vol. 2, no. 1), where the final vowel of "sonno" and the initial vowel of "ohimè" are separated in the musical setting, but count as a single syllable of the poetic line.

Sineresi and *sinalefe* may be taken as the norm for the treatment of consecutive vowels in Italian poetry. The opposite procedures (*dieresi* and *dialefe*), in which the two vowels are counted as two metrical units, are encountered less frequently. As far as poetic metre is concerned, *dialefe* virtually disappeared with the Petrarchan revival of the sixteenth century.[7] *Dierese*—the separation of two consecutive vowels within a single word—is, however, another matter. In modern editions its presence is indicated by placing two dots above the first vowel of the pair (e.g. äere). Some older sources employ an acute accent for the same purpose. More often, however, the presence of *dieresi* is not distinguished in the text and the reader (and editor) must decide whether to fuse or to separate the vowels. The choice is not always governed by a clear set of rules and may require a detailed knowledge of the style of a particular period or of the literary genre concerned. Elwert does, however, provide some valuable guidelines which we summarize here.[8]

1. When, at the end of a word, we find a dipthong consisting of an accented vowel followed by an unaccented vowel *(dittongo discendente)* as, for example, in the word *avea,* the dipthong will normally count as one syllable if the word occurs in the middle of the line, but as two syllables if it occurs at the end of a line or at a caesura:

   Fosse del sangue empir del popol mio
                                     10/11
     (Tasso, *Gerusalemme liberata,* III. 19)
   Mio fosse un giorno! e no 'l vorrei già morto
   1
     (Tasso, *Gerusalemme liberata,* III. 20)

   This rule applies to word endings which were bi-syllabic in Latin (e.g. aveva>avea) and to *dittonghi discendenti* in such monosyllables as *lui, fia, io, tuo, due, quei* whatever their derivation.

2. *Dieresi* became favored in pronouns when these were followed by a word beginning with a consonant, and particularly by a word beginning with *s impura* (i.e. *s* followed by a consonant), as, for example, *mïo spirto.*

3. *Dieresi* is permitted when the two vowels originally belonged to different syllables and the accent falls on the second vowel, as, for example, in *päura, vïaggio, päese, impetüoso, bëato, söave.*[9]

4. *Dieresi* is permitted when neither of the vowels forms the principal accent of the word (e.g. *trïonfante*).

5. Although a *dittongo discendente* occurring in the middle of a line will normally count as one syllable, exceptions are sometimes made in the case of proper names (e.g. *Pompëo*).

6. A pair of unaccented vowels appearing at the end of a word will normally count as one syllable only. This is almost invariably the case with unaccented vowel-pairs beginning with the letter *i*—*-̆io, -̆ii, -̆ia, -̆ie*—whether they are found in the middle or at the end of the line. Exceptionally, they are treated as two units at the end of a line; this happens when the poet requires to produce a large number of *versi sdruccioli* (see below, p. 22) and the context will usually make this usage clear. A rather different convention applies in the case of the vowel-pairs *-̆ao, -̆ai, -̆eo, -̆ea, -̆ee, -̆uo, -̆ua.* These are treated in the same manner as a *dittongo discendente:* that is, they normally count as a single syllable in the course of a line, but as two syllables at the end of a line or at a caesura.

In addition to the convention of fusing the final and initial vowels of two consecutive words *(sinalefe),* there are also a number of cases in which one of the vowels is suppressed altogether. If the final vowel is suppressed, the process is known as *elisione: io t'ho visto (= io te ho visto);* and if the initial vowel is suppressed, the process is known as *aferesi: che 'n (= che in).* These forms are a matter of custom and usage, both in spoken and written language, and when editing and translating Italian poetry one has to be alive to their meaning.

One has, also, to be alive to cases of apocopation *(apocope),* that is, to abbreviated forms in which the final vowel is customarily suppressed, even before a consonant. There are two main groups of apocopated words:

1. in which the final vowel is dropped after *-r, -l, -m, -n,* as, for example, in *parlar* < parlare;

2. in which the final vowel of a *dittongo discendente* is dropped (an Old Florentine usage), as for example, in the words *se'* < sei, *i'* < io, *que'* < quei.[10]

A third kind of apocopation involves the suppression of the entire final syllable, as in *fèr* < fiero, *passâr* < passaro. This usage, together with other archaic abbreviations, such as *medesmo* < *medesimo,*[11] can often, however, be identified with the aid of a good dictionary.

One last, but very important factor has a bearing on the number of syllables in a poetic line. This is the position of the tonic accent in the final word. The line can end in any one of four ways:

1. with the accent on the penultimate syllable *(verso piano);*
2. with the accent on the final syllable *(verso tronco);*
3. with the accent on the antepenultimate syllable *(verso sdrucciolo);* or
4. with the accent on the fourth syllable from the end *(verso bisdrucciolo).*

Since words stressed on the penultimate syllable predominate in the Italian language, the *verso piano* is the most characteristic line of Italian poetry. And for the purposes of poetic theory all lines are classified as though they were *versi piani:* that is, one counts the number of syllables up to and including the first unstressed syllable following the final accent. Thus, an *endecasillabo piano* contains eleven *syllables,* but an *endecasillabo tronco* contains ten, an *endecasillabo sdrucciolo* twelve, and an *endecasillabo bisdrucciolo* thirteen.

With the exception of various experiments in adapting Latin and French metres to Italian verse,[12] lines of more than eleven syllables are rarely found in Italian poetry. And of the available lines not all have been held in equal esteem. Dante seems to have been the first to enshrine a hierarchy of line lengths in poetic theory:

> ... But we do not find that anyone has hitherto used a line of more than eleven or less than three syllables. And though the Italian poets have used the lines of three and of eleven syllables and all the intermediate ones, those of five, seven and eleven syllables are more frequently used [than the others], and next to them that of three syllables in preference to the others. But of all these the line of eleven syllables seems the stateliest, as well by reason of the length of time it occupies as of its capacity in regard to subject, construction, and words; ... We say also that the line of seven syllables follows next after that which is greatest in celebrity. After this the line of five and then that of three syllables. But the line of nine syllables, because it appeared to consist of the line of three taken three times, was either never held in honour or fell into disuse on account of its being disliked. As for the lines of an even number of syllables, we use them but rarely because of their rudeness; .... [13]

Though Dante was, of course, speaking only of the poetry of his own and preceding generations and of the lines appropriate to the *canzone,* his judgments seem, very largely, to have remained valid for the poetic forms cultivated during the Renaissance. In the major forms, lines with an uneven number of syllables *(versi imparisillabi)* were preferred; and though the lines of five and three syllables (*quinari* and *ternari*) were little used, they are sometimes found as subdivisions of a longer line. The last *endecasillabo* of the *canzone* stanza "Vergine chiara" quoted below (p. 26), for example, is divided into *quinario* and *settenario* by the internal rhyme on the second word. Lines with an even number of syllables *(versi parisillabi)* seem to have been reserved during the sixteenth century for lighter, strophic verse.

The pride of place that Dante gave to the *endecasillabo* reflects not only such abstract qualities as the weight and stateliness of the line, but also the rich variety of rhythmic possibilities that it affords. In addition to the fixed accent on the tenth syllable of the line, the *endecasillabo* has one other principal accent which usually falls on the fourth or sixth syllable. Within this general framework, however, a number of rhythms are available, from the regular iambs of

> Il gran sepolcro adora, e scioglie il voto
>   2   4   6   8   10
> (Tasso)

to the more irregular structure of

> Quanto più desïose l'ali spando
> 1   3   6   8   10
> (Petrarch)

and

> Hai di stelle immortali aurea corona
>   3   6   7   10
> (Tasso).[14]

Three of the major poetic forms set to music during the sixteenth and early seventeenth centuries—the sonnet, the *terza rima,* and the *ottava rima*—employ hendecasyllabic lines only. The sonnet was the most important of the forms in the Petrarchan canon and, thus, of sixteenth-century lyric poetry, too. In structure it consists of a single stanza of fourteen lines divided into two groups of four, related by rhyme scheme (the octave), plus two groups of three, again related by rhyme scheme (the sestet).

The following sonnet, in which Petrarch thinks of his beloved Laura, was set as a duet by Dognazzi (1614) and Orlandi (1616). It employs the popular rhyme scheme ABBA/ABBA/CDC/DCD and is typical of many Petrarchan sonnets in that each of the quartets and tercets forms a self-contained unit. The subtlety of rhythmic structure available from a sequence of *endecasillabi* can be demonstrated by showing the pattern of accented syllables in the first quartet. The unexpected stress on the first syllable of the fourth line serves to focus attention on the important word "morte."

> Ite, caldi sospiri, al freddo core,
> 1   3   6   8   10
> Rompete il ghiaccio che Pietà contende,
>   2   4   6   8   10
> Et se prego mortale al ciel s'intende,
>   3   6   8   10

Morte o mercè sia fine al mio dolore.
1   4   6   8   10
Ite, dolci penser', parlando fore
Di quello ove 'l bel guardo non s'estende:
Se pur sua asprezza o mia stella n'offende,
Sarem fuor di speranza et fuor d'errore.
Dir se pò ben per voi, non forse a pieno,
Che 'l nostro stato è inquieto e fosco,
Sì com'è 'l suo pacifico et sereno.
Gite securi omai, ch'Amor vèn vosco;
Et ria Fortuna pò ben venir meno,
S'ai segni del mio sol l'aere conosco.

Go, hot sighs, to her cold heart; break the ice that hinders pity and, if a mortal prayer is heard in Heaven, death or compassion will put an end to my sorrow. Go, sweet thoughts, speaking aloud of that which her beautiful glance cannot see: if her harshness or my star still remain inimical, we shall be beyond hope or error. Tell her, though you cannot, perhaps, tell fully, that our state is as troubled and dismal as hers is peaceful and serene. Go now, with confidence, for Love goes with you; and ill-fortune may well diminish if I read aright the signs in her face.

Neither *terza rima* nor *ottava rima* belong to the group of Petrarchan lyric forms. *Terza rima (terzina)*, as its name implies, is a stanza of three lines. A sequence of *terzine*, linked by the interweaving of rhymes so that each rhyme after the first appears three times (ABA/BCB/CDC/etc.), was employed by Dante for the *Divina Commedia* and by Petrarch for the *Trionfi*.[15] From the fifteenth century, too, it became a characteristic scheme for eclogues. Sannazzaro, for example, used *terza rima* for several of the eclogues of *Arcadia* (first authorized publication, 1504). A section of one of these is quoted below on page 29.

The *ottava rima*, a stanza comprising six lines alternating in rhyme plus a rhyming couplet (ABABABCC), was the preferred stanza for epic and narrative poetry. Ariosto's *Orlando furioso* (published 1516) and Tasso's *Gerusalemme liberata* (1581), the two great epic romances of the sixteenth century, are both constructed from a sequence of ottavas, and from among these composers chose a number of individual stanzas to set as madrigals. The stanzas most frequently chosen were those that could easily be taken out of context to express a generalized idea or situation, stanzas of earthy eroticism like "Non rumor di tamburi" (*Orlando furioso*, XXV. 68), or with the pictorial imagery of "Vezzosi augelli infra le verdi fronde" (*Gerusalemme liberata*, XVI. 12). Occasionally, though, a composer chose to set a narrative or semidramatic sequence of stanzas. Monteverdi, for example, set the three stanzas beginning "Vattene pur, crudel" (*Gerusalemme liberata*, XVI. 59-61) in which the sorceress Armida curses Rinaldo as he deserts her. These were set as a cycle of three five-part madrigals and published in Monteverdi's third book of madrigals (1592).

Although the *ottava* was not usually employed for lyric poetry, Bernardo Tasso, father of the more famous Torquato, used the form for his fifteen *Stanze di lontananza,* poems addressed to his wife during a period of enforced separation.[16] Two of these stanzas became popular among the composers of the sixteenth century and were set again as duets during the early seventeenth. Monteverdi set one of them, the impassioned outburst "Ohimè, dov'è il mio ben?" (1619); the other, set by Cifra (*Secondo,* 1613), is more artificial in diction:

> Vostro fui, vostro sono, e sarò vostro
> Fin che vedrò quest'aere, e questo Cielo;
> Vili prima saran le Perle, e l'Ostro;
> Negre, et ardenti fian le nevi, e 'l gielo,
> Che 'l tempo spenga mai quest'ardor nostro
> Per cangiar clima, o variar di pelo;
> Anzi crescerà sempre il mio bel foco,
> Quanto andrò più cangiando etate, e loco.

> Yours I was, yours I am, and yours I shall be as long as I see this air and sky; pearls and purple shall first become worthless, snow and ice be black and burning before time will ever extinguish our ardor through changing climate or coat; rather will this fire of mine always increase, however long I go on changing in age or place.

The problem of balancing sincerity of emotion with artificiality of utterance was already inherent in the Petrarchan lyric, and it was to become more acute still in the madrigals of Guarini and Marino. Tasso, however, justified the artifices of the *Stanze* in a letter dated 1544. Writing to his patron, Ferrante Sanseverino, he said that in the *Stanze* he had employed

> the greatest artificiality, so that they may satisfy the world; for though I am no expert in music, I know at least what is expected of poems intended to be sung. They are smooth; they are amorous in their affection; they are colorful; and they abound in phrases suitable for music.[17]

It is not clear from the letter exactly what sort of musical setting Tasso envisaged for his poems, but we should note that, because of their regular structure and use of hendecasyllabic lines only, ottavas, together with sonnets and poems in *terza rima,* lent themselves to performance in musical formulae in which a single melodic and harmonic scheme could be used for any poem of similar structure.[18] This type of formula persisted into the seventeenth century. Einstein, for example, quotes an aria "per cantar sonetti" which is found in Biagio Marini's 1635 book;[19] and in the field of the duet Monteverdi's *Romanesca* setting of "Ohimè, dov'è, il mio ben?" and Cifra's *Ruggiero* setting of "Vostro fui" simply continue in a new guise the long tradition of setting ottavas to stylized melodies.

With the exception of the nine-syllable line *(novenario)*, whose rhythmic characteristics are akin to those of the *versi parisillabi*, the *versi imparisillabi* combine well with each other and, as we can see from Dante's hierarchy, were mixed freely in early Italian poetry. By the sixteenth century, however, the only two *imparisillabi* that were regularly combined were the *endecasillabo* and the *settenario* (the so-called *versi toscani*). A free mixture of these two lines had formed the basis of the second most important type of poem in Petrarch's *Canzoniere*—the *canzone* itself.

The *canzone* is one of the oldest and most illustrious of the Italian lyric forms. It is strophic, though with no fixed number of lines to the stanza. Each stanza comprises two parts, the *fronte* and the *sirma* or *coda*. The *fronte* itself is divided into two *piedi* which match each other in terms of number of lines and line-lengths employed. The rhymes of the two *piedi* do not necessarily correspond, though if one line is unrhymed in the first *piede* it is given a rhyming line in the second. The *sirma*, which is undivided in the Petrarchan *canzone*, is linked to the *fronte* by rhyming its first line with the last line of the *fronte* (the *verso chiave*). A typical *canzone* comprises between five and seven stanzas which correspond in terms of the number of lines, but not in rhyme scheme. It usually ends with a single stanza of different structure, termed the *commiato*. As an example of the *canzone* stanza, we quote here the sixth stanza of Petrarch's "Vergine bella," showing it division into *piede* and *sirma*. The first ten lines of this stanza were set as a madrigalian duet by Marco da Gagliano (1615).

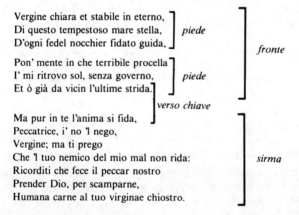

Vergine chiara et stabile in eterno,
Di questo tempestoso mare stella,
D'ogni fedel nocchier fidato guida,   *piede*

fronte

Pon' mente in che terribile procella
I' mi ritrovo sol, senza governo,
Et ò già da vicin l'ultime strida.   *piede*

verso chiave

Ma pur in te l'anima si fida,
Peccatrice, i' no 'l nego,
Vergine; ma ti prego
Che 'l tuo nemico del mio mal non rida: *sirma*
Ricorditi che fece il peccar nostro
Prender Dio, per scamparne,
Humana carne al tuo virginae chiostro.

Virgin bright, biding forever, the star of this stormy sea and the true guide of every faithful helmsman, take heed of this terrible tempest in which I find myself alone, without a rudder, and close to my last breath. But still in Thee my soul trusts, though it is laden with sin, I do not deny it, O Virgin; but I pray Thee, do not let Thy foe laugh at my suffering: remember that for our sin, to preserve us, God assumed human flesh in your virgin womb.

Of the other Petrarchan forms the *sestina,* a virtuoso variant of the *canzone* comprising six six-line stanzas of *endecasillabi* only in which word-rhymes are retrograded *a croce* (ABCDEF/FAEBDC/etc.) and a *commiato* of three lines in which all six of these words must appear, is encountered rarely, the most famous example in musical setting being Monteverdi's 'Incenerite spoglie', to a text by Scipione Agnelli (*Sesto Libro de Madrigali,* 1614); the *ballata* (see below, p. 29) was employed only infrequently by the sixteenth-century Petrarchists; and the Petrarchan madrigal was not imitated at all.

The sonnet and the *canzone,* then, were the main Petrarchan legacy to the sixteenth century and they remained the staple fare of *Canzonieri* until the early seventeenth. To them, however, we must add one other form of great importance—the new madrigal, which came into being during the early sixteenth century, its early development being closely bound up with the evolution of the madrigal as a musical type. As a poetic form, the new madrigal consisted of a single, freely constructed stanza of mixed *endecasillabi* and *settenari* with no fixed number of lines, but usually fewer than the fourteen of the sonnet. Unlike the sonnet, the madrigal in its earliest stages was used only for amorous subjects; it was only during the seventeenth century that it aspired to the philosophical, religious, and moral subjects that had originally been the province of the sonnet.

In appearance the new madrigal resembled a single *canzone* stanza and was, in fact, at first called *canzone* or *canzonetta*[20] though it soon acquired the name *madrigale,* the etymology of which has been the subject of much inconclusive discussion.[21] Some of the earliest of the new madrigals were written by Pietro Bembo himself and published in his series of dialogues on love, *Gli Asolani* (1505).[22] Einstein, however, pointed to Luigi Cassola as the first important poet of the madrigal's early literature, and he printed this example of Cassola's work:[23]

> Per far il mondo pien di meraviglia
> Quel buon fabro del cielo
> Vi fè si bella sotto un mortal velo,
> Che nessuna altra in terra vi sommiglia.
> O bellezze divine, o viso santo,
> O sacri, et bei costumi,
> Che fate al secol nostro haver cotanto:
> Felice è ben quel pianto,
> Ch'esce per voi da rugiadosi lumi:
> Felice chi vi mira:
> Felice l'alma che per voi sospira.

To make the world full of wonder, that good smith of the heavens made you thus beautiful under a mortal veil that no-one else on Earth resembles you. O, those divine beauties, that holy face, O, those sacred and fine manners that you bestow abundantly on our century: happy indeed are those tears that pour forth for you from dewy eyes: happy is he who gazes on you: happy the soul that sighs for you.

The subject matter and platonic tone of the madrigal are conventionally Petrarchan and the last line is, indeed, a quotation from Petrarch's *canzone* "Perchè la vita è breve" (line 67), but the text also contains the exclamations and elements of hyperbole that were to become the commonplace of later madrigal verse and the delight of composers.

The *versi parisillabi,* the lines of four, six, eight, and ten syllables, which were rejected by Dante as too "rude" for the noble *canzone,* differ from lines like the *endecasillabo* and *settenario* in lacking their fluid mobility of accent. And though some of the *parisillabi* exist in more than one rhythmic form, it is very unusual to find these combined in a single strophe. Poems employing *versi parisillabi,* then, tend to have fixed accents and a regular rhythm. This characteristic renders them particularly suitable for dance songs. During the late fifteenth century, *ballate* composed of regular eight-syllable lines—a type also called *frottola-barzelletta* or simply *canzone a ballo*—were written for the Florentine carnival by, among others, Lorenzo de' Medici. The form consists of a *ripresa* of four lines, rhymed xyyx or xyxy, and stanzas whose structure of two *piedi* and two *volte* resembles that of the early *canzone* stanza. At the end of each stanza of the *ballata,* however, the last line or last two lines of the *ripresa* are repeated. We thus have a strophic form with refrain whose structure and use of eight-syllable lines anticipates a popular aria type of the seventeenth century. Lorenzo de' Medici's *Trionfo di Bacco ed Arianna* is one of the most famous of these dance songs for the Florentine carnival. Its *ripresa* demonstrates quite clearly the regular rhythm produced by *versi parisillabi:*

> Quant'è bella giovinezza
> Che si fugge tuttavia.
> Chi vuol esser lieto sia;
> Di doman non c'è certezza.

> How fine is youth, but how fleeting. He who wishes to be happy should be, for tomorrow is uncertain.

During the mid-sixteenth century, *versi parisillabi* seem only to have been employed for lighter musical verse, for *frottole,*[24] and for the *canzone villanesca* or *villanella,* these latter terms denoting not a fixed poetic type (though such poems were often strophic), but one supposedly of rustic origin. Einstein quotes a number of texts of this kind that employ *versi parisillabi*[25] and others that employ the less usual of the *versi imparisillabi.*[26] It was not until the end of the sixteenth century, however, that the *versi parisillabi* were again elevated to the status of art-poetry in the new *canzonetta melica* of Chiabrera.

The Poets and Poetry of the *Concertato* Duet

In their choice of texts, some early seventeenth-century composers do seem to have been fairly conservative in taste, and Florentine composers such as Marco da Gagliano display a distinct leaning toward fine literature. We should remember, though, that a number of favorite texts were simply handed on from one generation of madrigalists to the next. The light-hearted *ballata* "Io mi son giovinetta, e volontieri/m'allegro e canto en la stagion novella," with which Boccaccio concluded the ninth day of the *Decamerone,* is a case in point. It was first set as a madrigal as early as 1546, by Domenico Ferabosco.[27] A corrupt version, beginning "Io mi son giovinetta,/E rido e canto la stagion novella," was still current in the early seventeenth century. Monteverdi set it as a five-part madrigal (*Quarto Libro de Madrigali,* 1603) and the otherwise unknown composer who styled himself Accademico Bizzarro Capriccioso set it as a madrigalian duet (1621).

Another instance is furnished by Sannazzaro's "La pastorella mia,"a text taken from the first eclogue of *Arcadia.* Cast in *terza rima* and given a deliberately "rustic" veneer by the use of *versi sdruccioli,* this passage introduces the figure of the unyielding shepherdess, unmoved by the complaints of her lover, a figure much beloved of later madrigalists and writers of strophic verse. The text was set as a polyphonic madrigal by, among others, Marenzio (*Terzo Libro de Madrigali a Cinque Voci,* 1582) and Giovanelli (*Gli Sdruccioli... Libro Secondo,* 1589)[28] and, in the seventeenth century, as a strophic duet, by two Florentine composers, Antonio Brunelli (1613) and Raffaello Rontani (1614). This is the section of the eclogue set by Rontani; Brunelli set two further *terzine.*

> La pastorella mia spietata e rigida,
>   Che notte e giorno al mio soccorso chiamola,
>   E sta superba e più che ghiaccio frigida.
> Ben sanno questi boschi quanto io amola;
>   Sannolo fiumi, monti, fieri et omini,
>   C'ognor piangendo e sospirando bramola.
> Sallo, quante fiate il dì la nomini,
>   Il gregge mio, che già a tutt'ore ascoltami,
>   O ch'egli in selva pasca o in mandra romini.

My shepherdess, pitiless and unbending, to whom I call for aid both night and day, remains proud and colder than ice. Well do these woods know how much I love her; well do rivers, hills, wild beasts and men know that, weeping and sighing each hour I long for her. My sheep know how many times each day I name her, for whether browsing in the woods or ruminating in the sheepfold they hear me constantly.

Petrarch

Petrarch's poetry, which was already declining in popularity during the late sixteenth century, enjoyed a short-lived revival in the hands of the monodists. For the composers of duets, however, it was a specialized taste. Of the amatory sonnets only two—"Ite, caldi sospiri" and "Vago augelletto" (S. Rossi, 1628) were set as duets. The more melancholy and spiritual aspect of Petrarch's work attracted two Florentine composers, Marco da Gagliano and Severo Bonini, though in Bonini's case this was in a wholly reactionary spirit. When he published his second book of madrigals in the new Florentine manner (1609), Bonini stated in his dedication that he had chosen to set serious poetry as an antidote to the lascivious madrigals and canzonettas currently being sung by young people. Thus, it was from among Petrarch's spiritual sonnets that he chose the text of his duet "I' vo piangendo i miei passati tempi."[29]

Sannazzaro

Sannazzaro fared rather better. Although the majority of early seventeenth-century composers looked rather to Guarini and Marino for the texts of their pastoral duets, the eclogues of *Arcadia* did provide Teofilo Gargari, a contralto singer in the Papal choir,[30] with the texts of two pairs of madrigals, "Si m'è dolce il tormento"/"Così vuol mia ventura" and "Per pianto la mia carne"/ "Hor pensate al mio mal" which were published, respectively, in the anthologies issued in 1621 and 1622 by Fabio Costantini.[31] These were drawn from the second eclogue, a source which had also provided Caccini with one of the first texts which he set as a monody—"Itene all'ombra degli ameni faggi" (music lost).[32] To a later eclogue, the twelfth, belongs the rather dubious distinction of having furnished Bartolomeo Barbarino with the text of the first duet with independent *basso continuo* (c. 1605)—"I tuoi capelli, O Filli, in una cistula."

Sannazzaro's *Canzoniere,* published in 1530, furnished composers with fewer texts. Two of its sonnets were, however, remembered by the duet composers of the early seventeenth century. The first of these, "Interdette speranze e van desir" (Pasta, 1626), was also the forerunner of Guarini's "Interrotte speranze, eterna fede," on which Monteverdi (1619) bestowed some of his finest music. The second, "Liete, verdi, fiorite e fresche valli" (Girolamo Ferrari in Ghizzolo, 1623), in which the poet calls on valleys, woods, and birds to hear his complaint, may have suggested to another Neapolitan poet, Luigi Tansillo (1510-1568), the theme of this darker-hued sonnet:

> Valli nemiche al sol, superbe rupi
> Che minacciate il ciel; profonde grotte,
> Onde non parton mai silenzio e notte;
> Sepolcri aperti, pozzi orrendi e cupi;
>
> Precipitati sassi, alti dirupi,
> Ossa insepolte, erbose mura e rotte,
> D'uomini albergo, ed ora a tal condotte,
> Che temen d'ir fra voi serpenti e lupi;
>
> Erme campagne, abbandonati lidi,
> Ove mai voce d'uom l'aria non fiede:

Ombra son io dannata a pianto eterno,

Ch'a pianger vengo la mia morta fede;
E spero, al suon de' disperati stridi,
Se non si piega il ciel, mover l'inferno.

Valleys, enemies of the sun, proud rocks that threaten the sky; deep caves, forever enveloped in night and silence; open graves, horrid deep wells; fallen rocks, towering crags, unburied bones, broken, overgrown walls, once the abode of men and now so desolate that even snakes and wolves fear to roam among you; lonely fields, deserted shores where no human voice disturbs the air: a shadow am I, condemned to eternal tears, for I come to lament my dead faith: and I hope that if Heaven will not yield to the sound of my desperate cries, then Hell will be moved by them.

An altered version of this sonnet, "Valli profonde," was set as a monody by Marco da Gagliano (1615). Seizing on the Gothic horror of the original poem, Martino Pesenti in 1628 produced a setting for two basses and continuo, painting the scene of towering rocks with virtuoso arpeggio figuration. On the whole, though, this darker aspect of nature attracted composers far less than the lighter and more erotic motives of *Arcadia*.

Ariosto and Tasso

The earliest texts which were set in any significant numbers by the composers of duets were stanzas from the epic poems of Ariosto and Tasso. Only one of them, however, formed the basis of a madrigalian setting (by Usper, 1623); the remainder were set either as free strophic variations or as variations over stylized basses.

From *Gerusalemme liberata* Eleuterio Guazzi (1622) elected to set a description of one of Armida's nymphs, "Qual matutina stella esce dall'onde" (XV. 60) and Sigismondo d'India (1615) this slightly sinister picture of the sorceress Armida herself:

Fa nove crespe l'aura al crin disciolto,
Che natura per se rincrespa in onde;
Stassi l'avaro sguardo in se raccolto,
E i tesori d'amore e i suoi nasconde.
Dolce color di rose in quel bel volto
Fra l'avorio si sparge e si confonde,
Ma ne la bocca, onde esce aura amorosa,
Sola rosseggia e semplice la rosa.

The gamesome wind among her tresses plays, And curleth up those growing riches short; Her spareful eye to spread his beams denays, But keeps his shot where Cupid keeps his fort; The rose and lily on her cheek assay To paint true fairness out in bravest sort. Her lips, where blooms nought but the single rose, Still blush, for still they kiss while still they close.[33]

Otherwise, the *Gerusalemme* seems to have been the sole preserve of one composer, the Roman-born Antonio Cifra. In the volumes of music that he published between 1613 and 1615, Cifra included some ten settings of stanzas from Tasso's epic, beginning with the famous "Vezzosi augelli" and ending with the stanza just quoted. He ranged widely through the epic. Only one of his books, however, *Li Diversi Scherzi... Libro Secondo* (1613), contains settings of three consecutive stanzas—XVI. 59 to 61—and these are set separately in the order 59-61-60, even though the first stanza requires the second to complete its sense.[34]

The 1615 book seems to have been a turning point for Cifra. Having, from his point of view, exhausted the possibilities of the *Gerusalemme* he now turned back to Ariosto's *Orlando furioso* and, between 1615 and 1619, set six of the favorite stanzas from the older work, including "Ruggier, qual sempre fui."[35] In its variant form, "Fedel qual sempre fui," this stanza was also set as a duet by Vitali (1618) and Usper (1623); and Vitali published, in 1618, a setting of a stanza ignored by Cifra—"Se 'l sol si scosta" (XVI. 38).[36]

Tasso, Guarini, and Marino

Though his *Gerusalemme liberata* had proved a popular source of madrigal texts, as a writer of madrigals proper, Tasso enjoyed only a rather limited, localized popularity even among the composers of the sixteenth century; and only four of his many madrigals were chosen for setting as duets during the early seventeenth. These were:

"Gelo ha madonna il seno"	(Anerio, 1611)
"Non è questa la mano"	(Capece, 1625)
"Amatemi, ben mio"	(Galeazzo Sabbatini, 1625)
"Bella e vaga brunetta"	(Vignali, 1640)

The verse of the poet's charming pastoral play *Aminta* (first performed 1573), which had provided a few late sixteenth-century composers with madrigal texts, did not interest the composers of duets at all.

The poetry of the early seventeenth-century madrigalian duet was, in fact, dominated by two figures, Giovanni Battista Guarini (1538-1612) and the virtuoso Neapolitan poet Giambattista Marino (1569-1625).[37] Both worked extensively in the form of the madrigal, though they also produced sonnets and longer literary works from which composers selected the more musicable passages for setting. And both seem to have exercised considerable influence over the lesser, anonymous writers of madrigal verse whose poetry was set during the early seventeenth century.

Like Tasso, Guarini was mainly resident at the Este court in Ferrara where he was, for a time, secretary to Duke Alfonso II. His pastoral play *Il pastor fido,* written between 1580 and 1589 in emulation of Tasso's *Aminta,* is now considered a lesser work than its predecessor, though it enjoyed greater contemporary success both in Italy and elsewhere. Composers certainly found the studied artificiality of its verse amenable to musical setting and quarried it endlessly for the texts not only of madrigalian duets, but also of monodies and polyphonic madrigals.

The composers of duets chose a variety of passages from the play, including Amaryllis' praise of the woods as places of peace and tranquillity— "Care selve beate" (Act II. 5; Mutis, 1613)—and Dorinda's sigh of regret as her love is ignored by Silvio—"O misera Dorinda" (II. 2; Turini, 1621; Rigatti, 1636). The passages which interested them most, however, were those in which Mirtillo, the "faithful shepherd" of the title, expressed his love for the shepherdess Amaryllis; and they chose, for preference, those passages which represent Amaryllis as the unobtainable or obdurate object of Mirtillo's desires. The most famous of these passages, a complaint beginning "Cruda Amarilli, che col nome ancora d'amar" (I. 2), had been set as a polyphonic madrigal long before it appeared in two-part settings by Visconti (1616) and Alessandro Costantini (in F. Costantini, ed., 1622). From the same scene came another complaint, "Ma poi ch'era ne' fatti ch'io dovessi" (Usper, 1623). Elsewhere, we find Mirtillo declaring his love *to* Amaryllis—"Ch'io t'ami" (III. 3; A. Costantini, loc. cit.)—invoking the spirits of the underworld to hear his lament—"Udite, lagrimosi spirti d'Averno" (III. 6; Grandi, 1615)[38]—and finally laying down his life to save his shepherdess—"Hor consolato, io moro" (V. 3; Ghizzolo, 1609).

The theme of the distant, unobtainable lady, familiar from Petrarch's amatory sonnets, formed the subject of many of Guarini's madrigals. Guarini was a madrigal writer *par excellence.* The first volume of his *Rime,* published at Venice in 1598, contains 151 madrigals as against 106 sonnets and a handful of *ottavas.* Only two of his sonnets, "Interrotte speranze, eterna fede" (Monteverdi, 1619) and "Vedovo fosco albergo" (Priuli, 1622), and one of his ottavas, "Così m'ha fatto Amor" (Cifra, 1615; Rontani, 1619), seem to have been set as duets, and even here the composers chose those works which most resembled the madrigals in subject matter and language.

Some fifty-three of Guarini's madrigals were set as duets during the early seventeenth century, many of them more than once. Even as late as 1640 two young composers, Pietro Andrea Ziani and Francesco Vignali, included settings of the poet's work in the books that they published in that year.

A brief glance at the texts of Guarini's madrigals immediately suggests the reason for their popularity in the period of declamatory song and the *seconda prattica.* They express the passions both of fulfilled and of thwarted love; they contain numerous exclamations like "Ahi" and "Ohimè";[39] the lovers who speak through them "burn," "sing," "languish,"[40] suffer "martyrdoms,"[41] and "die"; love and the loved one are usually "cruel."[42] Artificial and insincere though they may be, the madrigals seem to express the depths of human emotion and are full of imagery which could be translated into music through rhetorical and harmonic gestures rather than linear word-painting.

It has been said of Guarini that he never invented a new theme, only reworked old ones. We can see this process in a madrigal of his which was set as a duet by Ghizzolo (1609) and Anerio (1611). In this text Guarini serenaded his lady by taking up the two lines which formed the final "point" of the madrigal "Per far il mondo pien di meraviglia" by the earlier sixteenth-century madrigalist Luigi Cassola of Piacenza.[43] A comparison of the texts demonstrates some of the essential differences between early and late sixteenth-century madrigal verse. Guarini's madrigal is more concentrated than Cassola's and his lady is addressed in more sensual terms; the lines with which Cassola concluded his text are here used as the starting-point for a cumulative effect released in the fourth line and then capped by the "point":

> Felice chi vi mira,
> Ma più felice chi per voi sospira:
> Felicissimo poi
> Chi sospirando fa sospirar voi.
> Ben' hebb'amica stella
> Chi per Donna sì bella
> Può far contento in un l'occhio e 'l desio.
> E sicuro può dir, quel cor è mio.

Happy is he who gazes on you, but happier still is he who sighs for you: most happy, then, is he who, sighing, can make you sigh. His star was fortunate who, through so beautiful a Lady, can satisfy at once his eye and his desire and can say with certainty, "that heart is mine."

Another aspect of Guarini's verse, the exploitation of erotic ambiguity, is illustrated by this madrigal, set as a duet by Radesca (between 1606 and 1610) and Frescobaldi (in F. Costantini, ed., 1622):

> Era l'anima mia
> Già presso a l'ultim'hore,
> E languia come langue alma che more;
> Quand'anima più bella, e più gradita
> Volse lo sguardo in sì pietoso giro,
> Che mi ritenne in vita.
> Parean dir que' bei lumi,
> Deh, perchè ti consumi?
> Non m'è sì caro il cor ond'io respiro,
> Come sei tu, cor mio.
> Se mori, oimè, non mori tu, mor'io.

My spirit was already close to its last hour and languished as a soul which dies languishes; when a most beautiful and welcome spirit turned to me so piteous a glance that she kept me alive. Those beautiful lights seemed to say, "Ah, why do you consume yourself? The heart whence I breathe is not so dear to me as you are, my heart. If you die, alas, it is not you who die, but I."

Both poems illustrate Guarini's concentration on the central theme of the madrigal, his avoidance of contrasting or conflicting images, and the sharp focus provided by the "point" of the madrigal.

But there was, too, a lighter side to the poet's nature, exemplified in a long madrigal entitled *Mascherata di Contadine,* which was set by Anerio (*Diporti,* 1617), Biagio Marini (1635), and Rigatti (1636). I quote here only the opening lines:

Le più belle zitelle del contado
Noi siam, che i rozzi amori
Fuggiamo di Bifolchi, e di Pastori.
Qui ne treccia s'innesta, o crin si tinge,
Ne guancia si dipinge.
L'oro, i gigli, e le rose
L'alma natura di sua man vi pose.

The most beautiful maidens of the country are we, who fly from the rude embraces of Rustics and Shepherds. Here we neither tie up our tresses, nor dye our hair, nor paint our cheeks. The gold, lilies and roses were put there by the animating hand of nature.

When they wished to explore lighter, more playful, even more pictorial motives, however, the composers of the early seventeenth century generally turned away from Guarini to the work of Giambattista Marino and his imitators. Compare, for example, the intense, declamatory opening of Grandi's setting of Guarini's "O com'è gran martire"[44] with his light, tuneful approach to the setting of Marino's "Rose, rose beate."[45] Moreover, unlike Guarini, whose work belonged mainly to the late sixteenth century, Marino was a contemporary of many of the composers who wrote *concertato* duets and his work was thus the first choice for those composers who wished to appear up to date. He was, furthermore, the most admired and widely imitated poet of the first third of the seventeenth century. Fêted by the academies, knighted by Duke Carlo Emanuele of Savoy, he enjoyed a European reputation. The course of his brilliant career took him from Naples to Rome (1600-1606), to Ravenna (1606-1608), to the courts of Savoy (1608-1615) and France (1615-1623), and finally in triumph back to Italy, where "the Italian literary world, drunk with adulation, bestowed on him the kind of glory many Renaissance poets anticipated but few actually enjoyed."[46] His career was not, however, without its darker side, nor did he lack detractors. He was imprisoned three times; the threat of obscenity charges from the Inquisition hung constantly over his head; and he was described as "heretic, hermaphrodite, sodomist and pornographer" by the poet Gaspare Murtola, whom he displaced as court poet at Turin.[47]

Marino's reputation as a poet was established by about 1590 and was confirmed by the publication of the first two parts of his *Rime* (later called *La Lira*)[48] in 1602, the year which also saw the publication of Caccini's *Le Nuove Musiche*. The earliest two-part settings of his poems appeared four years later in Brunetti's *Euterpe*. These were followed, particularly during the second and third decades of the century, by numerous other settings of madrigals, and rather fewer settings of sonnets and excerpts from Marino's longer poems. Many composers—Grandi, Turini, Monteverdi, and Rovetta among them—struck a balance, in their choice of texts, between Marino and Guarini, but all the duets in Marc'Antonio Negri's *Affeti Amorosi... Libro Secondo* (1611) and Giovanni Valentini's *Musiche di Camera, Libro Quarto* (1621) and most of those in Ceresini's *Madrigali concertati* (1627) are settings of texts by Marino.

The earliest of Marino's poems to attract general notice, and the one that formed the springboard for his subsequent literary career, was a *canzone* entitled *Baci*, which was written in the period before 1590. It was set to music by Tomaso Pecci at some time before 1601, when Marino wrote a sonnet, "Quelle de' miei piacer," in thanks to the composer. In 1630, Delipari took the title of the *canzone* for that of his madrigal book *I Baci* and included as its first item a two-part setting of the first three stanzas of Marino's poem.

The *Canzone dei Baci*, as it is usually called, introduced a motive that was to become one of the hallmarks of Marinist poetry—the kiss. The motive itself was not original. It was drawn from the work of Ovid, and Guarini had employed it in madrigals like "Baciai, ma chi mi valse" (Radesca, 1605; Ziani, 1640) and "Un bacio solo a tante pene" (Radesca, between 1606 and 1610; Accademico, 1620; Locatello, 1628). It was, however, one which Marino made very much his own and one through which the platonic love of the Petrarchan amatory lyric was replaced by physical love.

The kiss motive lent a more explicit sensuality to the veiled eroticism that we find in some of Guarini's poetry, though it was itself sometimes used as a symbol for sexual consummation. In the following madrigal, set as a duet by Monteverdi (1619) and Colombi (1621), the motive is given a pastoral setting and mixed with the erotic life-death imagery much loved by Guarini:

> Perchè fuggi tra salci,
> Ritrosetta ma bella,
> O cruda de le crude pastorella?
> Perchè un bacio ti tolsi?
> Miser più che felice,
> Corsi per sugger vita, e morte colsi.
> Quel bacio che m'ha morto,
> Tra le rose d'amor pungente spina,
> Fu più vendetta tua che mia rapina.

Why are you fleeing midst the willows, reluctant but beautiful, O most cruel of the cruel, shepherdess? Because I wrenched a kiss from you? Wretched more than happy, I gave chase to sip life, but I culled death. That kiss which gave me death, among the roses of love a stinging thorn, was more revenge for you than theft for me.[49]

The kiss motive appeared in many other variations. In "Tornate, O cari baci" (Monteverdi, 1619; Accademico, 1621; Ceresini, 1627), kisses are life-giving; in "Al desio troppo ingordo" (Ceresini, 1627), they are biting; in "Vorrei baciarti, O Filli" (Monteverdi, 1619); Ceresini, 1627), the lover is uncertain whether to kiss his beloved's eyes or mouth. In "Tempesta di dolcezza" (M.A. Negri, 1611), kisses provided Marino with an opportunity to produce a characteristically witty conceit—a "storm of sweetness" is brought about by a "flood of kisses"—and the clever word-play in "Fer*i*tevi fer*ite*, *V*iperette mordaci" (Accademico, 1620; Pasquali, 1627; Ceresini, 1627) introduces as subjects the lips and tongue which offer kisses.

In "Feritevi ferite," the kiss motive is accompanied by military metaphors of a kind which Marino first introduced in the second and third stanzas of the *Canzone dei Baci.* Through this convention love becomes a war, the lips and mouth warriors. This type of imagery, which appealed to Monteverdi in his later years, stemmed, like the kiss motive itself, from Ovid. Its source can be traced through Rinuccini's "Ogni amante è guerrier," a verse translation from Ovid's *Amores*, part of which was set for two and three voices by Monteverdi and published in his 1638 book.

One final madrigalian context in which the kiss motive appears should be mentioned. This is the *lettera amorosa*, or love letter. Marino's own work in this genre, as seen in the following example, set as a duet by Radesca (1610), seems to have spawned a number of anonymous imitations, including one, "Se i languidi miei sguardi," set as a monody by Monteverdi (1619). Girolamo Preti's "Vanne, O carta amorosa," set as a duet by Valentini (1622),[50] and (to a lesser extent) the sonnet "Nude figlie del cor," set by Crivelli (1626),[51] are in similar vein.

Foglio, de' miei pensieri
Secretario fedel, tu n'andrai dove
T'aprirà quella man, che m'apre il petto.
O felice, o beato,
Se mai per grazie nove
In quel candido seno avrai ricetto.
Ma più, quando avrai poi,
S'avien ch'a te per sciorre i nodi tuoi
La bocca s'avicini,
Mille baci di perle e di rubini.

Letter, faithful secretary of my thoughts, you will go there where the hand that opens my heart will open you. Oh happy, oh blessed, if by an extraordinary grace you should be received within that snowy breast. But how much more you will have, if it happens that to loosen your knots she should bring her mouth close to you, in a thousand kisses of pearls and rubies.[52]

The poems in which Marino speaks of kisses, though numerous, do not by any means represent the entire repertory of themes in *La Lira,* nor were they the only ones to be set as duets. Marino was also the author of the graceful sonnet "Su la sponda del Tebro" (Rontani, 1614), a charming pastoral tribute to a Roman lady,[53] and he was equally capable of writing passionate madrigals in the manner of Guarini, as may be seen in "Ch'io mora, ohimè" (Torre, 1622; Locatello, 1628; Vignali, 1640) and "Se la doglia e 'l martire" (A. Costantini, in F. Costantini, ed., 1621). His delicate descriptive poetry, represented by "O chiome errante" (Grandi, 1615; Giovanni Ferrari, 1628) and "Rose, rose beate" (Grandi, 1622),[54] was also popular. And this little pastoral madrigal was set as a duet no fewer than six times:

Riede la Primavera,
Torna la bella Clori:
Odi la rondinella,
Mira l'erbette e i fiori.
Ma tu Clori più bella
Ne la stagion novella,
Serbi l'antico verno.
Deh, s'hai pur cinto il cor di ghiaccio eterno,
Perchè, ninfa crudel quanto gentile,
Porti ne gli occhi il Sol, nel volto Aprile?

Spring returns, and with it the beautiful Chloris: hear the swallow, see the grass and flowers. But you, Chloris, most beautiful, preserve old winter in the new season. Ah, if your heart is still girded in eternal ice, why, nymph as cruel as kind, do you bring the Sun in your eyes and April in your face?

Taken as a whole, those of Marino's madrigals, sonnets and *canzoni* which were set as duets are less passionate, more whimsical and artfully constructed than those of Guarini. They show a greater concern, too, for witty conceits and clever word-play; a concern which occasionally detracts from the force of the concluding lines. They are, in short, more, not less literary than Guarini's verses.

The years which he spent in Paris enabled Marino to bring to fruition a number of major literary projects, some of which he had been working on for many years. Among these were two which attracted the attention of musicians—*La Sampogna* and the *Adone.*

La Sampogna (published 1620) is a collection of eight mythological and four pastoral idylls, long poems in a variety of poetic meters and dealing with subjects drawn from classical antiquity and more recent traditions. In two of the pastoral idylls written in dialogue form, *La Bruna Pastorella* and *La Ninfa Avara,* Marino himself appears in the guise of the shepherd Filenus, just as Sannazzaro had figured in the *Arcadia.* Three of the mythological idylls,

Dafne, Orfeo, and *Arianna,* treated subjects that had already formed the basis of operatic libretti. The last of them may, indeed, have been suggested by the Mantuan performance of Monteverdi's opera which Marino attended in the retinue of the Duke of Savoy.[55] Marino himself was an ardent lover of music, as the quotation at the head of this chapter amply demonstrates; and his *Arianna* contains a fine lament which was set as a monody by Possenti in his *Canora Sampogna* of 1623.[56] Although the lament was never set as a duet, the devoted Marinist composer Valentini was quick to seize on two other lyrical passages from *Arianna,* "Silenzio, O Fauni" (a section of the text in regular five-syllable lines) and the song of the Bacchantes, "Beviam tutti, io beo, tu bei," which he published in his 1621 and 1622 books respectively. The only other passage from the idylls of *La Sampogna* to be set as a duet during the first forty years of the seventeenth century was "Baccia, Lidio gentile" (Rigatti, 1636),[57] taken from the pastoral dialogue *La Bruna Pastorella.*

The composition of the *Adone* had occupied Marino for more than twenty-five years before its publication in 1623. In the event, this was to be his only contribution to the genre of epic poetry and his major work, though he had earlier contemplated a poem, *La Gerusalemme distrutta,* in imitation of Tasso; and the *Adone* was the poem which most exercised the eighteenth- and nineteenth-century opponents of *secentismo.* Its subject matter—the love of Venus and Adonis—was, of course, erotic rather than heroic and Marino filled out the original myth to a total of twenty cantos by introducing all manner of episodic material including, in the seventh canto, passages in praise of poetry and music.

In view of its contemporary fame it is, perhaps, surprising that so few composers chose to set ottavas from the *Adone.* Sigismondo d'India, who must have known Marino well during his years at Turin, seems to have had access to a manuscript of part of the poem during the years of its composition. He set a group of eight ottavas, beginning "Ardo, lassa, o non ardo?", from the twelfth canto as a set of strophic variations for two voices and published it in his 1615 book.

Some composers, particularly those working in the Papal States, may have been dissuaded from setting the poem by the fact that it was placed on the *Index Librorum Prohibitorum* in 1625. Settings can, however, be found after this date. Gregori (1635) and Rigatti (1636) included *Romanesca* settings in their books, and Antonio Marastone, in his *Madrigali concertati* of 1628, included madrigalian settings of eight stanzas from the *Adone,* including two in praise of the rose that are among the finest in the poem. Here is the second of them (III. 157), which recalls Tasso's descriptive gift:

Quasi in bel trono imperatrice altera
Siedi colà su la nativa sponda.

> Turba d'aure vezzosa e lusinghiera
> Ti corteggia d'intorn e ti seconda;
> E di guardie pungenti armata schiera
> Ti difende per tutto e ti circonda.
> E tu fastosa del tuo regio vanto
> Porti d'or la corona e d'ostro il manto.

Like a lofty empress on a beautiful throne, you sit there on your native shore. A throng of charming and enticing breezes courts you from every side and follows you; and an armed band of sharp guards everywhere circles and defends you. And you, magnificent in your royal splendour, wear a crown of gold and a mantle of purple.[58]

Strophic Verse

The work of the poets thus far discussed accounts for approximately one half of the madrigal texts and a substantial number of the sonnets and ottavas set as duets during the first forty years of the seventeenth century. The themes and motives employed by Guarini and Marino in particular also permeate much of the (as yet) anonymous madrigal verse of the period.

When we turn to the lighter forms of the duet, the strophic canzonetta and aria, however, we find that only a small proportion of the texts set were written by identifiable literary figures and these mainly during the period up to 1625. In dealing with the lighter forms we are more clearly in the realms of *poesia per musica,* of purely functional and frankly popular texts descended from the frottolas and *canzoni villanesche* of the sixteenth century.

The strophic texts set as duets are often undistinguished as poetry, even silly, and they were treated with considerable licence by the composers, who felt free to set as many or as few stanzas as they pleased. Thus, while Alessandro Costantini (in F. Costantini, ed., 1621) set five stanzas of the anonymous canzonetta "Deh scoprite, colorite," Rontani (1618) set only three; and there are many other examples of this practice. At the same time, however, strophic texts were of seminal importance to the development of early seventeenth-century music since they allowed composers freedom to experiment with new formal designs and textural possibilities: with refrain and *da capo* structures, ostinato basses and alternations of solo and duet writing.

The anonymous writers of strophic texts explored a fairly limited repertoire of themes derived mainly from those of contemporary madrigal verse. The maritime imagery of "Spiega, spiega la vela Nocchiero," set by Falconieri (1616) and Kapsberger (*Terzo,* 1619), is a rare exception to the rule. Occasionally, the poets remembered the rustic origins of the *villanella,* as in "Dalla villa, e dal contado" (Anerio, 1619), or clothed their verses in a delightfully fresh pastoral garb, as in "Fortunata pastorella"[59] and "Al fonte, al prato."[60] For the most part, however, they were content to take over the commonplaces of the madrigal—the lover's complaint, for example, or his praise of the lady's appearance—and to produce a seemingly endless series of variations upon them.

A few examples will suffice to show the general level of achievement in these anonymous verses. In the first, set by Ghizzolo (1610), the poet apostrophises his lady in the conventional pastoral manner by addressing her as the shepherdess Chloris:[61]

O dolce mia Clori,
O Clori mia bella,
O chiara mia stella,
Speranza de' cori;
Tu l'alma ristori,
La vita mi dai.
Io solo mi straccio,
Mi struggo, e mi sfaccio,
O Clori mia bella,
O Clori mia bella.

Oh, my sweet Chloris, my beautiful Chloris, my bright star, the hope of hearts; you refresh my soul, you give me life. Alone, I destroy myself, I fret and pine away, oh my beautiful Chloris, my beautiful Chloris.

While the poet of this piece of doggerel, set by Giovanni Battista da Gagliano (1623), managed to mention two shepherdesses in the same stanza:

Se tu sei bella
Più d'Amarillide,
Non sia rubella
D'Amor mia Fillide.
Pietad'ei brama
Ama chi t'ama.

If you are fairer than Amaryllis, do not rebel against Cupid, my Phyllis. He desires pity, love him who loves you.[62]

Fortunately, however, not all pastoral verse decends to this level. On a more original note, the poet of Sances' "Mi fai peccato" (1633) addressed a few words of worldly wisdom to a languishing shepherd:

Mi fai peccato, o pastorel,
Vederti consumar
Per quella ria crudel.
Deh, lascia il lagrimar
Che se sapessi tu quel che so io,
Daresti all'amor suo l'ultimo adio.

I am filled with pity, oh shepherd, to see you consume yourself for that cruel, wicked woman. Ah, leave your crying, for if you knew what I know, you would bid love a last farewell.

The poet of this text worked into his verse just the sort of colorful words that Bernardo Tasso had advocated for musical poetry almost a hundred years earlier; the tears, sighs, and torment form the burden of many a canzonetta. Visconti's "Lacrime, perchè vi versate" is a good example.[63]

The theme of the anguished lover crying out for release is familiar from Guarini's madrigals. It found a paler reflection in the canzonetta "Io mi sento morire," set by Radesca (1605) and Cagnazzi (1608). When the poets turned to considering the features of the beloved's face, however, some of them seem to have shared Marino's attitudes. Thus, we find a preference for golden hair, not only in the well-known "Chiome d'oro" (Monteverdi, 1619), but also in a text like "O vezzosetta dalla chioma d'oro" set three years earlier by Falconieri. Marinesque, too, are the eyes whose darts pierce the lover's heart, as found in the texts "Quando vuol sentir mia voce" (Cecchino, 1616) and "O stelle omicide" (Possenti, 1623). As to the lips and mouth, the anonymous poet of Sigismondo d'India's "Voi, baciatrici"[64] provided a catalogue of their attributes—"mouths biting, challenging, piercing, wounding."

In this text we return to the familiar kiss motive of Marino's madrigals, which had entered the world of the canzonetta as early as 1609 in Melli's "Bocca amorosa". In another text from d'India's 1615 book, "Alla guerra d'amore", we find the associated image of the war of love. Both motives are united in this canzonetta set by Cecchino (1616):

> Baci, parto de l'alma,
> Bel legame de' cori,
> Dolce aura a dolci ardori,
> Cibo al desio vivace,
> Ne le guerre d'amor nunzi di pace.

> Kisses, the fruit of the soul, beautiful binders of hearts, sweet breezes to fan sweet ardors, food to lively desires, the messengers of peace in the wars of love.

Although strophic texts were rarely original in content, they inhabited, in one respect, a world quite different from that of the more sophisticated madrigal, a world in which ideas were less important than attractive, dance-like rhythmic patterns. A text like "O dolce mia Clori," for example, has regular stresses on the second and fifth syllables of each of its six-syllable lines; and "Se tu sei bella," with its varied *piano* and *sdrucciolo* line endings, alternates lines in which the stress falls on the second and fourth syllables with lines in which the stress falls on the first and fourth syllables. Regular poetic rhythms of this kind, which could be matched or contradicted by musical meters, fascinated composers of monody and duet alike during the early decades of the seventeenth century.

Chiabrera

For all their shortcomings as poetry, the strophic texts chosen by early seventeenth-century composers were undoubtedly more refined and graceful than their sixteenth-century counterparts, and they displayed a far greater range of rhythmic variety. That this was the case was due, in large measure, to the influence of the poet Gabriello Chiabrera (1552-1638) of Savona, near Genoa. Chiabrera's own canzonettas, which may themselves have been influenced by the French anacreontic lyrics of Ronsard and the Pléiade, first began to appear in print in 1579-80 when two of them, "O begli occhi, O pupillette" (later set as a duet by Biagio Marini, 1622) and "Quando l'alba in Oriente" (Rubini, 1610; Anerio, 1619; Priuli, 1625), were published anonymously at Venice.[65] Fuller collections, *Scherzi e canzonette morali* and *Maniere de' versi toscane,* were published in 1599.[66]

The first of these collections introduced a term—*scherzo*—that was soon to enjoy a vogue among composers who, like Monteverdi in 1607, frequently employed it to describe settings of strophic texts.[67] Chiabrera's own *scherzi,* however, were poems in a single stanza—madrigals, in fact. Three of them— "Con sorrisi cortesi" (Radesca, 1606; Peri, 1609), "Soave libertate" (Monteverdi, 1619), and "Messagier di speranza" (Salamone Rossi, 1628)—were set as madrigalian duets. The first two consist entirely of seven-syllable lines; the third also contains lines of eleven syllables.

The popularity among composers of Chiabrera's anacreontic canzonettas was, no doubt, stimulated by his close association with the founding fathers of the Florentine "new music." Caccini set to music his entertainment *Il rapimento di Cefalo* for the wedding celebrations of Henri IV of France and Maria de' Medici in 1600 and also included settings of his canzonettas in *Le Nuove Musiche.* In the preface to this latter volume he remarked that Chiabrera had supplied him with many canzonetta texts that were "very different from the rest, and provided ... great opportunity for variety."

The opportunities for variety of which Caccini spoke, and which appealed as much to the writers of duets as to the monodists, sprang from the wide range of metric schemes that Chiabrera employed in his canzonettas.[68] Two of these at least—the schemes 8:4:8:8:4:8 and 4:4:8:4:4:8—were derived directly from the work of Ronsard.[69] The first scheme may be illustrated by the text "Del mio Sol son ricciutegli," which was set as a duet by Radesca (between 1606 and 1610) and Cifra (1617). The diminutives with which it is filled, and which infect much of the lesser verse of the period, are virtually untranslatable. Their only function is a rhythmic one; and the stresses in this particular verse, on the third and seventh syllables, imply *hemiola* rhythm very strongly.

> Del mio Sol son ricciutegli
> I capegli
> Non biondetti, ma brunetti;
> Son due rose vermigliuzze
> Le gotuzze,
> Le due labbra rubinetti.

My beloved's hair is curly, not fair, but brown; her little cheeks are two vermilion roses, her lips are two little rubies.

The same scheme was used by Chiabrera for six further canzonettas that were set as duets. Among them was one of his most skilfully contrived, and popular verses—"Vagheggiando le bell'onde" (Calestani, 1617;[70] Vitali, 1620; Capece, 1625).

The only example of a poem employing the second scheme that I have found set as a duet is the drinking song "Damigella tutta bella" which is, perhaps, too well known to require quotation.[71] Saracini (1614) made a rather feeble setting of the first six stanzas of this delightful parody of madrigalian imagery. But Chiabrera also extended the basic scheme to include other line-lengths. Thus, in "Chi può mirarvi"[72] (Priuli, 1625) and "Un dì soletto" (Radesca, 1606), we find lines of five and seven syllables (5:5:7:5:5:7); and in "Apertamente, dicea la gente" (Radesca, 1605; Rubini, 1610; Anerio, 1619)[73] lines of five and eleven syllables (5:5:11 *tronco:* 5:5:11 *tronco*). The canzonetta "Girate occhi" (Notari, 1613), built on yet another scheme, employs lines of seven syllables only, but alternates one *verso piano* with two *versi sdruccioli:*

> Girate, occhi, girate
> A' miei, che tanto pregano
> Gli sguardi, che non piegano
> Giammai verso pietate;
> Che se da lor si tolgono,
> Occhi, a ragion si dolgono.

Turn, eyes, turn to mine which so implore your glances though they never show pity; for if your glances should be taken away, my eyes would have good reason to weep.

Chiabrera's innovations did not end here. He was one of the first Italian poets to make use of stanzas employing regular line-lengths of fewer than eleven syllables—five-syllable lines in "I bei legami" (Brunelli, 1613), for example, and eight-syllable lines in "Quando vuol sentir mia voce" (Rubini, 1610; Cecchino, 1616)—and he also made great play with *versi tronchi* of the kind which can be seen in "Apertamente."

The popularity of Chiabrera's own canzonettas began to wane during the early 1620s. The latest two-part settings of his verse are contained in the books which Priuli and Capece published in 1625. A residual influence can, however, be found in a canzonetta by the younger Genoese poet Anton Giulio Brignole Sale (1605-1665)—"Chi nel regno almo d'amore"—which employs a variation—8:8:4:8:4:8—of the first of the two basic Chiabreran rhythmic schemes outlined above. The composer Giovanni Felice Sances liked this text so much that he set it twice, first as a duet (1636)[74] and later as a monody in his *Capricci Poetici* of 1649. The lasting influence of Chiabrera's work is felt in later cantata texts in which passages of regular rhythm (arias) are contrasted with passages of *versi toscani* (recitatives).

Rinuccini

During the late sixteenth and early seventeenth centuries, Chiabrera's rhythmic structures can be detected in the work of his Florentine contemporary Ottavio Rinuccini (1562-1621), in the work of Isabella Andreini and Ansaldo Cebà, and in a number of verses penned by anonymous writers. His use of mixed eight- and four-syllable lines, for example, gave rise to a variant—8:4:8:4:8:4—which was employed in the anonymous canzonettas "La mia dolce pastorella" (Melli, 1609), "Vezzosetta pastorella" (Brunelli, 1614; Anon. in *I-Fn,* MS Magl. XIX. 25) and the rustic "Dalla villa e dal contado" (Anerio, 1619). And verses like "O luci belle" (Calestani, 1617) and "Non vi partite" (Frescobaldi, *Secondo,* 1630) follow the practice of employing regular short line-lengths.

Rinuccini, like Chiabrera, was one of the few poets working in the early seventeenth century who did not succumb to the rising tide of Marinism and he is, perhaps, best remembered for the gentle poetry of his pastoral operas *Dafne* and *Euridice.* Only three of his beautifully refined madrigals were set as duets, though one of them, "Intenerite voi, lacrime mie,"[75] was set no fewer than five times; and Monteverdi's setting of his Petrarchan sonnet "Zefiro torna" is one of the best known of all seventeenth-century duets.

Some ten of Rinuccini's canzonettas were set as duets between 1605 and 1623 by a small circle of composers, including Barbarino, Ghizzolo, Rontani, Albini and Kapsberger. Several of the texts—"Mille dolci parolette" (Ghizzolo, 1613) and "Sul mattin, quando colora" (Barbarino, 1616), for example— show quite clear evidence of Chiabrera's influence in their adoption of the rhythmic scheme 8:4:8:8:4:8. It would be an injustice, however, simply to view Rinuccini as a protegé of Chiabrera. His canzonettas, though they adopt Chiabreran devices, frequently inhabit a world far removed from the bouncing gaiety of the older poet's work. Texts like "Non havea Febo ancora" (Kapsberger, *Secondo,* 1619)[76] and "Alma mia, dove ten vai?"[77] (Marco da Gagliano, 1615) deal with the laments of the abandoned lover and the sorrows of parting. They are more tearful, more plaintive, even more erotic than any of the canzonettas of Chiabrera that were set as duets. Phrases like "guance smorte" (ashen cheeks), in the canzonetta "Tutte le viste, omai, son fatte accorte," were altogether too much for the Roman censor, who excised them from Rontani's setting (*Quarto*, 1620).

Operatic Libretti

With Rinuccini, we have returned to the cradle of the Florentine "new music" and the early operatic libretti form the last source of duet texts to be considered here. They were not, on the whole, a very fertile source, though Ghizzolo drew on the Chiabreran choruses of Rinuccini's two early libretti for the texts of his canzonettas "Bella ninfa fuggitiva" (*Dafne*, lines 398-403 and 416-21) and "Biondo arcier, che d'alto monte" (*Euridice*, lines 743-66),[78] both published in 1610. The Roman composer Borboni also employed part of the text of *Dafne* (lines 151-158) as the basis of a set of strophic variations, "Chi da lacci d'amor" (1618).

Rinuccini's libretto for Monteverdi's *Arianna*, which provided the monodists with one of their favorite lament texts, seems to have been ignored by the composers of duets. From Alessandro Striggio's *Orfeo*, however, an anonymous poet took the stanza "Ecco pur, ch'a voi ritorno" which begins act II and turned it into a strophic canzonetta by adding four stanzas of his own. The Roman composer Pietro Paolo Sabbatini set this as a strophic duet (*Quarto*, 1631). And Francesco Turini set Orpheus' plea to Hope, "Dove, ah dove ten vai?" (act III) as a madrigalian duet which he published in 1621.[79] Taken out of their original context, Striggio's lines seem more akin to Petrarch's more melancholy lyrics than to the madrigal poetry generally encountered in early seventeenth-century settings, and it is perfectly matched by Turini's rather old-fashioned chromatic setting.

In this survey of the poets and the poetry of the early seventeenth-century duet we have seen that, with only a few exceptions, the writers of duets seem to have had little interest in the poetry of the distant past. Petrarch's lyrics, which had played so important a part in the madrigal verse of the sixteenth century, were largely ignored. So, too, were the lyrics of his early and mid-sixteenth-century imitators. Moreover, the composers of duets seem to have chosen for their madrigalian settings rather fewer sonnets and ottavas—the weightier verse-forms—than did the sixteenth-century madrigalists. They preferred, rather, to concentrate on the shorter, more pointed, more sensuous madrigals of Guarini and Marino. Ottavas, even those of Marino, were more generally set as variations on stylized melodic patterns, a technique that had been used for solo settings in the sixteenth century.

Because of the popularity of the strophic duet, a substantial number of the texts set as duets during the early seventeenth century are simple strophic canzonettas. Most of these are anonymous and few have any literary merit.

They are, in short, *poesia per musica*. In terms of content, however, the seventeenth-century canzonetta tends to be a genuine "counterfeit" of the more literary madrigal and to be amorous rather than parodistic in character. And among the strophic texts whose authorship can be established, those of Gabriello Chiabrera and his imitators are notable for their distinctive rhythmic characteristics.

Although strophic verse can be readily identified as *poesia per musica*, the case of the madrigal is more debatable. Einstein, however, seems to have had no doubt in his mind when he wrote:

> At the beginning of the seventeenth century music demanded of poetry merely that it should be a poetic foundation for its fixed musical form. For more than two hundred years literary poetry is again divorced from "poetry for music"; and the "poet for music", including even Zeno and Metastasio, is but a hack writer of doggerel verse. The musician no longer disports himself in the garden of true poetry. An epoch is closed.[80]

Some of the evidence that we have adduced would seem to support this point of view. As we have noted, the composers of madrigalian duets were little interested in the poetry of Petrarch and the mid-sixteenth-century Petrarchists. And they had relatively less interest in setting sonnets than their sixteenth-century counterparts. This can, in part, be accounted for by the increasing interest shown in the madrigal as a lyric form by the poets of the late sixteenth and early seventeenth centuries. And inasmuch as the poets were increasingly concerned with a literary form—the madrigal—which had intimate associations with music, they can be said to be "poets for music."

In all probability many of Guarini's madrigals were written for music, for he worked at one of the most important centers of madrigal composition during the late sixteenth century. And the rhetorical gestures and evocative words which form his poetic vocabulary were very much in tune with the musical requirements of composers of the *seconda prattica*. Marino, we know, also loved music and was pleased when his poetry was set. The language of his verse, too, often has a musical quality of its own. But this is not to say that it lent itself readily to musical setting by a madrigalist brought up to seek musically translatable images. While it was relatively easy for a madrigalist to suggest the passions that permeate so much of Guarini's verse, it was far more difficult to find an exact musical equivalent for the physical kiss which is the central theme of many of Marino's madrigals. Marino's concern, too, with witty conceits and a virtuoso use of language mark him out as a poet who was, from the madrigalists' viewpoint, more literary, less a "poet for music" than Guarini.

4

Sixteenth-Century Madrigalian Duos

From our consideration of the sources, forms, and texts of the independent duet settings that were published during the early seventeenth century we must now turn back to try and trace their relationship with the music of the sixteenth century. Our discussion of the sixteenth-century musical background comprises two elements. In this chapter we look at the unaccompanied madrigalian duos which constitute the largest surviving body of sixteenth-century secular music specifically written for two voices. In the next, as part of the larger problem of the styles and techniques found in the early *concertato* duet, we shall examine the surviving evidence of sixteenth-century duets with instrumental accompaniment, and the trio textures in sixteenth-century madrigalian composition which, together with the models provided by Florentine solo song and opera, form the immediate background to the emergence of the early seventeenth-century *concertato* duet.

Although the majority of sixteenth-century madrigals were scored for four or more voices, some ten publications dating from the sixteenth century include, or are wholly devoted to, settings of Italian secular texts for two unaccompanied voices. These are listed below in chronological order of first publication.[1]

1. *Canzoni Frottole & Capitoli da diversi eccellentissimi musici ... Libro Secondo de la Croce,* Rome (Dorico), 1526 [?1523].[2] Includes one madrigal à 2, "Amor, che mi consigli?," by Costanzo Festa.[3]
2. Ihan Gero, *Il Primo Libro de Madrigali italiani et Canzoni francese a due voci,* Venice (Gardane), 1541 [Venice (Scotto), 1539/40];[4] 2 part-books (Canto and Tenore). The 1541 printing also contains Festa's "Amor, che mi consigli?"[5] and a villota by Willaert, "E se per gelosia." Reprinted 1543, 1545, 1552 (twice), 1562, 1576, 1581, 1584, 1588, 1593, 1596, 1609, 1622, 1625, 1629 (twice), 1632, 1644, 1646, 1662, 1672, 1677, 1682, 1687.
3. Girolamo Scotto, *Il Primo Libro de i Madrigali a doi voci,* Venice (Scotto), 1541; 2 part-books (Canto and Tenore). Also contains Latin motets. Reprinted 1551, 1558, 1562, 1572.[6]

4. G. Scotto, *Il Secondo Libro delli Madrigali a duoi voci,* Venice (Scotto), 1559; 2 part-books (Canto and Tenore).[7]

5. G. Scotto, *Il Terzo Libro delli Madrigali a due voci,* Venice (Scotto), 1562 (reprint; date of first printing unknown, though presumably between 1559 and 1562); 2 part-books (Canto and Tenore).[8] The madrigals in this book seem to have been reprinted from the first edition of Scotto's first book of madrigals for two voices. Also contains Latin motets and textless duos.

6. Giovanni Paien, *Il Primo Libro de Madrigali a due voci,* Venice (Gardane), 1564 (reprint; date of first printing unknown); 2 part-books (Canto and Tenore). Reprinted 1597.[9]

7. Bernardo Lupacchino & Joan Maria Tasso, *Il Primo Libro a note negre a due voci...con la nuova giunta di alcuni canti di nuovo ristampato,* Venice (Scotto), 1565; only one part-book (Tenore) survives. This, the only edition of Lupacchino and Tasso's book (first published 1559) to contain texted duos, includes six anonymous settings of Italian texts.

8. Giovanni Matteo Asola, *Madrigali a due voci accomodate da cantar in fuga diversamente sopra una parte sola,* Venice (G. Vincenti), 1587 (reprint; a printing of 1584, now lost, is mentioned by Vogel).[10] Reprinted 1600, 1604, 1624, 1665.

9. Filippo Nicoletti, *Madrigali a due voci,* Venice (G. Vincenti), 1588; 2 part-books (Canto and Tenore). Reprinted 1605.

10. Paolo Fonghetti, *Capricci et Madrigali...a due voci,* Verona (F. Dalle Donne & S. Vargnano), 1598; 2 part-books (Canto and Tenore). Also contains textless duos.[11]

Among the works published in these sources Costanzo Festa's "Amor, che mi consigli?," printed in Dorico's *Libro Secondo de la Croce,* is notable as an early, and apparently isolated example of a duo with a secular Italian text, and it is thus something of a curiosity. Assuming that it was, indeed, first issued in 1523, then its publication came almost twenty years before the next surviving collection of madrigalian duos. It was clearly not forgotten, though, for it was reissued in that collection—Gero's *Primo Libro de Madrigali italiani et Canzoni francese a due voci.*

The *Libro Secondo de la Croce,* which contains music mainly for three and four voices, offers no real clue to the reason for Festa's choice of a two-part scoring. It does, however, contain one other duo, an anonymous setting of the French chanson "Je le lerray puis quil me bat." Einstein was clearly puzzled by these duos and conjectured that both required to have two further voices added in canon, on the model of the motets and chansons "a quattro sopra doi" published by Andrea Antico in the *Motetti novi et Chanzoni franciose* of

1521.[12] There is, however, no indication in the print that such a solution is necessary; and, indeed, when "Je le lerray" was printed in the *Libro Primo de la Fortuna* during the same decade it was specifically labelled "duo." As far as "Amor, che mi consigli?" is concerned, canon simply will not work and there is no reason to suppose that it is not complete as it stands.

The tradition to which Festa's duo belongs is not easy to distinguish. Although duos with Italian texts do survive from an earlier period, they belong mainly to the realms of sacred music, for two-part scorings were popular among the *lauda* composers of the fifteenth century.[13] On the other hand, a quite considerable literature of two-part French chansons survives from the late fifteenth and early sixteenth centuries and it may have been to this tradition, rather than to a native one that Festa was looking. Lawrence Bernstein has summarised the characteristics of these early French duos as follows:

1.   Virtually every two-part chanson in the late 15th century and early 16th century utilizes preexistent material, most frequently a cantus firmus.

2.   These compositions constitute a repertory set apart from other polyphonic compositions. Duos may be relegated to a separate portion of the MS or may be characterized by some special device, such as the use of minute repeated fragments, quodlibet techniques, or proportions.

3.   Many duos were designed to fill a specific purpose, such as offering a means of teaching the proportional system.

4.   The borrowed material may occur in either part, and the free voice may provide a modest counterpoint to the cantus firmus or may become extremely florid.

5.   Some duos seem to be contracted versions of pre-existent three-part chansons (that is, essentially true replicas of the three-voiced pieces with the contratenor left out). Others are polyphonic elaborations of popular tunes.[14]

In order to establish that Festa's "Amor, che mi consigli?" follows this tradition we would have to show first of all that the duo was based on pre-existent material. This possibility cannot be ruled out, however unlikely it may seem at first sight; and we shall return to the tradition of the French *cantus firmus* chanson a little later in this chapter.

The internal evidence offered by the duo itself is inconclusive with respect to its stylistic antecedents. It seems to owe little either to the chanson or to the Italian frottola tradition in that both voices are closely integrated and of equal importance in the contrapuntal argument. Like the instrumental duos of

Eustachio Romano published at Rome in 1521[15] it seems, in fact, to owe most to the freely composed two-part sections of Mass and Magnificat settings by Josquin Desprez and his younger contemporaries.

Besides being the earliest known setting of Italian poetry by Festa, "Amor, che mi consigli?" is also interesting as one of the earliest settings of a genuine madrigal text.[16] Its musical structure is, however, rather old-fashioned in being closely tied to the form of the text, with a cadence for the end of each line; but its composition is a good deal subtler than Einstein allowed when he described the piece as "poverty-stricken."[17] The text consists of eleven lines which Festa treats in two paragraphs of five, leaving the last line as a separate entity. Each of the five-line paragraphs is defined by a Phrygian cadence. The last line, the "point" of the madrigal—"Amor, non so che far, che mi consigli" (a paraphrase of Petrarch's "Che debb'io far? che mi consigli, Amore?")—is set twice, ending each time with an extended roulade for both voices.

Within this rather formal framework Festa introduces some subtleties of phrase structure and even some word-painting. The declamatory opening of the madrigal and Festa's evident delight in the sonorities afforded by two equal voices (both are notated in Soprano clef), for example, are forward- rather than backward-looking traits. The easy fluidity of Festa's vocal writing can be seen in his treatment of lines 9 and 10 (ex. 1), where the interplay of voices on the word "sorte" leads to an effective climax at the dissonance in bar 38; and the exchange of notes a third apart in bars 41-43, a technique criticised by Einstein, is here used to build towards a dissonant climax in an attempt to create a musical image for the growing anguish of "tanti aspri perigli."

Example 1

The Duo as Educational Music

There is no evidence that Festa's duo was intended to serve as anything more than entertainment music. In view of its scoring for two high voices, however, it may well have been written as an exercise in singing for the two boys to whom Festa acted as music tutor at some time before 1517. The idea that the duo may have served at least a semieducational function is by no means far-fetched, for by the late fifteenth century unaccompanied duos were already a well-established educational tool, particularly in the teaching of composition and theory. As early as 1477 Tinctoris had included several textless duos in his *Liber de Arte Contrapuncti* for the purpose of illustrating contrapuntal procedures (and eighty years later Zarlino was still recommending two-part counterpoint as the starting point for greater things).[18] During the late fifteenth and early sixteenth centuries, too, duos were employed in treatises dealing with the problems of notation, and particularly with proportions. The earliest of these was Gafurius' *Practica Musicae* of 1496 and the most extensive collection of proportional duos is found in the manuscript *Regule de Proportionibus cum suis exemplis,* apparently copied at Venice in 1509.[19] Pietro Aron[20] and Glareanus[21] also included proportional duos in their writings.

The textless duos found in treatises clearly represent an academic use of the medium,[22] and they show that the duo, as the smallest unit of counterpoint, was ideal for illustrating the essentials of particular procedures and problems. There can be no doubt that they belong mainly to the realms of educational music. When we turn to independent duo collections, however, and particularly to those containing Italian madrigals, the case is by no means always as clear-cut. It is complicated, too, by the fact that the two-part madrigals published in Italy during the mid and later sixteenth century were not an isolated phenomenon. They form part of a much more extensive literature of duos which grew up particularly after the 1530s and which comprised not only madrigals and chansons, but also sacred music, music for instrumental ensemble and textless duos intended to serve as vocal and instrumental exercises.[23] Moreover, it was a literature that was international in character, for duos were also collected and published in France, Germany, the Netherlands, Spain, and England. They were particularly popular in Germany, where several collections were published expressly for use at the Lutheran music schools. One of the most important and influential of these, the *Bicinia Gallica, Latina, Germanica* (2 vols., Wittenberg, 1545) compiled by the publisher Georg Rhau, also bequeathed to the unaccompanied duo the Latinised name *bicinium* by which it is now often known.[24] The literature of German and other north European *bicinia* is larger than that of Italian duos and its traditions can be felt as late as the eighteenth century in the four duos that J.S. Bach included in the third part of his Clavier-Übung.[25]

The extent to which unaccompanied duos were intended as educational music varied from collection to collection and, to some extent, from country to country, and it is misleading to lump them all together under the heading *bicinia* as though all served precisely the same function. In his study of Italian textless duos Einstein was inclined to view all sixteenth-century duos as at least semieducational, but he neatly summarized the equivocal nature of the medium:

> The duo of the sixteenth century is one of the most striking examples of the ambiguity of a musical species wavering between vocal and instrumental use and between instructive and purely artistic intentions—not to say between didacticism and artistry.[26]

This dictum can, of course, be applied to individual duos, but it is more helpful to think of it first of all as applying to particular types of two-part music or to individual collections. As regards the balance between didacticism and artistry, each collection of duos requires to be examined in its own terms; and a distinction needs to be drawn between duos that were clearly intended to serve an educational function and those that may have been used, though not necessarily intended, as educational music.

In Italy, textless duos were the type most clearly associated with an educational function. The fullest early statement of the educational virtues of such pieces is found in the dedication to the second book of *Duo Cromatici* (Venice, 1546) addressed by the Cremonese composer Agostino Licino to Benedetto Guarna of Salerno. In his dedication Licino stated that his duos were intended to afford Guarna's sons and their friends a more profitable form of amusement than playing cards or other games. They were to serve as an "alphabet of music" and for practice in playing stringed instruments. Since the 44 duos contained in the two books of *Duo Cromatici* (the first was published in 1545) are all written in canon and arranged according to the church modes, "alphabet of music" may be interpreted as meaning that they could be used as primers in composition and music theory; but since the title page of each volume also bears the indication "da cantare et sonare" alphabet may also be taken as "a metaphoric substitute for *ut, re mi,*" thus indicating that the textless duos could be performed as solmization exercises.[27] Licino's canons are intended to be read from one book only. The composer did, however, provide a separate part-book containing the resolution of the canons in case the task of providing these at sight from the leading part only should prove too difficult.[28]

From the middle of the sixteenth century textless duos were variously seen as playing a part in the training of performers, whether singers or instrumentalists, and in the study of theory and composition. This role is confirmed, in whole or in part, by the dedications of Pietro Vinci's *Primo Libro della Musica* (Venice, 1560), Vincenzo Galilei's *Contrapunti a due voci* (Florence, 1584), and Antonio il Verso's *Primo Libro della Musica a due voci* (Palermo, 1596).

Textless duos were also the province of budding composers. Both Antonio il Verso, in his *Primo Libro,* and Giovanni Battista Cali, in his *Ricercari*

(Venice, 1605), for example, stated that these were their earliest compositions.[29] And when the Milanese publishers Tini and Besozzo issued, in 1598, a
volume of duos by Gastoldi and other experienced composers, they tactfully
included two duos by Hieronimo Baglione, the son of their dedicatee.[30] Even
Eustachio Romano, whose *Musica... Liber Primus* (Rome, 1521) was the
earliest published collection of duos for instrumental ensemble to appear in the
sixteenth century, remarked to his patron and dedicatee that the duos
represented his "first efforts."[31] They were not, however, intended so much for
the education of his patron, who was the Archbishop of Sipontina and Bishop
of Pavia, as for his amusement and refreshment "when tired from weightier
studies."[32]

Of the surviving madrigal collections listed earlier only the *Madrigali a
due voci accomodate da cantar in fuga* by the Veronese composer Giovanni
Matteo Asola can clearly be seen as educational music. The composer did not
specify this either on the title page or in the dedication. His collection, however,
follows the path opened up by Licino's *Duo Cromatici*. Each of his madrigals is
conceived as a canon for two voices, but only the leading voice is printed. The
point at which the second voice should enter is marked over the first together
with an indication of the type of canon to be employed. Example 2 shows the
opening of one of the simpler madrigals, though even here the second singer has
not merely to follow, but also to transpose the written part down a fifth. These
madrigals, then, provide a test, or a training in sight singing which is
demanding by any standards; and unlike Licino, Asola provided no separate
"Resolutio."

Example 2

Because of their canonic technique, Asola's madrigals lend themselves to
instrumental as well as vocal performance, though this possibility is not
advertised on the title page. His book clearly found a niche in the educational
literature, for it was reprinted several times up to the middle of the seventeenth
century, the last printing being issued in 1665.

None of the other collections of madrigalian duos bears any indication of
didactic intent on its title page; and none advertizes its contents as suitable for
instrumental as well as vocal performance. Nor do the extant dedications

suggest an educational purpose. The dedication to Gero's *Primo Libro de Madrigali italiani et Canzoni francese a due voci,* in fact, indicates that his compositions were intended as chamber music.

> I am convinced that this collection will be welcome to Your Excellency by reason of the convenient nature of music for two voices. This is music that is suited for princes and gentlemen; it is used by them when, withdrawn from the tumult of the crowd, they enjoy in the company of a few intimate friends the melodies born of the imagination of the best composers.[33]

The fact that Gero's madrigals and chansons were still being reprinted nearly 150 years after the date of their first publication and long after the styles which they represented had become outmoded does, however, suggest that they may have been used as educational music whether they were composed for that purpose or not. Furthermore, in eleven of the reprints issued during the seventeenth century—those of 1622, 1625, 1629, 1632, 1644, 1646, 1662, 1672, 1677, 1682, and 1687—the texts of the French chansons were omitted altogether, thus transforming them into the type of textless duos suitable for both vocal and instrumental use which are most readily identifiable as didactic music. It is, however, significant that the madrigals, which depend far more closely on the texts for their musical structure and sense, were left intact.[34]

In the case of the madrigal collections issued by the Venetian publisher Girolamo Scotto there is some circumstantial evidence of didactic intent. The madrigals of his first book all carry headings indicating the mode in which they are written. The pieces are grouped according to mode (see Table 1), but otherwise there seems to have been no further attempt at systematic ordering; certainly nothing like that found in Licino's *Duo Cromatici.* The order in which clef pairings appear seems fairly haphazard, both within the mode groups and within the book as a whole. Like the majority of mid and late sixteenth-century madrigalian duos, Scotto's are not scored for voices of equal range. The majority are for two adjacent voices, with canto/alto the favorite pairing.

Both Scotto's first and third books and Fonghetti's *Capricci et Madrigali* contain a mixture of genres, perhaps intended to provide the novice performer with practice in all the types of music that he would normally expect to encounter. Thus, Scotto's first book contains, in addition to madrigals, a group of Latin motets; and his third book includes madrigals, motets, and textless duos. Fonghetti's book contains madrigals and textless duos. The mixture of genres links these books with a didactic collection such as Rhau's *Bicinia.* No such circumstantial evidence is apparent for the collections of Paien and Nicoletti and we should, perhaps, consider these as educational only in the sense that, during the sixteenth century, duo collections were often understood to be useful for beginners in music.

Table 1.   Table of Contents from Girolamo Scotto's *Primo Libro de i Madrigali* (1541 edition)

Page	Incipit	Mode	Clefs
1	S'amor non e	5	C/A
2	Non v'accorgete	5	A/T
3	Pace non trovo	5	A/T
4	Solo e pensoso	5	C/A
5	Consumando mi vo	1	MezzoSop/T
6	Io son tal volta	1	MezzoSop/T
7	Piu lieta di me	1	A/T
8	Non son piu	1	C/A
9	Qual donna	1	C/A
10	Gentil mia donna	1	C/A
11	Ecco ch'un altra volta	1	C/T
12	Lasso ch'io ardo	1	C/A
13	Datemi pace	1	C/A
14	Fuggite hormai	1	A/Baritone
15	Sovra una verde riva	1	A/Baritone
16	Valle che di lamenti	1	MezzoSop/T
17	Vago augelletto	1	MezzoSop/T
18	Hai dispietato	1	MezzoSop/T
19	S'io credessi	1	A/T
20	Padre del ciel	1	A/T
21	Qual anima ignorante	3	C/A
22	Vergine bella	3	T/B
23	Poiche la vista	3	C/T
24	S'el mio bel sol	3	C/T
25	La vita fugge	3	C/T
26	S'io pensassi	3	C/T
27	O s'io potesse	1	C/A
28	Hogn'hor	1	C/A
29	Se del mio amor	1	A/Baritone
30	Quando penso	7	C/A
31	Rotta e l'alta colonna	7	C/A
32	Ardeva tutto	7	C/A
33	Piangete donna	7	A/T
34	Io son de l'aspettar	7	T/B
35	Amor quando fioriva	5	T/B
36	Che debb'io far	5	C/T
37	Lagrimando dimostro	4	B/A
38	Discolorato hai morte	4	T/A

The Duo as Publishers' Music: Arrangements

The stylistic antecedents of the duos written by Ihan Gero and his mentor Girolamo Scotto seem to have been, at least partly, French: the rhythm 𝅝 𝅗𝅥 𝅗𝅥 is commonly used as an opening gambit and the upper voice generally maintains a melodic identity. More specifically, they may be seen as the Italian response to a volume of *Canzoni francese a due voci* issued in 1539 by Scotto's rival at Venice, the French-born publisher Antonio Gardane. Gardane's collection of chansons consists largely of his own compositions and included twelve reprinted from the fourth volume of *Le Parangon des Chansons,* issued the previous year by Jacques Moderne at Lyons.

The rivalry between Scotto and Gardane in publishing duo collections lasted almost until the latter's death in 1569, and it produced several of the best known of all sixteenth-century duo collections. A comparison of the output of the two publishers during a twenty-five-year period around the middle of the century shows that the madrigal collections were not an isolated phenomenon. The list given below shows both newly-issued volumes (marked with an asterisk) and reprints.

*1539	Gardane, *Canzoni Francese*	(Gardane)
*?1539/40	Gero, *Primo libro de Madrigali Italiani et Canzoni Francese*	(?Scotto)
1541	Gero, *Primo libro*	(Gardane)
* 1541	Scotto, *Primo libro de i Madrigali*	(Scotto)
* 1543	Gardane (ed.), *Primo libro a due voci de diversi autori*	(Gardane)
1543	Gero, *Primo libro*	(Gardane)
1544	Gardane, *Canzoni Francese*	(Gardane)
1545	Gero, *Primo libro*	(no printer named, but contents as in Scotto's 1552 reprint)
* 1545	Licino, *Primo libro di Duo Cromatici*	(Gardane)
* 1546	Licino, *Secondo libro di Duo Cromatici*	(Gardane)
1552	Gardane, *Canzoni Francese*	(Gardane)
1552	Gero, *Primo libro*	(Scotto)
1552	Gero, *Primo libro*	(Gardane)
1553	Gardane (ed.), *Primo libro a due voci*	(Gardane)
* 1559	Lupacchino & Tasso, *Primo libro a due voci*	(Gardane)[35]
* 1559	Scotto, *Secondo libro delli madrigali*	(Scotto)
1560	Lupacchino & Tasso, *Primo libro*	(Scotto)
* 1560	Vinci, *Primo libro della Musica*	(Scotto)
1562	Gero, *Primo libro*	(Scotto)
* 1562	Scotto, *Terzo libro delli Madrigali*	(Scotto; reprint)
1564	Gardane, *Canzoni Francese*	(Gardane)
* 1564	Paien, *Primo libro de Madrigali*	(Gardane; reprint)

This comparison of the output of Gardane and Scotto does seem to confirm the idea that they vied with each other, or at least tried to keep in step in producing duo collections, for it is surely more than coincidence that both should have chosen to issue duos, after a break of several years, precisely in 1552. Both publishers pirated each other's work. Gero's madrigals and chansons, commissioned by Scotto, quickly became common property. And in 1560 Scotto apparently repaid this theft by producing his own edition of the *Primo Libro* of Lupacchino and Tasso.

Our comparison also shows that there seems to have been a fairly steady demand for two-part music which the publishers were concerned to supply by keeping a stock of duos in print. Until 1553 they catered for this market largely by printing and reprinting their own collections and Gero's commissioned book. During this period only Licino's two books of *Duo Cromatici* represent a composer working outside the publishers' circle. From c. 1559 to 1564 the number of new volumes issued suggests a renewed and increasing interest in duo composition and consumption and one that could not be satisfied merely by reprinting earlier publications. Scotto, however, seems to have tried to have things both ways, for the madrigals of his third book, ostensibly a completely new collection, seem all to have been reprinted from the first edition of his *Primo Libro,* now some twenty years old. As products of the rivalry between Gardane and Scotto, then, the two-part madrigals of Gero, Scotto, and Paien may be regarded as a self-contained group of sources; and this is reflected in similarities of approach and technique.

The active part taken by music publishers, both in Italy and elsewhere, in commissioning, composing, collecting and editing, printing and reprinting duo collections argues not only that there was a ready market available, but also that these collections were in some special way "publishers' music." This can, in part, be explained by the educational role of many duo publications. As we have seen, however, there is no evidence of educational intent in the case of Gero's madrigals and chansons, or Paien's madrigals; and in the case of Scotto's madrigals the evidence is, to say the least, ambiguous. Some, at least, of these mid-century collections may, however, be considered "publishers' music" in a quite different sense, that of being arrangements for a few voices of contemporary polyphonic madrigals. And in this respect they are quite clearly linked, through Gardane's chansons, with a French tradition.

One of the most interesting discoveries of recent years is that the two-part French chansons published in the mid-sixteenth century follow those of the late fifteenth and early sixteenth centuries in being based on pre-existent material. Viewed in this light, the dedication to Gero's book, which mentions "melodies born of the imagination of the best composers," takes on a new significance.

Lawrence Bernstein has identified most of the polyphonic models on which the two-part chansons in Gardane's *Canzoni francese* and Gero's *Primo Libro de Madrigali italiani et Canzoni francese* were based;[36] and he has shown that Gardane and Gero used different techniques in treating pre-existent material. Gardane uses strict *cantus firmus* technique for the upper voice of his chansons, though the *cantus firmus* may be drawn not only from the superius of the model, but also occasionally from the tenor or even the bass.[37] The lower voice often utilizes material from the lower voices of the model, usually the tenor, with new material being added only to suit the different requirements of a two-part texture. His duos are, thus, essentially a reduction to two voices of the polyphonic original.[38] Gero, on the other hand, always borrows the superius of the model for the upper voice of his duos and adds to this a newly-conceived lower voice. His *cantus firmus* chansons, then, are essentially new settings of a borrowed melody.

In referring to his use of the "melodies born of the imagination of the best composers," Gero did not draw a distinction between the chansons and the madrigals contained in his book, nor did he exclude from the implications of his statement Festa's "Amor, che mi consigli?" and Willaert's "E se per gelosia," both of which were included in the first extant printing of the book. This seems to suggest that the madrigals may also be based on *cantus firmi* in the upper voice.

This is certainly the case with respect to Willaert's "E se per gelosia." In a recent study,[39] James Haar pointed to the similarity between the canto part of Willaert's duo and those of four other settings for three, four, and five voices that survive from the 1520s and 1530s. He surmised that all might be settings of a monophonic tune (now lost) of which he attempted a reconstruction,[40] and concluded:

> it now appears that a two-voice Italian-texted piece may also be—as yet I do not know with what frequency—an arrangement of a well-known madrigal.[41]

Professor Haar's own research into concordances with Gero's madrigals has shown that none seems to be related very closely to a polyphonic model.[42] And the homogeneity of Gero's part-writing itself seems to argue against *cantus firmus* technique, as may be seen from the opening of the madrigal "Non volete ch'io viva" (ex. 3). Although this begins with the chanson-like rhythm 𝅝♩♩ (and a consequent misaccentuation of the text), the smooth progression from imitative opening to the homophony which paints the word "dolce" reflects the influence of the new Italian madrigal, as does the dovetailing of musical phrases to link two lines of text where the sense is continuous (see bars 8-9 of the example).

Example 3

Although a thorough search of concordances with the early madrigalian duos lies outside the scope of the present study, a comparison of the duos of Scotto's *Primo Libro* and the two duos from Paien's book edited by Bartoli with concordances available in modern editions and transcriptions shows that these two volumes, at least, do include madrigals based on pre-existent material drawn from contemporary polyphonic madrigals.[43] I list below the madrigals with identifiable *cantus firmi* and give the first published source of the model known to me.

Scotto, *Primo Libro*	Model (superscript numbers from *RISM*)
"Ardeva tutto a voi presso"	Canto of Arcadelt à 4 (1540[20])
"Io son tal volta"	Canto of Verdelot (attrib.) à 4 (1540[20])
"O s'io pensassi donna"	Canto of Berchem à 4 (1539[22])
"Qual anima ignorante"	Canto of Willaert à 4 (1540[20]) [also set à 5 by Willaert in 1544[17]]
"Quando penso al martire"	?Canto of Arcadelt à 4 (1599[22])

Paien, *Primo Libro*	
'Gravi pene in amor'	Canto of Arcadelt à 3 (1542[18])

As far as one can tell from so few examples, the technique employed by Scotto in reusing his borrowed material resembles that used in Gero's chansons, while that employed by Paien is nearer to Gardane's more thorough-going parody. Scotto's "O s'io pensassi [potessi] donna"[44] illustrates his technique at its simplest. In this setting he has merely taken over the canto line of Berchem's madrigal for four voices and presented it untransposed, and with very few rhythmic changes, as his own canto line. One or two notes are altered to accommodate new points of imitation; where there is a whole bar's rest in the original it has been omitted in the duo; and bars 20 to 23 of the model are also omitted. Otherwise the *cantus firmus* is a faithful reproduction of Berchem's original.

For the most part, the lower voice is newly composed, with points of imitation added by Scotto (ex. 4). Although the lower voices of the model are not generally used, at the two moments in Berchem's setting where the texture thins to the two upper voices (bars 12-14 and 31) Scotto simply takes over the notes of Berchem's alto line for his own lower voice part.

Example 4

Paien, on the other hand, treats his *cantus firmus* with rather more freedom. In "Gravi pene in amor" he maintains the general intervallic shape of Arcadelt's canto line,[45] but transposes it up a fourth and alters it rhythmically, adding new cadential ornamentation and often extending the cadence to cover a new point of imitation begun in the lower voice. Again, the lower voice is, for the most part, newly composed. In the first half of the setting (to bar 21), Paien has the second voice leading in the imitative points, even where this differs from the model. He begins the second half of the setting in the same way, but from bar 29 not only are the roles reversed, but the points of imitation are clearly modeled on Arcadelt's own (ex. 5), so that the lower line of Paien's duo is a compression of the alto and bass parts of the model.

Example 5

A different approach again is found in Scotto's "Qual anima ignorante," a sonnet setting in two sections which is the most ambitious piece in the *Primo Libro*. Here, the model seems to have been Willaert's setting for four voices published in *RISM* 1540[20].[46] Unless both Scotto and Willaert modeled their settings on another as yet unidentified source, then the canto part of Scotto's duo must be regarded as a very free paraphrase of Willaert's. There seem also to be one or two elements of parody, but these may be no more than coincidental.

Example 6

Usually, Scotto takes only the beginnings of Willaert's lines and continues them in a quite different way. Even so he does not use all the line openings, nor does he always keep those he does use at their original pitch.

And, at one point in the second section of the setting, he passes the *cantus firmus* from canto to alto (ex. 6). The opening of the second section itself departs completely from Willaert's original. It begins with a repetition of the imitative point used at the opening of the first section, though with the entries reversed. And in constructing his counterpoint here, Scotto places the tenor high in his register in order to explore the possibilities of dissonance between the two voices that this opens up (ex. 7). This is his writing at its best, and it is used to prepare us for the images of tears and laments, sighs and sorrow that follow. The setting as a whole, though, is over extended and shows Scotto's propensity for stolid, rather academic counterpoint in his duos as compared with the flexible alternation between imitation and homophony which characterises Gero's work.

Example 7

I have been unable to find any evidence of *cantus firmus* technique in the volumes of madrigalian duos published later in the sixteenth century.[47] Fonghetti's madrigals, written in a rather old-fashioned chanson style, are the most likely candidates, but concordances are elusive.

Late Sixteenth-Century Madrigalian Duos

In just the same way that the duos of Gero and Scotto reflect the more widespread French influence on the madrigals of their day, so later in the century, the growing popularity of a lighter, more graceful type of madrigal is reflected in the duos of Filippo Nicoletti. Nicoletti's *Madrigali a due voci*, first published in 1588, were probably written while the composer was resident at Rovigo, on Venetian territory. Certainly his book is indebted for its choice of texts to a Venetian model—Andrea Gabrieli's *Libro Primo de Madrigali a tre voci* of 1575. Nicoletti set almost all the texts chosen by Gabrieli for his publication, and he set them in the same order, beginning with "A casa un giorno," a text attributed to Tansillo, and continuing with a series of multisectional texts drawn from Ariosto's *Orlando furioso*.[48] Incidentally, his decision to include a setting of "A casa un giorno," a decidedly risqué text on the same sexual theme later explored in Guarini's "Tirsi morir volea," is a factor which may argue against the idea that his duos were intended for children. And the same argument can also be advanced with regard to Fonghetti's *Capricci et Madrigali,* for this volume also includes a setting of the same text.

Nicoletti's duos, scored for canto and tenore (though the last two have tenor/bass and alto/baritone clefs respectively), are the most immediately attractive of all the sixteenth-century two-part madrigals. And their light, canzonetta-like style also seems to owe something to Andrea Gabrieli.[49] The opening of "Dunque baciar," for example, a setting for soprano and tenor of a passage from *Orlando furioso* (XXXVI. 32-33) in which Bradamante remonstrates with Ruggiero, employs devices like close imitation and sequence to build short motives into tightly knit paragraphs (ex. 8). This approaches quite closely the style and type of vocal interplay to be found in many early seventeenth-century duets, though the freshness of style disguises, in Nicoletti's case, a rigorous, almost canonic use of imitation. His delight in painting individual words places Nicoletti in the mainstream of late sixteenth-century madrigalists, as does his occasional use of ornamentation; and it should be remembered that he was employed at the Ferrarese court certainly from April, 1588. The ornament shown in example 9, from the second stanza of "Ella non sa" is one which is often encountered in early seventeenth-century florid duets (see, for example, volume 2, no. 6, bars 32-34).

The style of Nicoletti's collection is the nearest that the two-part madrigal came to the lighter forms of sixteenth-century music, for the madrigalian duo, though slight in stature, was serious in intent.[50] This is clearly reflected in the literary nature of the texts set. Gero and Scotto included settings of poetry by Bembo, Sannazzaro, and Boccaccio in their collections; and almost half of the settings in Scotto's *Primo Libro* are of texts by Petrarch.[51] These include one stanza of the *canzone* "Vergine bella," which also appeared as a two-part *lauda* in Vogel-Einstein 1563[13]. A setting of the same *canzone* in its entirety was advertised on the title page of Paien's *Primo Libro* as one of its main attractions. Many of the other settings in Paien's book are also of texts by Petrarch. In contrast, the collections of Asola and Nicoletti, published much later in the century, contain none at all. Nicoletti's preoccupation with Ariosto has already been noted; and Asola's book, too, opens with a setting from *Orlando furioso*—the popular pastoral "Cantan tra rami gl'augelletti vaghi" (XXXIV. 50-51).

Example 8

Example 9

It is difficult to draw any hard and fast general conclusions about the role played by madrigalian duos in sixteenth-century musical life. The available evidence, though often no more than circumstantial, suggests that the collections of Gero, Scotto, Asola, and Fonghetti may have been used as educational music. We have seen, however, that Gero, at least, intended his madrigals and chansons as a form of chamber music to be enjoyed by the cultured amateur in the company of a few friends. Given the lack of an explicitly stated educational function in the other collections of madrigalian duos published in the sixteenth century it is probable that they, too, were intended to serve more experienced singers who required music for small ensemble. In those cases where it can be shown that madrigalian duos were based on *cantus firmi* drawn from polyphonic settings, then the intention seems to have been to provide amateurs with arrangements of well-known madrigals so that they could enjoy them even when a full complement of singers was not available.

Perhaps the most telling point in favor of the view that two-part madrigals were intended primarily for entertainment and only secondarily as educational music during the sixteenth century is that no new collections were issued after the emergence of the *concertato* duet, and only those of Gero and Asola were reprinted after the first decade of the seventeenth century.[52]

The virtual disappearance of madrigalian duos after the first decade of the seventeenth century is given added significance by the fact that a literature of unaccompanied duos did continue to exist in Italy alongside the newer idioms of the *concertato* duet. And it comprised not only reprints of sixteenth-century collections but also newly issued volumes. Most of these, however, contained textless duos only and were often instrumental in character, as such titles as *Ricercari, Capricci, Canzoni da sonar* imply. Others were intended for vocal use, but they were strictly didactic. The books of Giovanni Gentile (1642), and Pompeo Natale (1681), for example, both bear the word "solfeggiamenti" on their title page.[53] Earlier in the century the *Varii Esercizi* (Florence, 1614) of Antonio Brunelli contained a number of ingenious exercises on different syllables, scored for one and two sopranos, which were intended to produce a flexible technique suited to brilliant passage-work. One volume, issued in 1610 by Giovanni Battista Bianco, did include settings of Latin texts. Its title page, however, like those of so many of the volumes issued during the seventeenth century, reveals a quite clear didactic intention—*Musica a due voci utilissima per instruir i figliuoli a cantar sicuramente in breve tempo & commodi per sonar con ogni sorte di strumenti*. This bold claim was echoed on the title page of Cristofano Piochi's *Ricercari a due e tre voci* of 1671, which were described as "utilissimi a chi desidera imparare presto a cantare e sonare." These were, in short, accelerated courses in musical technique of a kind still in evidence today.

The seventeenth century, then, saw the beginnings of a split in the dual role that unaccompanied duos had served during the sixteenth century. The seventeenth-century unaccompanied duos inherited their educational mantle, but their entertainment function was vested in the new *concertato* duet. The sixteenth-century madrigalian duo, then, forms one of the traditions which lay behind the emergence of the *concertato* duet. More specifically, it may have suggested to composers like Radesca, Cagnazzi, and Rubini the idea of issuing books devoted wholly to duets. As we shall see in chapter 6, however, these composers rarely looked to the style or technique of the sixteenth-century duo in writing their duets for high voice and bass/*basso seguente*.

5

Emergence of the *Concertato* Duet I

Although madrigalian duos provide the most substantial body of evidence for a sixteenth-century tradition of secular duet writing in Italy, their importance for the stylistic and technical evolution of the new *concertato* duet is outweighed by other factors in late sixteenth- and early seventeenth-century vocal music. *Concertato* duets differ from duos in two fundamental respects. First, they involve an accompaniment that does not simply double the two voices; and second, the majority of *concertato* duets are not two-part textures at all, but three-part textures in which the two vocal lines are supported by a *basso continuo*. They are, moreover, three-part textures of a particular kind, for though the continuo line generally forms a complete harmonic unit with the two voices, it does not, on the whole, join in their contrapuntal interplay.

Nigel Fortune has pointed out, quite rightly, that in this latter type of duet "the relationship of the two voices to the continuo is exactly the same as that of the solo voice in monodies";[1] and, as we shall see, Florentine monody had an important part to play in suggesting both a technical and a stylistic basis for many early seventeenth-century duets. Nevertheless, both the concept of the accompanied duet and the type of three-part writing found in duets with *basso continuo* had already evolved independently of Florence by the late sixteenth century. Stylistically, too, the duets written in the early years of the seventeenth century represent a diversity of elements drawn from the late sixteenth-century madrigal and canzonetta as well as from the newer styles of Florentine monody.

Accompanied Duets

Most of the few duets with instrumental accompaniment that survive from the sixteenth century are original compositions for the medium. It is clear, however, from the scattered documentary evidence that the art of the sixteenth-century duet must, like solo song during the same period, have been largely one of *ad hoc* arrangement from polyphonic originals; and such activity, by its very nature, tends to leave little concrete evidence of its existence.

We can be reasonably certain that sixteenth-century madrigals were often performed with instrumental accompaniment. This might take the form of an instrumental consort, with melody instruments doubling the individual lines of the madrigal, or a reduction of the score might be played on a harpsichord or lute, using a tablature prepared by the performer himself or borrowed from another source.[2]

In the later part of the sixteenth century, several books of secular vocal music were published which included an instrumental transcription as well as the vocal parts. Perhaps the most notable of these, certainly among the most interesting for the stylistic and technical prehistory of the *concertato* duet, are the beautifully engraved canzonetta anthologies of Simone Verovio, published at Rome between 1586 and 1595.[3] Four of these—the *Diletto Spirituale . . . a 3 et a 4 voci* (*RISM* 1586[2]), the *Ghirlanda di Fioretti musicali . . . a 3 voci* (*RISM* 1589[11]), the *Canzonette a 4 voci* (*RISM* 1591[12]) and the *Lodi della musica a 3 voci* (*RISM* 1595[6])—were issued in choirbook format with the vocal parts of each piece, a keyboard score, and a lute intabulation printed on a single opening of the book. The instrumental transcriptions could, thus, be used either for solo instrumental performances or as accompaniments to a full or partial vocal ensemble. There is no evidence to show that the canzonettas in Verovio's anthologies were actually performed as duets with instrumental accompaniment, though many of them lend themselves fairly readily to arrangement as duets, taking either two upper parts or soprano and bass.

The impact of Verovio's publications was felt well beyond Rome. In 1591 the Venetian publisher Giacomo Vincenti reissued all but the anonymous pieces of Verovio's 1586 book in three anthologies entitled *Canzonette per cantar et sonar di liuto a 3 voci* (*RISM* 1591[14-16]). In the third of these he added five canzonettas by Orazio Scaletta which had first appeared in Scaletta's own *Villanelle alla romana a 3 voci* (Venice, 1590). The tag "alla romana" that Scaletta used seems itself to have initiated a new fashion in the title pages of canzonetta publications at the turn of the sixteenth century. When Angelo Gardano reprinted most of the contents of Vincenti's three books of *Canzonette per cantar et sonar di liuto* in a single volume, he called the collection *Canzonette alla romana de diversi eccellentiss. Musici romani a 3 voci* (*RISM* 1601[8]; and this publication was itself reprinted with the same title by Phalèse of Antwerp in 1607 (*RISM* 1607[14]). Meanwhile, in Italy, the Sienese composer Orindio Bartolini had published, in 1606, a volume of his own *Canzonette et Arie alla romana, a 3 voci per cantar come hoggidì si costuma* (the significance of the final phrase is not clear); and Enrico Radesca di Foggia had already issued at least the first two of his four books of *Canzonette, Madrigali et Arie alla romana* for two accompanied voices (in 1605 and 1606).

In describing the contents of their anthologies as "alla romana" it is clear that Gardano and Phalèse were simply acknowledging the place where the music was written. Scaletta and Bartolini, on the other hand, were not Roman composers and seem to have had a stylistic imitation in mind. Radesca, too, may have had a similar idea when he used the tag for his duets; and certainly the music of his duets for high voice and bass/ *basso seguente,* madrigals and arias alike, owes a great debt to the style and structure of the canzonetta. But it would appear that "alla romana" could also imply the use of an instrumental accompaniment. This seems to be the inference that we must draw from the canzonetta "Deh cant'Aminta un'Aria alla romana" which stands at the head of Orazio Vecchi's *Canzonette a 3 voci* (Venice: Gardano, 1597), a volume issued, apparently in imitation of Verovio's anthologies, with a lute tablature in addition to the vocal parts.[4] The first stanza of the canzonetta (vocal parts only) is given as example 1. The passage purporting to be an "aria a la romana" is not stylistically related to the canzonettas of Verovio's anthologies, but suggests rather that Vecchi saw the "aria a la romana" as a piece which was homophonic in character and suited to solo performance with instrumental accompaniment.

We know from various sixteenth-century sources that polyphonic compositions, including the lighter forms of the madrigal, were often arranged as solo songs with instrumental accompaniment and that they were enjoyed in this form by everyone from courtiers to courtesans. But how likely is it that sixteenth-century madrigals and canzonettas were arranged as duets?

Outside the field of dramatic music the available evidence is, admittedly, very slight. An isolated literary reference to duet singing, cited by Einstein[5] is found at the end of the third decade of Giambattista Giraldi Cinthio's novella *Hecatomithi* (1565) where the two girls Camilla and Cornelia sing a duet, "Poscia che tu benigno," to an accompaniment played on viols by their male companions. This is, of course, an imaginary incident, though it must reflect a contemporary practice. For more concrete evidence of polyphonic madrigals arranged as duets we have to look outside Italy to a publication issued by Phalèse—the *Pratum musicum* of Emanuel Adriaenssen (*RISM* 1584[12])—which contains arrangements of madrigals and chansons by, among others, Rore, Lassus, and Alessandro Striggio. Each of the madrigals in Adriaenssen's collection consists of two or three vocal parts (usually cantus and bassus) chosen from the original ensemble, together with an intabulation for one or more lutes.[6] Example 2 shows the beginning of Adriaenssen's arrangement for cantus, bassus, and lute of Berchem's "O s'io potessi donna." The lute part supplies an ornamented version of the inner parts. Berchem's madrigal is, of course, the same one from which Scotto, some forty years earlier, drew the *cantus firmus* of his own madrigalian duo.[7] A comparison of the two versions tends to support the idea that it is the arranged duet for cantus and bassus rather than duo writing that is the forerunner of early seventeenth-century duets for high voice and bass/ *basso seguente.*

Example I

Example 2

Although Adriaenssen's anthology was not published in Italy, similar arrangements were issued there, notably in two collections of lute music by Giovanni Antonio Terzi, published in 1593 and 1599.[8] The principle of using only selected voices with instrumental accompaniment was, however, one that could be applied by an intelligent musician to any suitable madrigal or canzonetta. If, for example, we applied Adriaenssen's selection of cantus and bassus to a canzonetta such as Felice Anerio's "Horche vezzosa e bella" from Verovio's 1591 anthology,[9] the resulting duet for high voice, bass, and instrumental accompaniment would be very similar indeed to one of Radesca's duets. And if we chose to perform the two upper parts of Vecchi's "Deh cant'Aminta" (ex. 1) as a duet with keyboard or lute accompaniment, then we would have a prototype continuo duet and one which has much in common with the strophic duets issued in the early seventeenth century. And in neither case would the arrangement be a violation of the original conception.

It seems probable, then, that collections like those of Adriaenssen and Terzi are only the visible remains of what was a well-established and quite widespread practice. And it was one that did not entirely die out in the early seventeenth century, as we can see from Angelo Notari's arrangements for two voices and continuo of five-part madrigals by Monteverdi (included in *GB-Lbm*, MS Add. 31,440)[10] and from the pieces apparently arranged for two voices in MS L. IV. 99 of the Biblioteca Queriniana of Brescia.[11]

One field in which arranged duets were used quite frequently during the later sixteenth century was that of dramatic music. And they were almost always used as a result of the dramatic situation: that is, either for passages in dialogue or at the resolution of a scene in dialogue. The one exception, in which two-part music seems to have been used for purely musical reasons—Andrea Gabrieli's choruses for the performance of *Edipo Tiranno* at Vicenza in 1585— is also exceptional in that the duos are without independent instrumental accompaniment. Gabrieli's duos, some of which are for solo voices, some for two-part chorus,[12] are largely homorhythmic in character, with the two parts moving mainly in parallel thirds and sixths to produce a type of dignified declamation appropriate to the choruses of a classical tragedy.

The other evidence of duets in dramatic entertainments comes from two centers of music making: Florence and Venice. At Florence, at least two of the groups of *intermedi* played for various court festivities—those of 1568 and 1583 (1582 Florentine style)[13]—seem from their description to have included dialogues performed by two voices, though the music of these is now lost. At the beginning of the second *intermedio* for Lotto del Mazzo's *I Fabii* (1568), with music by Alessandro Striggio, for example, Hercules (bass) and Lady Pleasure (soprano) sang a dialogue accompanied by four trombones, four *viole d'arco,* two recorders, a transverse flute, and a foundation group of three harpsichords and three lutes.[14] Though the music of the dialogue is lost, its text survives and it is clear from this that the two voices never meet in a genuine duet.[15]

At Venice, the music is again missing for Cornelio Frangipani's *Tragedia,* a drama with music by Claudio Merulo which was played before the Grand Council of Venice in 1574. The text, however, shows that a duet, "Spargiam pianti felici," was sung by Pallas Athene and Mars during the course of the dialogue.[16] We have been more fortunate in the case of the dramatic dialogue "O che felice giorno," performed for Doge Cicogna on St. Stephen's Day, 1585, for Denis Arnold has identified the duet with lute accompaniment performed at the end of the piece as a madrigal by Giovanni Gabrieli—"O che felice giorno."[17] In its published source—*Dialoghi musicali de diversi eccellentissimi autori (RISM* 1590[11])—the madrigal[18] is notated, conventionally, for two four-part choirs and it was probably sung in its choral version to round off the entertainment. From the outset, however, it is evident that the two canto parts are intended to complement each other so that they make complete musical and textual sense when the lower voices are performed instrumentally.

Given the existence of accompanied duets in the late sixteenth century, the question arises to what extent they can be considered the forerunners of the *concertato* duets of the seventeenth. In the field of sacred music, the relationship seems quite clear. The practice of playing an organ accompaniment to motets was widespread, and from 1595 shorthand organ scores giving only the superius part and the sounding bass *(basso seguente)* began to appear in print.[19] Motets were also arranged for solo voices and small ensembles with organ accompaniment, and it was the abuses of this practice that Lodovico Viadana sought to remedy with his *Cento Concerti ecclesiastici,* published at Venice in 1602. In the preface to the work he stated:

> I saw that singers wishing to sing to the organ, either with three voices, or two, or a single one by itself, were sometimes forced by the lack of compositions suitable to their purpose to take one, two, or three parts from motets in five, six, seven, or even eight; ....[20]

He went on to describe in amusing detail the disjointed and often nonsensical results of this practice before offering his own *concertato* pieces as a rationalisation of it. Both the melodic style of his concertos and his use of a continuo line which could have been sung as well as played, however, serve to emphasise their close relationship with the sixteenth-century motet.

In the case of the secular duet there is no single composer whose work illustrates quite so neatly the transition from arrangement to *concertato* duet. The duets of Luzzasco Luzzaschi, published in his *Madrigali . . . per cantare et sonare a uno, e doi, e tre soprani* (Rome: Verovio, 1601), can, however, be seen as an intermediate stage between the two.

Luzzaschi's duets, with their virtuoso ornamentation and fully written-out accompaniment, were composed for the Ferrarese *concerto delle donne* and belong, probably, to the second period of its history: that is, to the period after c. 1580 and the reign of the quasi-professional singers Laura Peverara, Livia d'Arco, Anna Guarini, and Tarquinia Molza.[21] But duet singing was not unkown at Ferrara even before this date. Significantly enough, the very first documentary reference to singing ladies at Ferrara mentions their performance of duets. The reference occurs in a dispatch dated 14 August 1571 written by the Florentine ambassador Canigiani. The entire Ferrarese court had traveled to Brescello to meet the two sons of the Emperor Maximilian II of Austria and provided them with a typically lavish entertainment. Canigiani wrote:

> from dusk till late at night there was feasting at court . . . and one of those great concerts, with about sixty voices and instruments, and behind a gravicembalo played by Luzzasco, the Signora Lucrezia and the Signora Isabella Bendidio sang by turns and together, so well and so delightfully that I do not believe that I shall ever hear anything better.[22]

This was the period at which the singing ladies were drawn from the noblewomen of the court. No music survives that was specifically written for them and almost nothing is known from other sources about the music that they sang. In a letter to the Duke of Ferrara dated 10 April 1580, the Neapolitan bass singer Giulio Cesare Brancaccio, who had lived at the Ferrarese court from 1577, mentioned two types of music—*arie* for reciting sonnets, and *villanesche*—that he considered appropriate for the singing ladies with whom he had worked.[23] Both types are well known in the history of sixteenth-century "pseudo-monody," but whether either formed the basis of duets must remain an open question. As I have already pointed out, however, the lighter forms of the madrigal, represented here by the *canzone villanesca,* often lent themselves to arrangement as accompanied duets.

There is no further documentary evidence relating to duets sung at Ferrara either before or after 1580.[24] The four madrigals for two voices included in Luzzaschi's *Madrigali* cannot, therefore, be dated precisely. They are, nevertheless, the only concrete evidence on which we can base our idea of the Ferrarese accompanied duet.

In terms of style and technique, Luzzaschi's duets are poised between two worlds. They were, in all probability, written in the mid 1580s; yet they were published in 1601 for a Roman public which must already have heard of, if it had not already heard, the songs of Caccini and the early operas in the new Florentine manner. It is unlikely, however, that they were published simply as museum pieces. Rome, in 1601, was an established center of virtuoso singing and it is probable, as Newcomb suggested, that Luzzaschi's madrigals were intended to serve the virtuoso singers employed there by various cardinals.[25] Certainly virtuoso ornamentation remained a characteristic of the duets written during the early seventeenth century by Roman and Roman-influenced composers. And though Luzzaschi's ornamentation is more exuberant than Caccini's it is deployed with some respect for the sense and structure of the text.

In other respects, too, Luzzaschi's madrigals anticipate elements of the continuo duet. They are scored for two sopranos, a favorite combination of voices during the early seventeenth century. They contain declamatory passages (ex. 3, from "Cor mio, deh non languire") and the bass and voices often form a self-sufficient harmonic unit (ex. 4, from "Stral pungente d'amore"). The chief differences lie in the nature of the accompaniment, and it is this that ties Luzzaschi's duets inextricably to the sixteenth century. The accompaniment is fully written out and maintains a consistent four-part texture. The two vocal lines are essentially ornamented versions of the upper lines of the accompaniment, though the ornamented version of the line often seems quite independent of its basic form. The bass and tenor parts of the accompaniment scarcely join in the motivic interplay of the two sopranos. The bass acts as an almost continuous harmonic support, differing from a typical Florentine continuo only because it often moves in rhythm with the voices, thus limiting their freedom to move according to the passions. The tenor line serves mainly as a harmonic filler, though at cadences it often provides the essential leading note; so that in example 5 (from "Deh, vieni ormai") we have the paradox of an imitative passage over a sustained bass which might easily be mistaken for part of a duet with continuo, followed by a cadence which could not.

In terms of musical style and technique, the most tangible legacy of the Ferrarese *concerto delle donne* seems to have been what Newcomb dubbed the "luxuriant" style: that is, a type of madrigal writing in which written-out virtuoso ornamentation plays an important textural role. The idea of the *concerto delle donne* itself, however, was also imitated: at the Florentine court of Francesco de' Medici from 1584 to 1587-88, where the *concerto* was trained and accompanied by Caccini, and at Mantua and in the Orsini household at Rome from 1587-88.[26] We can glimpse some of the types of music written for the Mantuan *concerto* in Monteverdi's madrigal books III to VI, and possibly in book VII. As far as the Florentine *concerto* is concerned, we know that by 29 July 1584, Alessandro Striggio had written a "dialogo con due soprani diminuiti e fugati per il concerto" which had been commissioned by the Grand Duke, though this is now lost.[27] Jacopo Peri's duet "Intenerite voi, lacrime mie," which is, in any case, scored for two tenors, seems to date from a slightly later period than the Florentine *concerto delle donne*. The first three musical ideas used in Peri's duet are borrowed from the five-part setting by Luca Bati (in *RISM* 1598[11]).[28]

As for Rome, Giustiniani has left a quite clear statement that imitation of the Ferrarese and Mantuan *concerti* there included the writing of duets:

> With the example of these Courts and the two Neapolitan basses [Giulio Cesare Brancaccio and Alessandro Merlo] who sang in the manner described above, in Rome they began to change the style of composition for several voices... and also for one or two voices, at most, with instruments.[29]

Example 3

Example 4

Example 5

The period to which he was referring seems to be the 1580s. By the time that Luzzaschi's duets were published at Rome, then, the ground had been well prepared for them.

Trio Textures

Accompanied duets, then, whether arrangements or original compositions, played a part in both the chamber music and the dramatic entertainments of the late sixteenth century. Of the surviving examples described above, however, only the duets of Luzzaschi begin to approach the type of three-part writing that is typical of most seventeenth-century duets, in which the two upper parts form a distinct contrapuntal unit supported harmonically by the lowest part.

This type of trio texture can be traced back to the early sixteenth-century frottola.[30] And it seems to have remained a characteristic of the lighter strophic forms in Italy during the mid-sixteenth century while the more serious madrigal for three or more voices followed a path closer to the polyphonic motet. In the later sixteenth century, too, the lighter forms provide the richest vein of incipient duet textures.

A few examples will serve to show that several of the characteristic idioms of ensemble writing in the early seventeenth-century duet were probably derived from the late sixteenth-century canzonetta. The most important of these is what Einstein called "the 'scherzando' of the canzonetta—its cheerful, lively play of motifs":[31] that is, the use of short points of imitation "lightly touched" (as Thomas Morley put it in his definition of the Italian canzonetta)[32] and often repeated sequentially to produce a quasi-canonic texture. We have already met with this sort of writing in a duo—Filippo Nicoletti's "Dunque baciar"[33]—but examples 6a-6d show several passages drawn from three-part canzonettas in which the interplay of the upper voices is supported by the lowest. Examples 6b and 6d also illustrate, in contrast to the cadences found in Luzzaschi's madrigals, the more typical 4-3 cadence of the continuo duet in which one of the upper voices has the leading note. Two further idioms of the continuo duet, often used in contrast to *scherzando* imitation, can be seen in Vecchi's "Deh cant'Aminta" (ex. 1), which includes homophonic writing (bars 10-20) and opens with a passage in which the upper voices move in parallel thirds supported by a more slowly moving bass.

Example 6

Since late sixteenth-century canzonettas absorbed many of the mannerisms of the more serious madrigal, it is not surprising that we can also find some of the affective and declamatory gestures of the *seconda prattica* represented in passages of trio writing. Felice Anerio's "Fiamme che da begl'occhi" (*RISM* 1589[11]), which has already provided us with examples of the *scherzando* of the canzonetta, also contains rhetorical sighs for the word "ohimè" (ex. 7). And we can compare the opening of Ruggiero Giovanelli's "Jesu summa benignitas" (*RISM* 1586[2]), shown as example 8, with the more extended and impassioned version of the same idea used at the beginning of Grandi's "O come è gran martire."[34] Or compare a passage from Simone Verovio's "Giesu, sommo conforto" (*RISM* 1586[2]) (ex. 9) with analogous passages in Monteverdi's "O come sei gentile" (bars 12-13)[35] and Galeazzo Sabbatini's "Ohimè, misero, io canto" (bars 49-51).[36]

Example 7

Example 8

One of the most striking idioms of Monteverdi's duet writing is the combination of close imitation and suspensions. This can be seen at bars 39-47 of "Soave libertate,"[37] where the "chain" of suspensions suggests the chains that bind the lover, and the close entries the tightness with which he is held. It can also be seen at the end of the duets "Perchè fuggi tra salci?"[38] and "Armato il cor,"[39] where the successive entries, piled one on the other, are used to suggest multiple entries at the climax of a polyphonic madrigal. Even this device was anticipated in the canzonetta: by Monteverdi himself, in "Tu ridi mai," from his 1584 book (ex. 6c, bars 5-9), where the simple harmonic bass of bars 1-4 is transformed through the use of syncopation into an affective series of suspensions, and by Vecchi, in his canzonetta "S'udia un pastor l'altr'hieri" (ex. 10). And in Monteverdi's work it can also be traced in the five-part madrigal "Ah dolente partita,"[40] where a duet is the leading group in the intense climax of the madrigal.

Example 9

Example 10

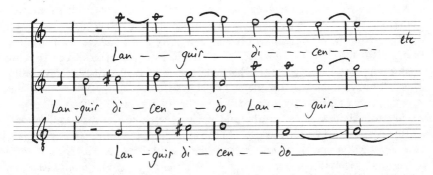

Just as it is possible to trace the antecedents of the duet in the three-part writing of the sixteenth century, so, conversely, it is also possible to trace the legacy of three-part contrapuntal writing in some continuo duets. Peri's "Intenerite voi"[41] is an example. In bars 3 to 5, for instance, the bass imitates the rhythm of the upper voices and could easily have the words "lacrime mie" underlaid. At bar 6 the bass moves in rhythm with the voices and has an uncharacteristically angular line, suggesting an underlying vocal concept; and at bar 18 the lower voice and bass are paired in parallel thirds in a manner often found in sixteenth-century three-part madrigals and canzonettas. This last example comes from a passage (bars 17-25) which is the most curious in the whole of Peri's setting, for at bars 20-21 he allows the bass to rest—a feature rarely found in later duets. Although the bass does not re-enter with motivic material, the technique of thinning the texture and then bringing back the bass as the climax to a set of entries is clearly derived from the polyphonic madrigal and suggests that Peri was thinking in terms of a vocal rather than an instrumental bass at this point.

In terms of both style and technique, then, it was only a small step from the three-part canzonetta to the fully fledged *concertato* duet, and canzonettas are among the most important immediate forerunners of the duets considered in this study. Their influence, moreover, was not confined to strophic settings. The light, canzonetta-like rhythms and *scherzando* imitation of Peri's "Intenerite voi," for example, show how closely related to canzonetta style even a serious madrigalian duet could be; and the bipartite structure of the piece, with a repeat sign at the end of bar 30, is also typical of a late sixteenth-century canzonetta.

In certain respects, however, the emergence of the duet with *basso continuo* had also long been preparing in the style and scoring of the late sixteenth-century polyphonic madrigal, particularly through the work of those composers, like Marenzio, who abandoned the consistent contrapuntal texture of the classic madrigal in order to explore the structural and expressive possibilites of contrasts in vocal scoring. This process may itself have owed something to the influence of the lighter forms and it is, perhaps, significant that the first example chosen by Einstein to illustrate Marenzio's new approach to madrigal writing—the opening of "Nel più fiorito Aprile," from the first book of six-part madrigals (1581)—makes prominent use of two contrasting trios written in concise, canzonetta-like styles.[42]

There has, fairly recently, been an attempt to classify the types of trio texture found in late sixteenth- and early seventeenth-century polyphonic music generally.[43] For the purposes of the present study, however, it is perhaps more interesting and pertinent to trace their use in the madrigals of a single composer—Monteverdi—whose output runs the whole gamut from *a cappella* madrigal to *concertato* duet.

A consideration of Monteverdi's *a cappella* madrigals again suggests the crucial role played by the canzonetta as a vehicle of stylistic and technical change at the end of the sixteenth century. Monteverdi himself began his career in secular music with a volume of three-part *Canzonette,* published in 1584 when he was only 17 years of age; and it is clear that the experience of this essentially Italian type of vocal music helped to shape and determine at least his early approach to madrigal writing.[44]

From the very outset of his first book of five-part madrigals (1587), one aspect of this experience is evident in the trio passage with which the madrigal "Ch'ami la vita mia" opens. The jaunty, quasi-declamatory homophonic writing of this trio is clearly derived from Monteverdi's canzonetta writing and can be compared, for example, with the opening of a work such as "Chi vuol veder" from the 1584 book.[45] Trio openings in styles derived from the canzonetta remained a consistent characteristic of the more anacreontic of Monteverdi's madrigals, furnishing a concise, emotionally neutral, but ear-catching opening gambit, and one which was fundamentally different from the imitative openings of many mid-sixteenth-century settings. Their use can be traced as late as the seventh book of madrigals, as the opening narration of "Dice la mia bellissima Licori" shows.[46] It was a type of opening, too, that Monteverdi was able to expand by using vocal roulades to suggest such pictorial images as the flowing of a stream (in "O rossignuol"),[47] or singing and flying (in "Quel augellin che canta").[48] At the beginning of "A un giro sol," in the fourth book of madrigals, he even combined the "turning" motives of the two soprano parts with a slowly moving bass to produce a quasi-continuo-duet texture.[49]

To a great extent, the function of trio sections in Monteverdi's early madrigals was structural rather than expressive. A structural function could, nevertheless, be an important part of the interpretation of a text, as we can see from the setting of "La giovinetta pianta," the opening madrigal of book III (1592).[50] Here, Monteverdi reserves the full five-part texture for the two points of focus of the madrigal, at the lines "L'intern'ardor che la radice accoglie" and "Ch'ardente è la radice de la vita."[51] The remainder of the setting is built almost entirely of overlapping three-part textures, partly imitative, partly homophonic in style, which prepare the way to the climactic points.

Although both halves of the text are exactly the same length—seven lines—Monteverdi chose to make the second part of his setting longer than the first in order to lend added weight to the final "point." If we look at the beginning of the second part,[52] we can see that one way in which he achieves this added length is by repeating the text in contrasting vocal colors. First of all, he sets lines 8, 9, and 10 of the text for a trio consisting of the three upper voices of the ensemble. Then, with a nicely judged contrast of color, he repeats the setting of lines 8 and 9 an octave lower, using the lower three voices. This is interrupted briefly by a new trio of two sopranos and tenor, who emerge suddenly from the dark colors of the lower trio to emphasise the notion that "love makes a girl beautiful," before the three lower voices continue to complete line 10. The trio writing itself might well have been taken from one of Monteverdi's early canzonettas, and in this passage, as in the madrigal as a whole, we can see Monteverdi growing confidently into the extended canvas and palette of the five-part madrigal without abandoning his early experience in the canzonetta.

Later in the same volume, the madrigal "Perfidissimo volto"[53] shows Monteverdi using bold contrasts of color to match the rhetoric of Guarini's text. After the opening lines of the madrigal, he sets a quite extended passage of text for the three lower voices in a subdued declamation. The exclamation "Ahi, ch'è spento il desio"[54] is then thrown into high relief by introducing the two sopranos in contrast. The effect is quite distinctively Monteverdian and the forerunner of other similar potent uses of contrast in "Era l'anima mia" and "Ohimè, il bel viso." It shows, too, how closely an imaginative composer of the late sixteenth century could approach the ideals of the Florentine "Camerata" without abandoning the traditional medium of the five-part madrigal.

In the madrigals of his fourth, fifth, and sixth madrigal books, the products of his years at Mantua, Monteverdi gradually moved away from the simpler canzonetta styles that had characterised his earlier pastorals. He now had a group of highly skilled professional singers at his disposal; he also had to write madrigals for a sophisticated audience and one accustomed to the music of Giaches de Wert, court choirmaster at Mantua until 1596; and he was now regularly setting the rhetorical and epigrammatic texts of Guarini and his imitators. These factors produced, in Monteverdi's middle-period madrigals, an increasing concern for clear declamation of the text and a search for new, more concise and intense ways of expressing their substance.

Example 11

Example 12

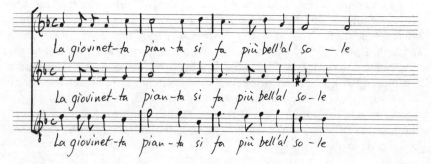

Although canzonetta style as such plays a diminishing role in the Mantuan madrigals, trio writing does not, and in the trio opening of a madrigal like "Cor mio, mentre vi miro"[55] we can see something of the new, weightier style of declamation that Monteverdi cultivated in the serious works of this period. The contrast with his earlier style can be illustrated vividly if we compare the rhetoric of a trio from "Anima mia, perdona" (ex. 11) with the dance-like rhythm of the opening of "La giovinetta pianta" (ex. 12). In the example from "Anima mia perdona" we find the prototype of the rich declamation which was later to characterise the opening of a duet like "Non vedrò mai le stelle."[56]

Contrasts in scoring, too, become sharper and more poignant in the middle-period madrigals as Monteverdi sought new ways to highlight details of the text in his music. The madrigal "Ohimè, il bel viso,"[57] the setting of a sonnet by Petrarch, illustrates the end-point of this process, and at the same time parallels the contrast of two voices and chorus which characterises several of Monteverdi's *concertato* madrigals. In the opening paragraph of the madrigal, Monteverdi makes use of the fact that five out of the first seven lines of Petrarch's sonnet contain the word "Ohimè" to bind together the first thirty-five bars of his setting. The two sopranos are the only voices to sing "Ohimè"; and for the first thirty-five bars they sing nothing else, while the three lower voices enumerate the well-remembered features of Petrarch's beloved, but now dead, Laura.

During the first twenty bars of the setting, the two sopranos take it in turns to punctuate the sombre-hued trio of lower voices with the word "Ohimè", sung usually at the correct points in the poetic line.[58] From bar 20, the beginning of the second quartet of the sonnet, in which Petrarch recalls Laura's smile, the two sopranos repeat the initial words "Et ohimè" over and over again in a duet comprising a chain of acrid dissonances, while underneath them the lower voices share the remainder of lines 5 and 6. And the way in which they do this demonstrates Monteverdi's new ability to dramatize human emotion within the bounds of the madrigal. First the tenor enters, but can only utter the words "il dolce riso." After two bars in which only the two sopranos are heard, the bass makes his attempt, but gets only a little further before breaking off. Finally, in a climactic effort, the alto manages to sing the whole of the sentence, dying away to silence as the sopranos complete their last "Ohimè."

This is one of the most protracted and powerful images of pain in Monteverdi's work. It introduces a harmonic sequence— $\frac{6}{4}$ resolving to $\frac{5}{3}$ —which was to become a cliché of Baroque music.[59] And it also shows Monteverdi working with a (sounding) bass line that moves independently of the two upper parts while supporting them harmonically. This arises from his combining in one concentrated musical image two musical ideas for two separate ideas in the text—a technique obviously denied to the poet. And, paradoxically, it was through the use of such double motives, a technique rarely used in his genuine duets, that Monteverdi first explored the world of writing for two voices and independent bass.

As with trio writing in general, the double motive is a technical feature that can be traced back in Monteverdi's own work to the *Canzonette* of 1584. It can be seen, for example, at the beginning of the second section of "Chi vuol veder"[60] and also in the single stanza of "Tu ridi sempre mai," a canzonetta in which we have already noted the clever way Monteverdi turns the resigned, slowly descending bass of the first four bars into an affective duet by presenting it as a syncopated duet against its own inversion (ex. 6c). At the beginning of this example we again find Monteverdi telescoping two lines of text, and most of the double motives found in his later madrigals are of this sort. Occasionally though, in his early madrigal writing, and specifically in response to the concrete imagery of Tasso's pastoral poetry, we find him using a double motive for a single line of text. An example can be seen in bars 7-12 of "Ecco mormorar l'onde"[61] at the words "A l'aura mattutina e l'arboscelli." Here, the upper voices moving in parallel suggest the gentle undulation of the waves, while the faster-moving tenor line seems to represent the breeze among the leaves.

Example 13

Sometimes Monteverdi uses a double motive for purely structural reasons as when, at the beginning of "O dolce anima mia,"[62] he turns the second half of his setting of line 1 into an invertible counterpoint for the first half, producing, with the addition of a third voice, the kind of trio writing with two voices moving in parallel over a "walking bass," that we also find at the beginning of the strophic duet "Chiome d'oro."[63] For the most part, however, he seems to have been more interested in the potential of the double motive as an interpretative device. In "Sì ch'io vorrei morire," from the fourth book of madrigals, for example, he was able to cap the eroticism of the text by bringing two lines of it into a new juxtaposition (ex. 13). As the two sopranos sing, in close imitation, "Ah, hold me close until I expire," the lover (bass) cries out "Ah mouth, ah kisses, ah tongue," falling silent before the duet is complete.

The double motive came into its own as a musical vehicle for the epigrammatic final point of the Guarinian madrigal. "A un giro sol,"[64] mentioned earlier for its opening trio, again furnishes an example. In the text of this madrigal, the lover's inner torment is thrown into relief by contrasting it with the joy that he sees around him: the beloved looks about her and the air laughs, the sea and the winds are quieted and the heavens filled with a new light; only the lover has tears in his eyes because of her cruelty. Monteverdi's setting falls into two clearly defined sections, matching in musical terms the contrast in the text. The second section consists, almost entirely, of the last three lines of Guarini's text:

> Certo quando nasceste
> Così crudel e ria
> Nacque la morte mia.

Certainly, when you were born so cruel and wicked, my death was born [with you].

Monteverdi sets the first two of these lines for alto and tenor, who begin by declaiming the first line on a monotone, building a tension which is only released as the alto rises a semitone to begin a sequence of acute dissonances, suggesting the beloved's cruelty. This in itself was a device to which Monteverdi returned with powerful effect in the duet "O sia tranquillo il mare";[65] and, as Fortune noted,[66] it also has its equivalent in the declamation of "Interrotte speranze."[67] In "A un giro sol," however, the idea also leads to a double motive. As the alto and tenor complete their statement, Monteverdi repeats their declamatory idea an octave higher, using the two sopranos. And this time he also introduces the final line of the text in a second motive sung by the bass. The beloved's cruelty and its consequence—the lover's death—are, thus, brought into sharp juxtaposition (ex. 14).

This method of encapsulating the "point" of a madrigal in a single musical image finds its zenith in Monteverdi's setting of "La piaga c'ho nel core,"[68] where the double motive for the final couplet of the text (surely the initial inspiration for the setting) is stated first as a trio, then in various combinations of three, four, and five voices, in its original form and with the counterpoint inverted, to create a musical paragraph which makes up half the length of the setting in a manner analogous to the aria section of a recitative and aria.

One last type of trio writing must be mentioned in the present context. In several of the Mantuan madrigals, Monteverdi displays a tendency to isolate a "leading group" of two voices and supporting bass within the full four-, five-, or six-part texture. This may, as Fortune suggested, have resulted from a concern to project the text clearly,[69] or it may have resulted from a desire to concentrate on particular voices within the *concerto*. And although the leading group often comprises two sopranos and bass, this is not always the case. At the end of "Ah, dolente partita,"[70] for example, a leading group of two sopranos and bass used for the line "Per far che moia" is immediately followed by a pair of tenors singing the same material.

This "leading group" technique is also found at the end of the lively pastoral "Io mi son giovinetta,"[71] in the opening plaint of "Cruda Amarilli,"[72] and, with a "walking bass," in the refrain of the *concertato* madrigal "E così a poco a poco."[73] In passages such as these, the function of the inner parts, though they may have a certain motivic independence, is largely to complement the rhythm of the "leading group" and to act as harmonic fillers. In short, they act as a continuo-like accompaniment to the duet. There is a clear parallel here with the texture and technique of Luzzaschi's duets; and the similarity is particularly striking when, as at the end of "Io mi son giovinetta," Monteverdi ornaments the two soprano lines to produce a climax for the madrigal.[74] With this type of "leading group" trio, Monteverdi stood on the threshold of the genuine duet with *basso continuo* accompaniment just as Luzzaschi did in his madrigals for two sopranos.

Example 14

In this chapter we have seen that there is clear evidence that accompanied duets, whether newly composed or arranged from polyphonic originals, did play a part in the musical life of late sixteenth-century Italy. We have seen, too, that the type of three-part texture characteristic of most seventeenth-century *concertato* duets had already evolved by the late sixteenth century. Examples are found most readily in three-part villanellas and canzonettas, and it can be no accident that the lighter forms dominated the early history of the *concertato* duet. But many examples can also be found in *a cappella* polyphonic madrigals, where trio textures were increasingly explored during the late sixteenth century for variety in scoring, for structural reasons and as the bearers of musical imagery. In Monteverdi's output quite obvious parallels can sometimes be drawn between techniques explored in the trio sections of his *a cappella* madrigals and passages found in his later duets. The ground from which the *concertato* duet was to spring at the beginning of the seventeenth century was, then, well prepared in the music of the late sixteenth.

6

Emergence of the *Concertato* Duet II

Well prepared though the ground may have been, there can be little doubt that it was the seminal influence of Florentine continuo-accompanied song that hastened the emergence and publication of a new type of *concertato* duet at the beginning of the seventeenth century. The early history of Florentine-style solo song in published sources is characterized by the appearance of a model publication—Caccini's *Le Nuove Musiche*—followed by fairly obvious imitations. The early history of the *concertato* duet, on the other hand, is characterized by the appearance of duets in several quite disparate sources, no one of which can be said to have provided the model that other composers followed, and by two distinct types of duet, the one with a genuinely independent *basso continuo,* the other with a continuo line that doubles the lower voice.

In this chapter, I shall review the various published sources in which duets are found during the first decade of the seventeenth century, and trace some of the characteristics of the independent duet settings found in duet books, volumes of villanellas, and monody books (together with such related sources as d'India's *Musiche a due voci* of 1615 and Valentini's *Musiche a doi voci* of 1622). The year 1623, which forms a terminal date for this chapter, provides a convenient turning point in our discussion of the stylistic and technical development of the duet and also marks a change in the content of monody books. After 1623, very few madrigalian duets appeared in monody books, and duets with *basso seguente* virtually disappeared from published sources.

Duets in Monteverdi's *Concertato* Madrigals

Monteverdi was one of the first composers to turn to the new medium of the *concertato* duet. Typically, though, he did so within the context of the larger-scale polyphonic madrigal, and his early duets are a striking mixture of a Mantuan love of sonority, ornamented vocal writing, and the languid, affective declamation typical of the Florentine solo madrigal.

The *concertato* madrigals of Monteverdi's fifth and sixth madrigal books

(1605 and 1614 respectively) occupy a special position in the composer's output and one which is comparable to that of the madrigals for one, two, and three sopranos in Luzzaschi's, for they seem to represent some of the more advanced practices of the Mantuan *concerto* with regard to virtuoso singing. The "luxuriant" style that Monteverdi employs for both solo and ensemble passages in these madrigals is an unmistakable sign of Ferrarese influence. And more important still, the decorative figuration that he uses is no longer simply an extension of the sinuous windings of the Marenzian pastoral, such as we find in the *a cappella* madrigals, but also incorporates the semiquaver divisions and dotted rhythms that were the stock-in-trade of early seventeenth-century virtuoso performers.

Monteverdi's fifth book of madrigals includes six madrigals with a genuine *basso continuo,* two of which—"Ahi, come a un vago Sol" and "E così a poco a poco"—are effectively duets with choral refrain. Monteverdi seems to have published these madrigals in response to the new seventeenth-century fashion for *concertato* music. Whether they were actually composed during the early years of the seventeenth century is, however, another question. Since a *concerto* of singers on the Ferrarese model had been in existence at Mantua from as early as 1587-88, it seems unlikely that Monteverdi would have waited until the early seventeenth century before experimenting with the full potential of the "luxuriant" style. It is possible, then, that some, or all, of the *concertato* madrigals in book V might have been written several years before their date of publication and even before the turn of the century. The nature of the continuo line and its relationship with the voices would not preclude a fairly early date in most cases. There is no musical evidence, for example, that Monteverdi was acquainted at this stage with Peri's recitative style. The first hint of this in a *concertato* madrigal comes in bar 27 of "Batto qui pianse" (1614), in which Monteverdi uses a recitative-like accented dissonance at the words "Deh mira."[1] The fairly static basses of "Ahi, come a un vago Sol" and "E così a poco a poco" may however, suggest that Monteverdi was acquainted with Caccini's solo songs.

At all events, the transition from *a cappella* to *concertato* madrigal in Monteverdi's work was not a simple one in terms of chronology. Rather, the two types of madrigal seem to represent complementary aspects of musical life at Mantua, an idea which is confirmed by the fuller information that we have on the chronology of the madrigals included in book VI.[2] Certainly the transition was not a simple one in terms of style and technique, and in the duet writing of his fifth and sixth madrigal books we can see Monteverdi coming to terms with two idioms not familiar from his *a cappella* madrigals—virtuoso ornamentation and the art of constructing extended paragraphs of melody over a continuo bass.

The latter problem—the fundamental one for seventeenth-century continuo madrigalists—is as evident in Monteverdi's duets as in his writing for solo
voices. And his experience of trio writing within the *a cappella* madrigal seems
at first to have suggested few viable solutions. The madrigalian technique of
juxtaposing a series of ideas generated by textual images was not in itself a
guarantee of success in duet writing, as we can see in the long and rather loosely
formed duet "Qui con meco s'assise" from the madrigal "Qui rise, O Tirsi."[3]

The duets of "E così a poco a poco," too, are not wholly successful. The
madrigal begins promisingly enough, with lines that blossom out "little by
little" into elaborate *fioriture* on the penultimate syllable of the line. But the
passages beginning "E nel fallace sguardo"[4] and "Quando si cura più"[5]
degenerate into a rather uninteresting parallelism. Their shortcomings seem
particularly marked when we compare them with the shapely and purposive
trio writing at the beginning of the *a cappella* madrigal "Era l'anima mia" in the
same book.[6] The duet sections of "E così a poco a poco" are scored throughout
for soprano and tenor and it may be significant that Monteverdi never returned
to this combination of voices in his later duets.

The most successful of Monteverdi's early duet writing is found in the very
first of the *concertato* madrigals of book V—"Ahi, come a un vago Sol."[7] And
it also contains some of the most forward-looking passages in his early duets.
At "Torn'al mio core" (bars 16-18), for example, he uses for the first time the
technique of stating an idea in one voice and then repeating it with the two
voices in parallel. This is one of the basic form-building techniques of his later
duets. At the word "lasso" (bars 33-35) he discovers the pleasure of allowing the
two voices to intertwine before resolving at the cadence. And at "non val
ascondersi" (bar 37) he pioneers the device of having both voices sing the same
note before making the first tenor fall an affective diminished fifth to hasten the
cadence.

Example 1

In this duet, too, we find early evidence of distinctive melodic idioms
generated by the use of a slowly moving continuo line. Thus, the melodic shape

of the initial point of imitation, with its repeated notes and characteristic under-third inflection before the accented syllable (ex. 1). This was to become a commonplace of continuo declamation in the Monteverdian circle, and instances of its use may be seen in the work of Galeazzo Sabbatini[8] and Giovanni Rovetta.[9] Thus, too, the use of semiquaver declamation and triadic figures, as in the setting of "Sì pront'a sospirar" (bars 15-16).

Above all, though, Monteverdi solved here the problem of constructing extended musical paragraphs in the new medium by creating successful antecedent-consequent relationships between relatively short phrases. This can be seen in the opening paragraph, where an imitative duet of four bars is immediately balanced by two bars of parallel writing. The whole process is then repeated, with a new imitative duet and a new passage of parallel writing. Rhythmically and melodically, each phrase implies the one that follows and requires it for the sake of completeness. Moreover, the whole paragraph of four phrases has a strong sense of unity since each pair of phrases is constructed over a similar harmonic pattern (ex. 2).

Example 2

Stylistic and technical considerations apart, Monteverdi's *concertato* madrigals are also marked by a degree of formalism not apparent in the *a cappella* madrigals. In the three madrigals "Ahi, come a un vago Sol," "E così a poco a poco," and "Qui rise, O Tirsi," for example, Monteverdi takes the last line of the text out of context and sets it as a choral refrain which he uses to punctuate and unify the setting. In "Ahi, come a un vago Sol" this produces a quasi-dramatic setting in which the choral refrain functions like the chorus of a classical tragedy, standing apart from the protagonists, commenting on their predicament and pointing the "moral" of the madrigal. It may be that Monteverdi had some such conception in mind. Certainly, until the end of the madrigal the two tenors and the chorus of soprano, alto, and bass are treated as two separate entities. Since they sing the final line of the text out of its correct order at bars 24ff. and 46ff., the chorus represent a stage of awareness that the tenors (the protagonists) have not yet reached. And it is only after the final line has been sung in its correct order by the tenors (bar 56ff.) that they are allowed to join the remainder of the ensemble in reiterating the "point" of the madrigal.

Duets in Early Opera

In some respects "Ahi, come a un vago Sol" resembles the complex of solos, ensemble, and choral refrain that concludes the messenger scene of Peri's *Euridice*. And, indeed, most early operatic ensembles, duets included, fulfill a choral function. Only two of the operas first performed during the first decade of the seventeenth century include duets sung by the named protagonists of the drama. The first of these is Cavalieri's *Rappresentatione di Anima e di Corpo,* in which Body and Soul sing two duets, the first in act II (no. 51), when they resolve to cast off the desires of earthly life, and the second in act III (no. 83), where they initiate the finale by calling on the chorus to praise God. Cavalieri's duet writing is essentially an outgrowth of monody. For although the voice parts and continuo are notated on three staves, the continuo simply doubles the lower voice, which is notated in bass clef.[10] Stylistically, the duets seem quite closely related to canzonettas, with a lyrical outline and only short-breathed points of imitation.

The other exceptional case is found at the end of Monteverdi's *Orfeo* where, in the new apotheosis scene substituted for Alessandro Striggio's original ending, Apollo and Orpheus rise to the heavens singing, as befits the gods of song, a florid duet. In both Cavalieri's and Monteverdi's operas the duets are duets of resolution in which the two characters share the same musical material. The idea of conflict in an operatic duet was, as yet, unknown: arguments, or disagreements were presented in dialogue form.

In most cases, however, duets formed part of the choruses of the early operas, where they developed quite naturally from a desire for musical variety. And, as in Andrea Gabrieli's choruses for *Edipo tiranno,* we can find both duets for two solo voices and two-part choral writing.

In the early pastoral operas the chorus plays an essential role in the *mise en scène,* providing the audience with essential information and commenting and elaborating on the emotions expressed in the recitatives of the principal characters. It plays, too, a crucial role in articulating the structure of the operas. The libretto for *Euridice,* for example, has no act or scene divisions, but it can be seen to fall into a prologue and five scenes, most of which end with a chorus. The texts for the choruses, in contrast with the generally free scheme of the libretto, are strophic, thus allowing the composer a range of musical possibilities, from choral dances to settings in which the scoring is varied from stanza to stanza. Both possibilites are exploited in Peri's setting.

The chorus which ends "scene 2" of *Euridice* is used to intensify the most tragic moment of the opera, for this is the scene in which the messenger Daphne tells Orpheus of Eurydice's death. The text of the chorus consists of seven stanzas, and the last two lines of the first—"Sospirate, aure celesti/ Lagrimate, O selve, O campi"—reappear as a refrain after each subsequent stanza. Peri set the first stanza in unison and the refrain for five-part chorus. The next five stanzas are set as two alternating solo arias for nymphs of the chorus, and the last stanza is set as a declamatory trio.[11] However, it was not Peri's setting of the chorus that was given at the first performance of *Euridice* on 6 October 1600, but rather a version composed by Caccini and subsequently published in his own version of the opera, for as Peri himself tells us in the preface to his score:

> although...I had composed the work exactly as it is now published, nonetheless Giulio Caccini (called Romano), whose extreme merit is known to the world, composed the airs of Eurydice and some of those of the shepherd and of the nymphs of the chorus, also the choruses "Al canto, al ballo," "Sospirate," and "Poi che gli eterni imperi," and this because they were to be sung by persons under his direction.[12]

For the most part, the outline of Caccini's setting of the messenger scene chorus follows Peri's exactly, and is a most shameless piece of plagiarism. In place of a declamatory trio, however, Caccini set the seventh stanza of the chorus as a lyrical duet, the only duet in either setting of the opera. He can thus add to the list of his claims for priority that of having composed the first operatic duet.

The duet itself is rather interesting. Unlike Peri's trio setting it is aria-like rather than declamatory and it employs an imitative technique that is so strict as to be almost canonic. In this respect it reminds us of Nicoletti's duo "Dunque baciar." Moreover, lines 2 and 4, which rhyme in the text, are also rhymed musically, though the ornamentation applied to the setting of line 4 moves at twice the speed of that for line 2 and concludes with a written-out *trillo* before leading back to the choral refrain (ex. 3).

In the version of Rinuccini's *Dafne* set by Marco da Gagliano in 1608,[13] we find yet another tragic chorus with refrain. The chorus in question—"Piangete Ninfe"—which follows the news that Daphne has been transformed into a laurel tree, is cast in stanzas of irregular length and meter, unified only by the refrain "Piangete, Ninfe, e con voi pianga Amore." In Marco da Gagliano's setting, prepared for performance at Mantua in 1608, the second stanza of the chorus is given to a two-part choir. Gagliano intended a specific visual effect to be employed at this point in the drama, as he explained in the preface to the published score:

> when they [the chorus] sing together the duo "Sparse più non vedrem di quel fin oro," if they look in each other's face on singing those exclamations it will be very effective...[14]

The duo mixes homophonic writing with short points of imitation, and on two occasions we find short, quasi-canonic passages which are settings of exclamations (exx. 4a and 4b). The second of these is the beginning of the refrain, for which Gagliano created one of his most telling musical ideas.

Example 3

['Sospirate'. Chorus à 5]

Example 4

Gagliano's *Dafne* also illustrates very well the way in which choruses were used to lend musical variety to an otherwise largely static scene and, at the same time, to provide the audience with the information it needed to orientate itself to the action of the opera. This was, clearly, a technique well suited to the opening scenes of an opera. In scene 1 of *Dafne,* a chorus of nymphs and shepherds, together with individuals of their number, occupy most of the scene, and their solos are punctuated by three ensembles. In the first of these—a setting of a strophic text beginning "Se la sù gl'aurei chiostri"—they call on the gods to save them from the monster that has been ravaging their lands. Gagliano set the four stanzas as a set of strophic variations, pairing stanzas 1 and 4 for solo voice, and 2 and 3 for two-part choir, who sing in parallel over a slowly moving bass. The whole complex is unified by a four-part choral refrain, "Odi il pianto." The two-part writing in this chorus, as in the duo in hemiola rhythm with duple-meter instrumental bass—"Se germoglian frondi, e fiori" which is found at the end of scene 1,[15] is of the simplest, consisting of little more than a melodic line reinforced by a second voice moving largely in parallel. Gagliano was a potent melodist, however, and he seems to have been particularly fond of the aria that he created for the duo sections of "Se la sù gl'aurei chiostri," for he used it again, to a different text, for the strophic duet "Alma mia, dove ten vai?" that he published in his *Musiche* of 1615.[16]

From the outset, librettists made use of the possibility of allowing one member of the chorus to speak for all, a possibility admitted by late Renaissance commentators on classical tragedy:

> the chorus served in two ways in tragedy, that is, either as an actor, with one of the chorus speaking in place of all, or with all singing together.[17]

This accounts for the appearance, in all the early pastoral operas, of individual, but unnamed nymphs and shepherds whose function as commentators and scene-setters is the same as that of the chorus as an ensemble. This device for articulating the plot, once admitted, opened the door to composers to experiment with other possibilities. Caccini's duet for two nymphs of the chorus is an early example of the results to which this could lead. But it is with Monteverdi's *Orfeo* that the technique of using two and even three individual members of the chorus in ensemble writing really came into its own.

In writing the text of *Orfeo*, Alessandro Striggio followed the same general precepts with regard to the use of the chorus that had guided Rinuccini in writing *Euridice*. The chorus, then, plays a major role at the end of each act and in shaping and binding together those parts of the opera in which there is little interaction between the principal characters. In *Orfeo* this means that it is used most extensively in act I, to portray the rejoicing on Orpheus's wedding day, and in act II, where the friends of Orpheus react to the news of Eurydice's death; and it is in these acts that all the duets sung by individuals from the chorus appear.

Like the choral duos in Gagliano's *Dafne*, the duets of *Orfeo* are all settings of strophic texts; and like Gagliano, Monteverdi set these texts both as simple strophic duets and as sets of strophic variations. At the beginning of act II, for example, two shepherds from the chorus sing three stanzas of poetry beginning "In questo prato adorno."[18] The first two are treated as a simple, unaffected strophic duet characterised by parallel writing and a lively triple meter. A ritornello introduces and separates the stanzas. The third stanza is given new musical material, in duple meter, which is then taken over by a five-part chorus. The result, typical of much of Monteverdi's writing in the first two acts, is to disguise the straightforward strophic nature of the choral complex, producing a sense of organic development which Peri and Caccini never quite achieved.

In contrast with this, a much more formal plan can be seen in the chorus "Alcun non sia che disperato in preda" from act I.[19] Here Monteverdi treats eight eleven-syllable lines with the seriousness due to an *ottava rima* by setting them as three stanzas of strophic variation (3 lines + 3 + 2), setting the first and last stanzas for two voices and the central one for three (he does not specify solo voices). The two-part writing here shows Monteverdi putting his recent experience as a writer of *concertato* madrigals to good use in developing balancing phrases of contrasting homophony and close imitation, as in "veste di fior ... ," where he also uses a bass line moving mainly in fourths and fifths to create a satisfactory sense of harmonic progression.[20]

It is in the choral complex at the end of the messenger scene in act II, however, that we find the most interesting of the duet writing in *Orfeo,* for here Monteverdi manages to integrate Peri's concept of declamatory recitative with his own experience as a madrigalist. The chorus which begins "Chi ne consola, ahi lasso?" is both simpler and more sophisticated than the corresponding choruses in *Dafne* and *Euridice:* simpler, because the chorus proper[21] consists only of two duets each followed by a choral refrain; more sophisticated because the material of the refrain has already been heard several times during the messenger scene.

It is, however, the duet writing that is our main concern here. The two duets are again conceived as a set of strophic variations, though their basses follow a similar pattern only for the first few bars. This time, however, they are of a declamatory rather than an aria-like character. Peri's influence can be seen most clearly in the opening bars of the second stanza, with its parallel writing, truncated phrases and accented dissonances. The chromaticism of passages like "pietosi a ritrovarle" and "da poter lagrimar,"[22] on the other hand, is a throwback to the style of an earlier Mantuan madrigal, "Rimanti in pace."[23] And in the second of these two passages Monteverdi uses the continuo as though it were the third voice of a three-part madrigalian texture. It may be that this passage suggested to Francesco Turini the chromatic basis of his madrigal "Dove, ah dove ten vai?,"[24] which is itself a setting of a text drawn from the libretto for *Orfeo.*

Example 5

At the same time, these duets can themselves be seen as the source of several idioms found in Monteverdi's own later duets. The use of declamatory recitative is one, of course, but so is the use of dotted rhythms to suggest happiness and innocence, as in "Io son pur vezzosetta."[25] And the curiously disjointed effect of introducing a point of imitation at the approach to a cadence, seen at the words "Ch'oggi è partita in sul fiorir de' giorni" (ex. 5) is a device which Monteverdi was later to employ at the beginning of duets like "Non è di gentil core"[26] and "Vorrei baciarti, O Filli."[27] There is a clear similarity of conception, too, between the declamatory style of strophic variation found here and that of the *Romanesca* variations "Ohimè, dov'è il mio ben" included by Monteverdi in his seventh book of madrigals.[28] And finally, moving outside the realm of the duet for a moment, it is worth noting that the final bar of the first stanza anticipates the more famous opening of the lament of Arianna.

The duets found in the early operatic scores and *concertato* madrigals are important for a number of reasons. First, in a field like the *concertato* duet, where there were no obvious models for imitation such as those provided for monodists by the songs of *Le Nuove Musiche,* these sources must be taken into consideration as a possible stimulus to duet writing among the composers of chamber music. We should not imagine that seventeenth-century composers share the historian's tendency to think of different genres as mutually exclusive.

Second, a study of the operatic duets in particular shows that two composers who were later to make important contributions to the published literature of independent duet settings—Monteverdi and Marco da Gagliano—were already working in the medium during the first decade of the seventeenth century. In Gagliano's case, too, we have clear evidence of self-borrowing from an operatic source in the case of the aria "Alma mia, dove ten vai?" (1615). In the case of Monteverdi, the duets both of the fifth book of madrigals and of *Orfeo* reveal him as a masterly writer in all three of the forms—madrigal, strophic duet, and strophic variation—that dominate the early history of the duet. And the more serious of these compositions show that he had already realized the potential of the duet as a vehicle capable of expressing the most powerful and intense emotions. In the changing aesthetics of the early seventeenth century this was a potential which was realized by only a few of Monteverdi's contemporaries, but it produced in his own work such masterpieces as "Interrotte speranze," "Non vedrò mai le stelle," and "O sia tranquillo il mare."

Most important of all, however, these early *concertato* duets provide us with a substantial proportion of the earliest datable examples of duets with a genuine *basso continuo.* For although duets were published in quite large numbers during the first decade of the seventeenth century, only a few of the independent settings actually have a genuine *basso continuo.* The total, in fact, amounts to no more than twenty-six settings, of which more than half are simple strophic duets, with only a handful of madrigals (most of them in one source—Brunetti's *Euterpe* of 1606) and strophic variations.

Duets with *Basso Seguente,* 1604-1623

The overwhelming majority of the duets published up to 1610 are scored for high voice and bass, printed in score on two staves with the bass part also serving as an instrumental *basso seguente.* This type of duet fills the early duet books of Radesca, Cagnazzi, and Rubini and is also found in volumes of unaccompanied villanellas and a number of monody books. Some early monodists—Jacopo Peri, for example—published no other kind of duet. In most monody books, though, and particularly in those published after 1610, duets for high voice and bass appear together with duets having an independent *basso continuo.* Viewed solely in this context they might appear simply to be continuo duets for soprano or tenor and bass notated in a shorthand manner.

In fact, duets for high voice and bass/*basso seguente* form a quite distinct group of early settings. They were published in quite large numbers during the early years of the century and their scoring sets them apart from the mainstream of later continuo duets, which were written for two equal voices. In the majority of duets for high voice and bass, too, the upper voice is the more important in terms of melodic interest, with the bass part being conceived primarily as a harmonic support. These duets are, in short, song-like, and in Brunetti's *Euterpe* and one or two other monody books they are advertised as being suitable for performance by either one or two voices. Given these facts and that duets for high voice and bass began to appear in print from as early as 1604, it seems fair to assume that their composition was directly influenced by the publication of Caccini's solo songs in 1602.

The extent of each composer's debt to Florentine monody, however, varies greatly. Many of Enrico Radesca's madrigals, for example, with their melodious character and fast rate of harmonic change, owe more to the sixteenth-century canzonetta than to the Florentine solo madrigal. On the other hand, in a declamatory madrigal such as "Hor consolato i' moro" (1609) by Giovanni Ghizzolo, we can reduce the bass part to a continuo line which closely resembles the relatively static basses of Caccini's madrigals (ex. 6). And in the madrigal "Alma afflitta" (1606) by Domenico Brunetti we find written-out *trilli* of a kind which seems to come directly from Florence (ex. 7).

For the most part, the composers who published duets for high voice and bass during the first decade of the century worked outside Florence and the other main centers of virtuoso singing. And with only one possible exception— the Paduan lawyer Domenico Maria Melli[29]—they were all professional musicians. At the time that they published their duets, Montella and Lambardi were musicians in the viceregal chapel of Spanish-dominated Naples. Radesca worked at Turin. Two further composers—Cagnazzi and Ghizzolo, the latter a Franciscan friar and a pupil in music of Costanzo Porta—came from towns near Milan. From centers nearer Florence came figures like Nicolò Rubini of

Example 6

Example 7

Modena, a pupil of Orazio Vecchi and the author of a treatise on counterpoint, and Domenico Brunetti of Bologna who, in 1609, was organist at the church of San Domenico. But the only Florentine to publish such duets during this period was, as we have seen, Jacopo Peri.

Song-like though they may be, duets for high voice and bass, with their frequently imitative texture, represent a rather equivocal response to Florentine monody as such. And like the madrigalian duos of the sixteenth century they may have been aimed primarily at amateur singers. In dedicating the first two of his books of *Canzonette, Madrigali et Arie alla romana,* for example, Radesca made it quite clear that he expected his noble patrons to sing his duets and not merely to listen to them being performed by professionals. The style of the duets is correspondingly simple, often with only one note for each syllable of the text.

The link between the duet for high voice and bass and the sixteenth-century duo, though perceptible, is rather tenuous in most cases. As we saw in chapter 4, many of the madrigalian duos of the sixteenth century were stylistically related to the French chanson, and most were of a rather serious nature even when, as in the case of Nicoletti's madrigals, we can find some evidence of canzonetta influence. The spiritual legacy of the duo can be traced only in a few of the more serious madrigalian duets for high voice and bass, works like Rubini's "Una tempesta ria" (1610), which begins with a wide-ranging line reminiscent of some of Giaches de Wert's writing (ex. 8), or his "Mentre la Donna mia" (1610), with its long opening point of imitation (ex. 9).[30] Despite their superficial similarity to madrigalian duos, however, Rubini's madrigals were not intended to serve any educational function. And even though his settings involve genuine two-part counterpoint they are intended to be accompanied by chordal instruments such as the harpsichord and theorbo. Their consistent scoring for soprano[31] and bass, too, links them closely to solo song. The Venetian publisher Alessandro Vincenti certainly had no doubt of this, for in the catalogue that he issued in 1621 he listed Rubini's duets, together with those of Radesca and Cagnazzi, in the section devoted to monody and opera and not under the heading "Musica a due voci" that he reserved for unaccompanied duos.[32]

Example 8

Example 9

The madrigals in Rubini's collection are through-composed, but the majority of duets for high voice and bass, madrigals and arias alike, are cast in a bipartite or tripartite structure in which the sections are marked off by double bars or repeat marks, a characteristic that serves to link them directly to the canzonetta and villanella literature of the sixteenth century. Even the exceptions to the rule—the single-section madrigals and arias in Brunetti's *Euterpe,* for example, Jacopo Peri's aria "Al fonte, al prato" (1609),[33] and his delightfully fresh madrigal "Con sorrisi cortesi" (actually a setting of one of Chiabrera's *scherzi*) from the same book—are related stylistically to the canzonetta, though they follow Caccini's practice of leaving canzonetta settings undivided.

The most prolific composer of duets for high voice and bass, and perhaps the most influential in popularizing this sort of duet, was Enrico Radesca di Foggia, whose four books of secular *Canzonette, Madrigali, et Arie alla romana* were published between 1605 and 1610. As a young man Radesca had served with the Venetian army in Dalmatia. Only later did he turn to a musical career. He was appointed organist of Turin cathedral in about 1597 and held this post until 1615, when he became choirmaster. By 1605 he was also working as a chamber musician to Don Amedeo, son of the Duke of Savoy. On 20 June 1610 he became a musician at the ducal court and by 1615 he had also attained the position of choirmaster of the court chapel.

Soon after his arrival at Turin, Radesca had published a volume of three- and four-part canzonettas (*Thesoro amoroso,* Milan, 1599) and the duets that he published six years later seem to have evolved as the reduction to the two outer voices of a fairly homophonic canzonetta texture. There is, then, more than passing significance in the fact that Radesca himself referred to his duets simply as canzonettas in the dedicatory letters to his publications, even though his books contain madrigals as well as strophic settings.

This is not to say, however, that there is no distinction between Radesca's arias and his madrigals, though the latter belong, even at their most serious, to the world of the light madrigal. The simplest settings in the collections are the strophic arias in triple meter which are note-against-note settings of rather inconsequential verse. And here, it is the regular stress pattern of the verse that dictates the rhythm of the musical setting. A stanza like the following, for example,

Dopo che tu
Mi vuoi tradire
Per te languire
Non voglio più.
Poichè la fè
E i giuramenti
Son già mai spenti
Fuggo da te.

with its regular pattern of *tronco* and *piano* lines, falls naturally into triple meter, and Radesca's musical setting (between 1606 and 1610) follows this slavishly.

Most triple-meter arias of this sort are notated in C $\frac{3}{2}$, but in two settings notated under the mensuration sign C—"Apria Urania" (1610) and "Regia Infante gloriosa" (between 1601 and 1610)—Radesca employs hemiola rhythm of the kind that can also be seen in Giovanni Ghizzolo's "Biondo arcier" (1610).[34] The second of the settings by Radesca is, incidentally, an occasional piece dedicated to Margherita of Savoy on her "navigating the River Po."

Rather more interesting from the technical point of view are those arias which involve changes from duple to triple meter or *vice versa*. These changes are always suggested by some facet of the text. Occasionally Radesca changes meter to lend emphasis to a particular phrase as when, in "Mi parto, ahi, sorte ria" (1606), he writes two bars in $\frac{3}{2}$ to emphasise the phrase "Ne morrò no." More often, though, he introduces rhythmic changes to accommodate a new type of poetic line. We can see this in his setting of Chiabrera's "Un dì soletto" and the anonymous "Mentre pomposa" (both 1606), both of which employ a scheme in which two five-syllable lines are followed by one of seven syllables:

> Un dì soletto,
> Vidd'il diletto,
> Ond'hò tanto martire.
> E sospirando,
> Tutto tremando,
> Così le presi à dire.

In both cases Radesca adopts the same procedure, setting the five-syllable lines in triple meter and the seven-syllable line in duple meter.

A more unusual verse-form still is found in "Come vuoi c'habbia in te" (between 1606 and 1610), in which two eleven-syllable lines are followed by two of five syllables and one of seven *(tronco)*. Here, Radesca sets the first two lines in duple meter as the first section of a bipartite structure. Then, at the double bar, and with the first of the five-syllable lines, he changes to triple meter (ex. 10).

Example 10

With the exception of the *balletto* "Per voler d'Amore" (between 1606 and 1610), Radesca's arias in duple meter—all of them settings of texts employing the more usual seven- and eleven-syllable lines—differ little in style from his madrigals. And their texts approximate quite closely to the high-flown sentiments of the Guarinian madrigal. Unlike the arias in triple meter, those in duple meter make use of short points of imitation, and we can find various examples of madrigalian word-painting, as in the fine opening of "Occhi dolci e soavi" (between 1606 and 1610), though the raising of B flat to B natural for "dolci" and the graceful figuration for "soavi" become of purely musical interest in the second and subsequent stanzas (ex. 11).

Example 11

The arias in duple meter abound in rhythmic subtleties; and so do Radesca's madrigals, as we can see from his setting of Guarini's "Non miri il mio bel Sole."[35] At the beginning of this setting, Radesca exploits the rhythmic ambiguity available under the mensuration sign C. He sets the first two lines twice, in hemiola rhythm, as though he were beginning an aria. Then, at bar 9, as the poet begins to speak of himself, Radesca cleverly changes direction in the music: harmonically, through an abrupt change of chord, and rhythmically by having the singers chant the next line as if in *falso bordone,* a technique which Monteverdi had already used in the madrigal "Sfogava con le stelle" (*Quarto Libro de Madrigali,* 1603). And just as Monteverdi had done, so Radesca concludes the free declamation with a bar of measured rhythm.[36]

The setting of "Non miri il mio bel Sole" modulates fairly freely, though always to cadences closely related to the basic G major. And apart from a little mild chromaticism, such as that found at the beginning of his setting of "Ohimè, se tanto amate" (1606), this is the pattern of most of Radesca's madrigals. So, too, is the way in which almost all the melodic interest is concentrated in the upper part.

The connection with solo song is even more apparent at the beginning of "Ahi, ch'io mi svegl'ohimè,"[37] where the first phrase, complete with ornamental rising third, might have been taken from one of Caccini's songs. But the dialogue-like exchanges on the word "ohimè" seem to show that Radesca was thinking in terms of a genuine duet texture.

Unlike "Non miri il mio bel Sole," which is written almost entirely in a note-against-note style, "Ahi, ch'io mi svegl'ohimè" contains short points of imitation which are used to build toward points of climax. In bars 25-29, for instance, Radesca extends a short melodic phrase (first heard in bars 23-24) by means of imitation and sequential repetition as he builds to the cadence at bar 29 and the key word "gioia." And again, in bars 29-40, he extends a short initial phrase into a long sequence, releasing the tension in the long-drawn-out setting of the word "amaro," the languid bitter-sweetness of which perfectly matches the mood of the text.

Although Radesca's madrigals are unpretentious in scale and scoring they are, nevertheless, imaginative and well made. But the madrigal for high voice and bass was, at best, an uneasy compromise between solo song and duet. For since the bass had always to act as a harmonic support, the composer was severely limited in the range of sonorities and contrapuntal devices that he could employ.

After the last of the early duet books was issued, in 1610, far fewer duets for high voice and bass/*basso seguente* were published in Italy. It was some time, however, before they disappeared entirely from monody books. Indeed, several of the Florentine and Pisan composers who were active in publishing monodies during the second decade of the century—Rontani (1614 and 1618), Brunelli (1614), and Calestani (1617)—wrote duets of this kind. These were, for the most part, strophic, and even the Sienese nobleman Claudio Saracini, now better known for his unconventional solo madrigals, included three rather undistingushed note-against note canzonettas in triple meter for soprano and bass in his 1614 book.

Given the song-like qualities of duets for high voice and bass it is, perhaps, not surprising to find that strophic duets of this kind outlived madrigalian settings. During the second decade of the century, madrigals were published mainly by rather minor figures—composers like Ercole Porta (1612), organist and choirmaster of the Collegiate Church of San Giovanni at Persiceto, near Bologna, Giulio Santo Pietro de' Negri [hereafter abbreviated as G.P. Negri] (1613 and 1614), an amateur composer who, in 1613-14, seems to have been living first at Correggio and then at Lecce, and Giulio Romano (1613), once identified with Giulio Caccini, but now thought to have been a priest or monk rather than the eminently worldly Florentine.[38]

Outside Italy, one composer—Tomaso Cecchino, who held posts as choirmaster of Spalato (Split) Cathedral and later at Lesina (Hvar)—devoted himself mainly to duets for high voice and bass, which were advertised on the title page of his 1612 book as "facili per cantare et sonare." His 1612 book contains only madrigals; and though he included two arias with continuo in his 1616 book, the majority of the madrigals and strophic duets that it contains are also scored for high voice and bass. As we can see from his duet "Lilla, un bacio ti chiesi" (1616),[39] neither the passage of time, nor the adoption of a fashionable new poet—Marino—did much to change the basic nature of the madrigal for high voice and bass. Cecchino's setting, though it contains some affective writing in bars 6-9, is, if anything, more genuinely contrapuntal, and thus more duo-like than the madrigals of Radesca.

The last publication to contain madrigals for high voice and bass in any significant number is Fornaci's *Amorosi Respiri Musicali* (1617), which includes seven. Only three further madrigals—"Sù Ninfe leggiadre" in Marini's 1622 book and "T'inaspri, mio core" and "Perchè pieta" in Kapsberger's *Libro Secondo d'Arie* (1623)—are found after this date. Arias for high voice and bass, on the other hand, continued to appear regularly until the early 1620s, most notably in the publications issued in 1620 and 1622 by Biagio Marini.

Marini had been a violinist in the orchestra of St. Mark's, Venice, from 1615 and had published at Venice his *Madrigali et Symfonie a 1,2,3,4,5* (1618), a volume which, though now incomplete, probably contained only continuo duets, as befitted its status as a madrigal book. By 1620, however, when Marini published his *Arie, Madrigali et Corenti,* he was installed as choirmaster of Santa Eufemia at Brescia and as "capo della musica" of the Accademia degli Erranti. The 1620 book, which is printed in score, contains three madrigalian duets and an aria with continuo, but it also includes two strophic duets—"Al fonte, al prato" and "Amor, che deggio far?"—for one or two voices. The first of these is, of course, a setting of the strophic canzonetta that Peri had also set for soprano and bass.[40] A comparison of the two settings, however, reveals quite striking differences of approach. Peri's setting is a simple, but graceful melody and accompaniment, equally apt for all four stanzas. Marini's is more madrigalian in approach. It is bipartite in structure, with quasi-canonic writing at the beginning of each of the sections. The roulades at the end of the first section, and the tempo marking "presto" and use of close imitation at the beginning of the second are clearly intended to illustrate the word "correte," which is repeated several times at this juncture (ex. 12). It does not, however, recur in the other stanzas, which are very difficult to underlay satisfactorily.

Example 12

Marini's decision to write imitative canzonettas for high voice and bass after he had already had experience in the field of the genuine continuo duet may be explained by the popularity which this kind of duet seems to have enjoyed in the part of Italy to which he had moved from Venice. For it is noticeable that several of the composers of duets with *basso seguente* worked in towns and cities in northwest Italy—Radesca at Turin; Cagnazzi at Lodi; Ghizzolo at Novara; G.P. Negri at Milan. Sigismondo d'India, too, who worked at Turin from 1611 to 1623, published three arias for high voice and bass in 1618, even though he had previously published a number of continuo duets and had, indeed, devoted a whole book to the medium in 1615.

Example 13

Whatever the truth of the matter, it is certain that only a year after leaving Brescia, Marini included no fewer than six duets for high voice and bass (all the duets in the book, in fact) in his *Scherzi e Canzonette* of 1622; and only one of these is advertised as being suitable for either one or two voices. All are light in style and bipartite in structure. And each has an extended ritornello for violin and chitarrone which is also cast in two sections with each repeated. The length of the ritornellos suggests that these duets were intended as dance songs. Certainly they reflect Marini's grounding as a violinist and his interest in writing independent instrumental music. And he produces some interesting and idiomatic instrumental writing here. In the ritornello that he wrote for the last of the duets in the book—"Una vecchia sdentatt'e bavosa"—for example, he uses a bass line running consistently in quavers and forming cadential patterns of a kind that was not to become commonplace in vocal music until much later in the century (ex. 13). In several of the duets, too, we can trace the interpenetration of vocal and instrumental idioms. "Tra bei cristalli," for example, is a duple-meter aria consisting largely of note-against-note writing and short points of imitation. In this respect it is not radically different from many earlier duets for high voice and bass. But in setting the line "Par che l'ombra involvi il Sol," Marini employs an idiosyncratically patterned exchange in semiquavers (ex. 14a) which is also used for the motivic interplay of the first section of the ritornello (ex. 14b).

Example 14

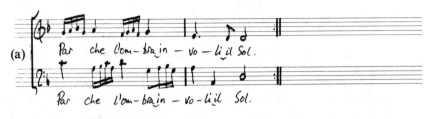

(a)

Par che l'om-bra in — vo — li il Sol.

Par che l'om-bra in — vo-li il Sol.

(b)

   Following the publication, in 1623, of Giovanni Ghizzolo's *Frutti d'Amore* and Kapsberger's *Libro Quarto di Villanelle,* even strophic duets with *basso seguente* all but disappeared from published sources as continuo duets became the order of the day. Of the stragglers, Nicolò Fontei included two arias—"Tante volte" and "Sò che finto"—marked "a 2 se piace" in his 1635 book; and in the same year Giovanni Battista Abbatessa published a guitar tutor, *Cespuglio de varii fiori,* in which he included three arias for soprano and bass. This is, however, the exception that proves the rule, in that it is a didactic work directed specifically to beginners.

Continuo Duets in Monody Books and Related Sources, c. 1605-1623

Although duets for high voice and bass/*basso seguente* are found in various types of publication at the beginning of the seventeenth century, duets with independent *basso continuo* are found mainly in monody books, at least until the early 1620s. Nevertheless, most of the pioneers of the continuo duet worked outside Florence—Barbarino at Pesaro and Padua, Brunetti at Bologna, Bellanda probably at his native town of Verona, and Ghizzolo at Novara. The only Florentine to have published a continuo duet before 1610 was, in fact, Caccini's pupil, Severo Bonini. We know, however, that Sigismondo d'India, who became musical director to the Duke of Savoy in April, 1611, and who is one of the most important figures in the early history of the continuo duet, visited Florence in 1608, where some of his earliest songs were performed by Vittoria Archilei and by Caccini himself.[41] And it can safely be assumed that Domenico Maria Melli had some personal contact with Florentine monody at its formative stage since his first book of *Musiche* appeared some months before Caccini's *Le Nuove Musiche.*

During the second decade of the century, however, Florence came into its own as a centre of duet writing. Marco da Gagliano, Domenico Belli, Domenico Visconti, Piero Benedetti, and Francesca Caccini all published their duets during these years. So did Vincenzo Calestani and his teacher Antonio Brunelli, who from 1612 was choirmaster to the Grand Duke of Tuscany at the Church of the Knights of St. Stephen at Pisa. And Gagliano's younger brother, Giovanni Battista, added his contribution to the genre in 1623. Two more Florentines, Filippo Vitali and the popular monodist Raffaello Rontani, also published their earliest duets in their native city before moving to Rome, the city whose composers began to rival the Florentines after 1620 in the production of monody books and, hence, in publishing strophic duets. Like Vitali and Rontani, the Neapolitan lutenist Andrea Falconieri, who was temporarily attached to the Medici court as a musician in 1615, seems to have spent a period at Rome, though he must have returned to Florence by 1619, when his *Quinto Libro delle Musiche* was published there.

Venice, soon to become the focal point of madrigalian duet writing through the work of Grandi and Monteverdi, could only boast one rather minor figure working during the formative years of the continuo duet. This was Marc'Antonio Negri, who was assistant choirmaster at St. Mark's from 1612 to 1620. And Rome, the third main center of Italian music making during the early seventeenth century, is represented by only five composers who published duets in monody books before 1620. These are Paolo Quagliati, organist of S. Maria Maggiore, the self-styled German nobleman Johann Hieronymus (Giovanni Girolamo) Kapsberger, Giovanni Francesco Anerio, Nicolò Borboni, and Giovanni Boschetto Boschetti. And of these, Anerio published his *Recreatione Armonica* (1611), which contains the largest early collection of two-part madrigals, while he was choirmaster of Verona cathedral. Quagliati, however, was among the very first composers to cultivate the new medium, for he included duets in his dramatic entertainment *Carro di Fedeltà d'Amore,* which had first been given in the streets of Rome in 1606. A sixth composer, Antonio Cifra, who was choirmaster of the Holy House of Loreto from 1609 to 1622 and the most prolific composer of two-part *ottava* settings during the second decade of the century, was also Roman trained.

After 1620, the balance was redressed somewhat in favor of Roman composers by the anthologies issued at Rome by the publisher Giovanni Battista Robletti (1621 *bis,* 1622, 1629). And the anthologies edited by Fabio Costantini and published at nearby Orvieto in 1621 and 1622 should also be mentioned here. Although they were issued in part-book format, and contain more madrigals than arias, Costantini's anthologies share a certain common ground with Robletti's including, in the 1622 book, works apparently borrowed from Robletti's publications.

Four composers working outside their native country in the early seventeenth century were quick to adopt the new medium. In Austria, Bartolomeo Mutis, Count of Cesana [Bartolameo Cesana], who was *Hofkaplan* and a tenor singer at the court of the Archduke Ferdinand at Graz,[42] and Camillo Orlandi, a native of Verona who was in the service of the Archbishop of Salzburg, both included duets in their monody books, in 1613 and 1616 respectively. And Giovanni Valentini, Mutis's colleague at Graz, who followed the newly created Emperor Ferdinand to Vienna in 1618 as imperial court organist, was among the earliest composers to issue a book devoted entirely to continuo duets. His *Musiche* (1622) was considered by Schmitz to be a particularly important document in the early history of the duet.[43]

Much further afield, in London, an expatriate Venetian, Angelo Notari, published his *Prime Musiche Nuove* in 1613.[44] With Sigismondo d'India, Marco da Gagliano, and Filippo Vitali, Notari is one of the finest and most imaginative of the early duet composers, as may be judged from his intense setting of Rinuccini's "Intenerite voi."[45] And his *Prime Musiche Nuove,* including as it does three madrigals and two strophic duets with continuo, a set of variations on the Romanesca and two strophic duets for high voice and bass/*basso seguente,* contains an almost complete conspectus of the types of duet being written in Italy during the early years of the seventeenth century.

Scoring

As far as scoring is concerned, the continuo duets published in monody books before 1623 set the pattern that was to obtain until the middle of the seventeenth century. That is, the majority are scored for two voices of equal range, usually for two sopranos, though there is also a substantial body of duets for two tenors. Other equal-voice pairings are also encountered, though more rarely.

The two most popular of these equal-voice scorings are already familiar from the trio textures of late sixteenth-century canzonettas and madrigals. It seems possible, however, that one reason for the continuing popularity of equal-voice duets is that they afforded a certain amount of flexibility with regard to transposition, so that a duet for two tenors could easily be turned into a duet for two sopranos or *vice versa,* providing always that the lower voice did not then stray below the continuo line. It could even be turned into a duet for two altos, though this transposition was never suggested in the printed sources.

It should be said, however, that as far as the duets in monody books are concerned, the evidence for this practice is not very substantial. Our conclusions with regard to the scoring of these duets has largely to be based on the evidence of the clefs used. Few composers actually specified in words the voices for which their duets were written. Of those who did, however, several suggest alternative scorings. All the madrigals by Mutis (1613), for example, and both the continuo arias in Brunelli's 1614 book may be performed either by two sopranos or by two tenors. But other sources make it clear that composers occasionally preferred one scoring to the other.

Comparatively few early continuo duets are scored for two different voice ranges. Of those that are, most are written for soprano, or tenor and bass. They represent a midway stage between duets with *basso seguente* and those with a completely independent continuo and are often a compromise between monody and duet. Andrea Falconieri was particularly fond of this scoring, and something of its ambiguous nature may be judged from his strophic duet "Soccorso, ahimè, ben mio" (1616). Here, the bass sometimes assumes an independent role, sometimes merely doubles the continuo in providing a harmonic support for the soprano line, which begins in madrigalian style as though it were the opening of a declamatory solo song (ex. 15).

Example 15

Other early composers who, like Falconieri, employed this rather ambiguous scoring include Bellanda (1607), M.A. Negri (1611), G.P. Negri (1613 and 1614), Albini (1623), and Quagliati (1623). And all of Francesca Caccini's duets (1618) are scored for soprano and bass. Perhaps not surprisingly, since he worked at Maleo Lodigiano, near Milan, in that corner of northwestern Italy which had seen the publication of so many duets with *basso*

seguente, Francesco Ugoni scored both of the bipartite madrigals in his *Giardinetto di Ricreatione* (1616) for high voice, bass, and continuo.

There are, in fact, more madrigals than strophic duets of this type. Many, however, are found in one book—G.F. Anerio's *Recreatione Armonica* of 1611. Only the last nine of the madrigals in the book are actually scored for soprano and bass, but the first ten, for soprano and tenor, also have a continuo part which is essentially a *basso seguente.* The madrigals in Anerio's collection cannot, unfortunately be reconstructed since the canto part-book is lost. But, like the majority of madrigals with *basso seguente,* they are all bipartite or tripartite in structure and would, thus, seem to be related to the sixteenth-century canzonetta and villanella.

The other possible combinations of unequal voice ranges are fairly thinly represented in monody books. There are, however, several duets for soprano and tenor and for alto and tenor, among the latter two interesting sets of variations on the Romanesca by Filippo Vitali—"Lasso, ch'io mi credea" and "Fedel, qual sempre fui" (both 1618). The remaining scorings found in early monody books are soprano and alto, treble and soprano, and treble and tenor.

Strophic Duets

Just as the solo songs of Caccini's *Le Nuove Musiche* were not wholly innovatory, so the styles, techniques, and textures that we find in early continuo duets represent various degrees of compromise between the stylistic concepts of Floretine monody and older traditions of composition.

We have already noted that while duets with *basso seguente* were published in quite large numbers during the first decade of the seventeenth century, only a small number of continuo duets were published during the same period outside the context of opera and the continuo madrigal. Few composers were involved, and in some instances their first efforts were very tentative indeed. Such is the case with Barbarino's "I tuoi capelli, O Filli," which was the earliest continuo duet to be included in a monody book. This work is unusual among continuo duets in that it can be performed by either one or two voices. It seems to have been conceived primarily as a set of strophic variations for solo tenor, the second tenor part being added only as an afterthought. Moreover, in contrast to Barbarino's solo songs, which are clearly modeled on those of Caccini, the duet is an uneasy compromise between Florentine monody and the sixteenth-century tradition of improvised solo song on a stylized bass. The text, from Sannazzaro's *Arcadia,* is cast in *terza rima,* and each line is sung to one phrase of the bass pattern. The necessity of extending the musical line to fit this artificial scheme occasionally leads Barbarino to ornament, and thus to misaccentuate unimportant syllables in a quite un-Florentine manner (ex. 16).

Example 16

Most of the early composers of continuo duets included only one or two pieces in each of their monody books. Of the three books containing continuo duets that were published in 1609, for example, Severo Bonini's *Secondo Libro de Madrigali, e Motetti* includes only the sonnet setting "I' vo piangendo";[46] Sigismondo d'India's *Musiche* includes two duets, the one—"Fresche erbette novelle"—a brief madrigalian setting, the other—"Dove potrò mai gir"—a quite substantial set of variations on the *Aria di Ruggiero;* Domenico Maria Melli's *Le Terze Musiche* includes three duets, but all of them are short strophic arias. In contrast to the small number of duets contained in these volumes, however, Bonini's book contains seven solo songs, Melli's twenty, and d'India's no fewer than forty-five.

The only early books in which these proportions are significantly reversed are Kapsberger's *Libro Primo di Villanelle* of 1610 and G.F. Anerio's *Recreatione Armonica* of 1611. Anerio's book contains nineteen duets and twelve solo songs. However, since all the duets are essentially of the *basso seguente* type, their relatively large number is less remarkable than might at first appear. Kapsberger's duets, on the other hand, have a genuine continuo. And his 1610 book, which contains ten strophic duets as against only two solo arias, may be considered a quite important document in the early history of the continuo duet.

Its importance lies not so much in its musical merit as in the way that it illustrates how straightforward was the transition from sixteenth- to seventeenth-century idioms for the composer working in the lighter forms. Kapsberger's book is, in fact, scarcely a "monody book" at all, for it is devoted mainly to music for two and three voices with continuo. It is, rather, the equivalent in the "new music" of a late sixteenth-century collection of villanellas or canzonettas for three and four unaccompanied voices. Stylistically, too, Kapsberger's duets owe little to Florence, but a great deal to the sixteenth-century three-part canzonetta. There is little difference in style, for example, between the opening of his "Poichè senti il mio dolore" (ex. 17) and the openings of either Vecchi's "Deh cant'Aminta" or Felice Anerio's "Fiamme che da begl'occhi," shown as chapter 5, examples 1 and 6a respectively. The parallel between Kapsberger's book and those late sixteenth-century canzonetta collections that included a lute tablature appears even closer when we see that he included not only a continuo accompaniment, but also a tablature for chitarrone and an alphabet for Spanish guitar.

Example 17

In view of the similarity in texture between the late sixteenth-century canzonetta for three voices and the continuo duet it is not, perhaps, surprising to find that simple strophic duets, in which the same music serves for each stanza of the text, form the largest group of continuo duets published in monody books, even before 1623. Many monody books include a few duets of this kind, and several individual publications—those of Kapsberger (1610; *Secondo,* 1619; *Quarto,* 1623), Barbarino (1616), Rontani (1618), Ghizzolo (1623), and the *Stravaganze d'Amore* (1616) [see J. Chater, "Castelletti's 'Stravaganze'" for a borrowing from Marenzio in this book] of Flamminio Corradi, an amateur composer working at Venice—contain them in quite large numbers. Corradi's book, like Kapsberger's of 1610, also includes a tablature for the chitarrone.

Strophic duets appear in the sources under various headings— *aria, canzonetta, scherzo,* and *villanella*—or with no heading at all. We should not, perhaps, attach too much significance to the particular terms used since they seem often to have been a matter of personal taste rather than precise indicators of style, structure, or textual type. The terms *aria* and *canzonetta* are those most generally encountered. They seem to have been interchangeable, though the former was also used to designate the more complex sets of variations based on the *Romanesca, Ruggiero* and other stylized "arias."

Only two composers seem to have used the more old-fashioned term *villanella,* and both were Roman. One was Kapsberger. His seven surviving books of villanellas, published between 1610 and 1640, certainly include one or two texts, like "Alla caccia" and "Correte pescatori" (both 1610), which suggest the rustic associations of the villanella, and the music of his 1610 book in particular has a rather old-fashioned flavor. But he also concerned himself with more serious and pathetic texts like Rinuccini's "Non havea Febo ancora" (1619)[47] and "Alma, che scorgi tu?" (1623). The other composer was Quagliati, who used the term for two settings—"Aure vaghe" and "Vedi l'alba"—in his 1623 book.

The term *scherzo,* which had been employed by the poet Chiabrera for a type of madrigalian text, enjoyed a fairly limited vogue among the composers of duets. Some scherzos, like Cifra's "Del mio Sol son ricciutegli" (1617)[48] and Calestani's "Vagheggiando le bell'onde" (1617),[49] are actually settings of Chiabreran verse, though not of his scherzos.[50] The use of the term as an up-to-date substitute for *canzonetta* seems to follow the usage of Monteverdi's *Scherzi Musicali* of 1607. G.P. Negri was attracted by the term and used it in his 1613 book seemingly to indicate settings of a lightweight nature, while in 1614 he used the designation *canzonetta* for the more serious "Ahi, chi mi fa languire." The only stylistic feature that links Negri's scherzos to Monteverdi's, however, is his use of paired notes to set single syllables in the duet "Amorosa Fenice" (1613). This feature, apparently a novelty of seventeenth-century canzonettas, is, however, also found in duets not specifically labelled *scherzo,* works like Kapsberger's "Flora più vaga e bella" (1610), or his "Per pietà delle mie pene" (*Secondo,* 1619), or Marco da Gagliano's "Fanciulletta ritrosetta" (1615).[51] It is, too, a stylistic feature that may be associated with the concept of "Canto alla francese," since it is also found in Monteverdi's seven-part setting of Petrarch's "Vago augelletto" (1638) and in the final ensemble of the first of Francesco Rasi's *Dialoghi rappresentativi (1620),*[52] both of which are labeled "alla francese."

Most of the strophic duets found in sources published before 1623 are short, unpretentious pieces intended to entertain rather than to edify. Though they could not have existed without the stimulus of Florentine monody they remain essentially the spiritual successors of the three-part canzonettas written in the late sixteenth-century. With only a few exceptions they are, like their forerunners, ensemble pieces in which extended solo writing and virtuoso ornamentation play no part.

In terms of repetition schemes, too, most early strophic duets follow the bipartite division of the canzonetta. The double bar is generally placed at a convenient point of articulation somewhere near the middle of the stanza, but there is no rule about this. In Kapsberger's "Non havea Febo ancora," for example, the double bar simply marks off the refrain, dividing the piece into two very unequal sections. A few Florentine duets, like Visconti's "Lacrime, perchè vi versate?,"[53] follow the through-composed outline of the canzonettas in *Le Nuove Musiche*. And another small group of pieces are cast in A B B form. In the case of Brunelli's "Care Luci" (1616), the repeat of the B section is fully written out. But in most, like d'India's "Voi baciatrici,"[54] it is simply indicated by the sign 𝄋 . Very few early strophic duets seem to be in A B A form. Quagliati's "Aure vaghe" (1623) is one, but here the second A section, beginning at bar 26, is suggested by a repeated line in the text.

A few composers attempted to make their settings longer and more varied. Anerio, for example, gave each of the four stanzas of "Scherzava un giorno" (1619) a different setting. Falconieri did the same for his setting of "Spiega spiega la vela nocchiero" (1616), but he linked the four sections of the aria with the triple-meter refrain "Spiega spiega...," which appears at the beginning of the setting and recurs in the middle of each of the subsequent sections. A comparison of Falconieri's aria with the simpler setting of part of the same text in Kapsberger's third book of villanellas (1619) shows that the refrain originally appeared at the beginning and end of the stanzas and that Falconieri has divided and elided the original verse to produce his own more complex structure.

The most pretentious of all early aria settings are to be found in Valentini's *Musiche a doi voci* (1622). "Poichè la cruda e fera" is the only one of these which qualifies as an ensemble duet (the others contain extended passages of solo writing). Even so, it is a quite complex setting. Stanzas 1, 2, and 3 are each set to different music in duple meter and separated by two different "Sonatas" for one instrument and continuo. Stanza 4 is introduced by Sonata 1 and set to the music of stanza 2. All four stanzas are linked by a refrain in 6/4 (ex. 18) which is reworked for the conclusion of the piece.

Example 18

The instrumental passages that Valentini uses to separate the stanzas of his arias were already a familiar feature of strophic duets. Florentine composers, in particular, were fond of gracing their work with ritornellos for one or two unspecified instruments. In none of the strophic duets published in monody books, however, do melody instruments play with the voices, though we do occasionally find instrumental interjections between vocal phrases within an aria. Marco da Gagliano made a particularly subtle use of this device in "Fanciulletta ritrosetta" (1615).[55] The piece begins in a dance-like rhythm which is maintained throughout the first statement of what appears to be the ritornello. This is, however, followed by a new, affective setting of the last phrase of the verse before the ritornello proper is heard.

Most of the ritornellos found in strophic duets are quite modest affairs, with melodic lines which the continuo player could easily accommodate under his fingers. Some, however, like the two-part ritornello for Visconti's "Lacrime, perchè vi versate?,"[56] seem to demand the use of other instrumentalists.

Dance songs were the obvious context in which instrumental music could blossom forth, and Calestani's attractive "Vagheggiando le bell'onde" (1617)[57] includes both a ritornello to be played twice between each verse and instrumental interjections between the phrases, all of them heavily accented to suggest the beating of the "Turkish Drum." Though there is no formal relationship between ritornello and aria in "Vagheggiando le bell'onde," Calestani links them by means of similarities in rhythmic and melodic shape. This is a technique which he probably learned from his teacher, Antonio Brunelli. All three of the strophic duets in Brunelli's 1616 book, for example, have lively ritornellos for two instruments which are based on a sequential elaboration of short motives drawn from the arias themselves.

By far the greater proportion of early strophic duets are written in duple meter, and they range from light-hearted villanellas of the type written by Kapsberger to works in which the composer sets the first stanza as though it were a miniature arioso madrigal. Visconti's "Lacrime, perchè vi versate?" is a work of this latter kind. Its powerful declamatory opening phrase is, in fact, very similar to that of Notari's madrigal "Intenerite voi,"[58] whose subject is also that of weeping. The two vocal lines of Visconti's duet are cast in a declamatory arioso style with the second soprano line forming an almost exact rhythmic canon with the first.

This is, perhaps, an extreme example of a madrigalian approach to writing strophic duets and, fortunately for Visconti, the texts of the second and subsequent stanzas, with their rhetorical apostrophes, will also support the weight of his musical setting. But the danger of incongruity between the music and the text of later stanzas was ever present for those composers who included elements of word-painting in their strophic duets. If we look back to Marco da Gagliano's "Fanciulletta ritrosetta," for example, we can see that one of the reasons for the change of style introduced at the end of the aria was to create a musical image for the words "e i cori ancidi." The declamatory line and strident dissonance that Gagliano uses form a striking image which is also, as it happens, appropriate for the concluding words of the second stanza, but is quite meaningless for those of the third.

In practice, though, we are not really aware of the discrepancy since the final phrase of Gagliano's setting also serves a purely musical function as a broad, coda-like conclusion to the aria. Most of the examples of word-painting that we can point to in strophic duets function both as imagery and as an integral part of the musical line. Thus, the Lombard rhythms used in Barbarino's "Corri Filli" (1616) to depict the words "Nover danze e guidar balli" or the C minor chord that Brunelli introduces into his "Care luci" (1616) for the word "soffrir" (ex. 19). Or the words of the first stanza might suggest changes in meter. Notari, for example, sets most of the text of "Girate occhi" (1613) in triple meter, but changes to a broader duple meter for the last line, "Occhi, ragion vi dolgano," which he sets twice to emphasise its more dolorous nature.

Example 19

Many of the instances of word-painting that we find in strophic duets are harmonic in nature or exploit the sonorities available from the use of two voices. In the middle of "Alma mia, deh che farai?" (1614), for example, Brunelli abandons the bouncing dotted rhythms and vocal writing in parallel thirds which characterise the opening of the duet to write a broader cadential phrase in parallel seconds for the words "ai tuoi tormenti." And the opening of Giulio Romano's "Bella Filli crudele" (1613), with its awkward chromatic modulation and parallelism of harmony might be seen as a musical image for Phyllis' cruelty. Equally, though, it could simply be a product of the composer's limited ability.

No such charge can be leveled at Filippo Vitali, who was particularly skillful at introducing harmonic acerbities into his strophic duets without destroying the sense of line. In the duet "Più di stral che d'arco scocchi" (1617), for example, a phrase like "ancide e fere" is enough to spark off a chain of suspensions (ex. 20); so, too, the phrase "Il dolor della partita" in the duet "Rimirate, luci ingrate" (ex. 21). Here, Vitali uses dissonance between the two voices to suggest the image of sorrow while at the same time creating a broad

arch of melody; and when he immediately repeats the phrase a fifth lower, the
picture of the lover's life ebbing away is vividly conjured up as his cries die away
towards the cadence. In a work like this, aria writing and the technique of the
two-part arioso madrigal approach each other quite closely.

Example 20

Example 21

Like the canzonetta textures discussed in chapter 5, most strophic duets
are characterised by the interplay of two vocal lines over an independent and
more slowly moving continuo. It is not difficult, however, to find echoes of
other textures characteristic of the sixteenth-century canzonetta. Passages of
homophonic writing are perhaps the most common, while at the opposite
extreme we find occasional passages of three-part counterpoint, such as the

phrase "che languir non vuoi" in Vitali's "Se tu vuoi" (1617; ex. 22), which is
also used as the basis of the instrumental ritornello. Other duets have passages
in which the second voice and continuo are grouped together as a contrapuntal
unit. Usually, this technique is used only in passing, as it is in bar 7 of Marco da
Gagliano's "Fanciulletta ritrosetta." Sigismondo d'India, however, employed it
at much greater length in his triple-meter aria "La mia Filli crudel" (1615), in a
passage in which the second soprano and continuo move in parallel tenths,
producing a sort of pseudo-canon with the first soprano (ex. 23).

Example 22

Example 23

Just as in the case of solo arias, melody is the mainspring of most strophic
duets, whether in duple or triple meter, and homorhythmic writing between the

voices, usually interspersed with short points of imitation, their most characteristic texture. Imitation is scarcely ever used as the building block for large-scale structures and it is rare, even at the beginning of a piece, to hear a complete statement of a thematic idea in one voice before the other enters; many strophic duets, in fact, begin homophonically. Among those that do begin with an imitative idea, a favorite gambit was to have a rising line in one voice, followed at a short interval by the second voice. Rontani used this device in his setting of "Deh girate, luci amate" (1614; ex. 24) and Brunelli in his "Accorta lusinghiera" (1614; ex. 25). More learned counterpoint than this would have been out of place in an essentially light form.

Example 24

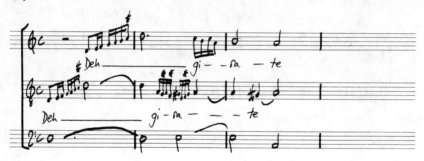

Example 25

After the opening phrase, short points of imitation are generally used to articulate the phrase structure and to lend variety to the composition. A new type of texture is often introduced at the double bar. Angelo Notari used this technique to particularly good effect in his "Su la riva del Tebro" (1613) to suggest a distinction between narrative and direct speech, even though none actually exists in the text. The setting begins with homorhythmic writing, as the poet describes the scene: a shepherd was standing one day on the banks of the

Tiber (ex. 26). After the double bar, however, when the shepherd's cries and laments are described, the words are set in a weightier imitative style, complete with affective intervals, the juxtaposition of unrelated chords and, once again, our rising, pseudo-canonic motive (ex. 27). Needless to say, however, the distinction which Notari draws is not nearly as appropriate for the other stanzas of the text.

Example 26

Example 27

A number of strophic duets employ homorhythmic writing throughout the setting. These are, effectively, augmented solo songs in which the second voice is used simply to add another layer of sonority to the melody. And, quite often, the two voices simply move in parallel thirds. Paradoxically enough, this group of duets includes some of the most attractive and the most powerful of the early strophic settings for, freed from the constraints of imitative technique, composers were able to give free rein to their melodic gifts and to explore declamatory styles.

Parallel writing is a technique characteristic of many of the settings in Kapsberger's second (1619), third (1619), and fourth (1623) books of villanellas and, as far as one can speak of stylistic development in the duple-meter aria, Kapsberger's later strophic duets are certainly more urbane that those of his

1610 book, as we can judge from his setting of "Non havea Febo ancora" (*Secondo,* 1619).[59] Raffaello Rontani, too, is at his most attractive in this vein, as we can see from the opening of his "Alma, che scorgi tu?" (1620; ex. 28).

Example 28

Few duple-meter arias employing parallel writing are as fine as Marco da Gagliano's "Alma mia, dove ten vai?" (1615)[60] though some of the characteristics which set it apart—the use of accented dissonances, for example—are directly traceable to its operatic origins. Piero Benedetti provided worthy successors to this work in the two strophic duets that he included in his 1617 book. The first of these, "Sento Filli," with its brief but exquisite second section (ex. 29) is homorhythmic throughout and has a bass which moves largely in crotchets. The second, "Serenatevi, O stelle," has a short passage of imitative writing at the end of the setting, but it opens with a passage of declamatory recitative, complete with written-out ornamentation, for two voices in parallel (ex. 30).

Example 29

As we can see from Calestani's "Vagheggiando le bell'onde," the technique of writing in parallel thirds was by no means confined to duets written in duple meter. It was particularly suited to dances and to dance-like pieces of the kind represented by Barbarino's delightful *hemiola* setting of "Se bel rio, se bell'auretta" (1616). More interesting still, though, are those *hemiola* settings in which the composer uses the two voices to create cross-rhythms by combining one line in 3/2 with another in 6/4. Cifra's "Del mio sol son ricciutegli" (1617)[61] is one of these and practically every bar of the setting from bar 4 onward has its share of cross-rhythms. Moments such as those provided in bar 6, where the continuo pursues yet a third rhythm, are particularly delightful.

Example 30

In using this technique, though, Cifra was only following a path opened up by Melli with the two settings "Dispiegate, guancie amate" and "A che sguardi amorosetti" which he included in his 1609 book. The third setting in Melli's book—"La mia dolce pastorella"—is again in triple meter, but it is written in a much broader style, with both the vocal lines and the continuo moving in conjunct motion (ex. 31). And it is this type of setting, rather than dance-songs or duple-meter arias, that held the key to the future development of the strophic duet, for it anticipates the *bel canto* style cultivated during the late 1620s and the 1630s.

Example 31

The tendency towards a broader style of triple-meter writing is continued in the six strophic duets of Sigismondo d'India's *Musiche a due voci* (1615). Some of these settings are anything but light-hearted, and their exploration of motives like the kiss and the war of love is a reminder that the poet Giambattista Marino was resident at the Torinese court when d'India was preparing this book. "Voi baciatrici,"[62] with its refrain in which the kisses are "biting, challenging, piercing, wounding," is a setting of one of these Marinesque texts, possibly even of a text by Marino himself. In terms of musical style it is curiously hybrid. The opening of the duet, with its equal rhythmic stress on each minim, is reminiscent of the light-hearted canzonetta; but the refrain, with its broad sweeping line and emphasis on the first of each group of three minims, is much closer to the type of *bel canto* writing that we can see, for example, in Francesco Manelli's "Ti lascio empia, incostante" (1636).[63]

Several of the earliest examples of *bel canto* writing in duets are found in Florentine and Roman sources, in works like Francesca Caccini's "O vive rose" (1618) and Rontani's "Tanto sdegno ha 'l core" (*Quarto*, 1620). "O vive rose," with its gracefully decorated line and asymmetrical phrase-structure (ex. 32), has something of the same quality of "dignified and tranquil melody" which Fortune distinguished in the earliest *bel canto* aria for solo voice—Calestani's "Folgorate" (1617).[64] Exactly the same description can be applied to the style of Rontani's duet, and his work may have helped to shape the tastes of the younger and lesser-known Roman composers who are represented with him in Robletti's anthologies of 1621.

Example 32

In Robletti's *Raccolta,* for example, we find the earliest work of Domenico Mazzocchi, including a lyrical *bel canto* duet for alto and tenor, "Filli, da tuoi bei sguardi." Mazzocchi's duet, however, like the triple-meter villanellas of Quagliati published in 1623,[65] retains the symmetrical phrase-structure of earlier canzonettas. In Robletti's other anthology, the *Giardino*

Musicale, we encounter one work, "La mia leggiadra Filli," by the otherwise unknown Francesco Cerasolo, which begins like a very ordinary duple-meter duet, but ends with a telling little recitative and arioso (ex. 33).

Example 33

Cerasolo's is not, however, the first duet to be cast in this type of composite form. For this, we have to look back to Falconieri's *Libro Primo di Villanelle* of 1616, the source book for several new departures in the strophic duet, including the use of refrain structure that we noted earlier. The text of the duet "Quel bacio" comprises two five-line stanzas, of which I give the first below:

> Quel bacio che mi dai,
> Da me bramato tanto,

Per premio del mio canto,
Premio non è, ma pena,
Perchè 'l cor m'avelena.

That kiss which you give me (and that I desired so much) as a reward for my singing, is not a
reward, but a punishment, for my heart is poisoned by it.

In setting this verse, Falconieri reverses what might be the expected procedure.
The first three lines, which contain words like "bramato" and "canto," and
which might well have suggested triple meter, are, in fact, set as ten bars of
duple-meter arioso. The final couplet, which speaks of the lover's pain, is,
however, set as a broad, slow triple-meter arioso in which the lines of the text
are repeated to produce a setting of no fewer than twenty six bars of 3/2 (ex.
34).

Example 34

Sonnets, *Terza Rima,* and *Ottava* Settings

Most of the sets of two-part strophic variations published before 1623 are, like
Barbarino's "I tuoi capelli, O Filli," of a more artificial kind than the variations
for solo voice found in *Le Nuove Musiche;* and they were occasionally used as
the vehicles for complex virtuoso ornamentation. These settings belong, in

fact, to a much older tradition than the variations of *Le Nuove Musiche,* a tradition stemming from the improvised solo performance of sonnets, *terza rima,* and ottavas on stylized arias. This was a type of improvised performance cultivated during the late sixteenth century by the singing ladies of the Ferrarese court. And as a type of composed music in the early seventeenth century, it seems to have been particulary favored by Roman composers; indeed, one of the most famous of the stylized arias, the *Romanesca,* took its name from the city of Rome.

Apart from Barbarino's "I tuoi capelli, O Filli," apparently written on a bass invented by Barbarino himself, I know of only one other stylized setting of *terza rima,* d'India's "Porto celato il mio nobil pensiero" (1615). This is set as an *Aria sopra Zefiro,* a bass which is not encountered elsewhere, but which has certain elements in common with the *Gazzella* bass which Cifra used for *ottava* settings. Stylized settings of sonnets, too, are rather rare in the duet literature. Both Dognazzi (1614) and Orlandi (1616) set Petrarch's "Ite caldi sospiri," Dognazzi using the Neapolitan *Aria di Ruggiero* and Orlandi a bass of his own devising which he also used for the *ottava* "Lassa diceva" (1616). Otherwise, only Raffaello Rontani seems to have favored this type of setting. In his 1618 book, for example, he included a setting of the octave of Chiabrera's sonnet "Su questa riva," treating it as though it were an *ottava* in two sections. His setting of Marino's exquisite "Su la sponda del Tebro" (1614) is, however, more interesting.[66] It employs two arias with a similar harmonic outline, one for the two quartets of the sonnet, the other for the two tercets. The setting is written in an attractive Florentine arioso style with restrained ornamentation. But the principle of using two arias as the basis of a sonnet setting can be traced back to the beginning of the sixteenth century, as we can see from Andrea Antico's setting of "Io mi parto, Madonna," published in 1509.[67]

Stylized two-part *ottava* settings, on the other hand, are encountered quite frequently in monody books; and Monteverdi included one in his 1619 madrigal book, though such pieces are comparatively rare in this format.[68] Fortune observed that there are more two-part *ottava* settings than there are *ottava* settings for a solo voice.[69] It would be idle to speculate on the reasons for this, though the fashion for coordinated ornamentation in ensemble music set by the Ferrarese *Concerto delle donne* and by the publication of Luzzaschi's madrigals may have contributed to their popularity. In fact, though, most of the two-part *ottava* settings are the work of a few composers—d'India, Cifra, and Vitali—who seem to have made them a speciality. The greater part of d'India's *Musiche a due voci* (1615) is made up of ottavas.

By and large, the settings are of stanzas from the two epics *Orlando furioso* and *Gerusalemme liberata,* and we have already noted the way in which Cifra worked his way through the favorite stanzas of Tasso's epic before turning back to Ariosto's in his 1615 book.[70] Other poets were also set, though.

Rinuccini was the author both of Notari's imaginative "Piangono al pianger mio" (1613) and of Borboni's "Chi da lacci d'amor" (1618), an octave from the libretto to *Dafne*. Cifra (1613) and Monteverdi (1619) set two of Bernardo Tasso's *Stanze di Lontananza*. And d'India (1615) even managed to set some stanzas from Marino's *Adone* before that work had appeared in print.[71]

Four different "arias" are associated with two-part *ottava* settings. Two of them—the *Romanesca* and the *Aria di Genova*—have obvious geographical associations. A third, the *Aria di Ruggiero,* was Neapolitan in origin, but seems to have acquired its name by association with the stanza of *Orlando furioso* which begins "Ruggier qual sempre fui."[72] The fourth, the *Aria del Gazzella,* which was used only by Cifra, still eludes precise indentification.

Of these four "arias," the *Romanesca* was the most popular, and it was celebrated in literary as well as musical sources. The Venetian poet, Giulio Strozzi, praised it in the twelfth canto of his *La Venetia edificata* (1624), and Giustiniani described it as:

> unique and considered to be most beautiful...[it] is sung by everybody with the greatest delight as something exquisite and most suitable for every sort of embellishment and [it] is accompanied with great facility in every mode.[73]

Palisca has shown that the *Romanesca* was not, as was long thought, simply a bass pattern over which the singer would improvise, but that it had an associated melodic line (ex. 35).[74] He has shown that this melodic line can be traced even in a two-part setting like Monteverdi's "Ohimè, dov'è il mio ben";[75] and it can be detected, too, in the outline of Cifra's "Vattene pur, crudel."[76] These are, then, variations on the "Aria" of the *Romanesca* and not simply variations over its bass; and we should note that the bass used by Monteverdi is similar to Cifra's only in harmonic outline, not in detail.

Example 35

It seems probable that a melodic pattern was also associated with the *Aria di Ruggiero* and, possibly, with the other "arias" as well. In his 1609 book, d'India drew a distinction between his setting of "Vostro fui, vostro son," which is a set of variations "sopra il Basso dell'Aria di Ruggiero di Napoli" and the duet "Dove potrò mai gir?," which is "sopra l'Aria di Ruggiero." It is, however, impossible to deduce from the two-part texture what the original melodic pattern might have been.

As far as the relationship between words and music is concerned, all *ottava* settings conform to one general principle: that each phrase of the "aria" is used to set one line of text. It was this principle which defeated Barbarino, who was forced to misaccentuate the text of "I tuoi capelli, O Filli" in order to make it fit the pattern of the bass. But the very restrictions of the form may themselves have attracted the more able composers. Monteverdi, in particular, excels in overcoming the apparent limitations of the *Romanesca* to provide a dramatic and passionate depiction of Bernardo Tasso's pain at the separation from his wife.

In Cifra's settings, as we can see from volume 2, no. 33, the bass remains the same from stanza to stanza, and the composer has to use all his (fairly limited) skill to provide new musical ideas over the same bass to match different pictorial or emotional images in the text (compare, for example, bars 9-12 with bars 57-60). Both Monteverdi and Sigismondo d'India, however, took liberties with the rhythmic structure of the bass. D'India does this for two reasons: either to make room for ornamentation, or, as we can see from a comparison of the opening of the first two stanzas of "Ardo, lasso" (1615) to convey different affective states in the text (exx. 36a and 36b).

Example 36

The *Aria di Romanesca* and the *Aria di Ruggiero* are both used to set two lines of text per "stanza" of music. Each "aria" consists of two phrases, the second of which is usually repeated; and here the composer takes the opportunity to show off his skill by providing a new working for the repeated phrase. Most *Romanesca* and *Ruggiero* settings are of one *ottava* only, divided into four fairly short sections.

The *Aria di Genova* and the *Aria del Gazzella* are rather different. Both are used to set four lines of text, and both are generally used for rather longer settings than the *Romanesca* and *Ruggiero*. Cifra's *Gazzella* setting "Misera non credea" (1614) for example, is a setting of two ottavas. And in each of the four stanzas Cifra produces an A B B[1] structure by repeating the last two lines (ex. 37). The *Aria di Genova* which d'India uses for Marino's "Ardo, lasso" is more succinct, but since he sets no fewer than eight ottavas, "Ardo, lasso" is a very substantial work indeed.

Example 37

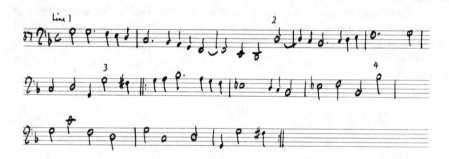

It is also the finest of d'India's *ottava* settings, a work in which the composer exploits to the full the equivocal nature of the duet medium, mixing affective declamation (ex. 38) with madrigalian dissonances (ex. 39) to capture the exaggerated ardors of Marino's verse. At the same time, we are conscious that the mainspring of the setting is the art of virtuoso singing, and though d'India generally relegates ornamental passages to the ends of the stanzas, several of these stanza endings are very florid indeed (ex. 40). The tendency towards florid song had been quite pronounced, even in d'India's earliest two-part *ottava*, "Dove potrò mai gir?" (1609)[77] but it reaches its zenith in the *ottava passeggiata* "Argo non mai" (1615). This *Romanesca* setting contains passage work of extraordinary difficulty, suggesting that the court at Turin must have boasted very expert singers during d'India's years there as director of music. It suggests, too, that in matters of musical taste Turin may have been closer to Rome than to Florence.

Example 38

Example 39

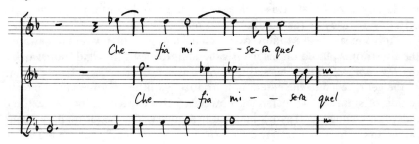

Example 40

D'India's "Argo non mai" represents an extreme of virtuosity. Most two-part ottavas are, like those of Cifra, much simpler arioso settings, using only a few stock ornaments. Of these less ornate settings, the Romanescas are certainly the most attractive. Filippo Vitali included no fewer than four of them in his 1618 book, though he only gave the title "Romanesca" to the first two—"Io vissi un tempo" and "Lasso, ch'io mi credea." These use a bass which is very similar to that of Cifra's "Vattene pur, crudel." The other two settings—"Se'l Sol si scosta"[78] and "Fedel, qual sempre fui" (here divorced from its usual

Ruggiero bass)—though undesignated, do nevertheless employ a variant of the *Romanesca* bass. The usual repetition of the second phrase is, however, omitted, and their stanzas are, consequently, shorter and less pretentious than those of the so-called "Romanescas." Vitali's settings are marked out from the average by his melodic gift. The rather sweet chain of dissonances with which "Se'l Sol si scosta" ends, however, scarcely matches the bitter images of Ariosto's text.

As if to prove that the *Romanesca* was capable of bearing a greater emotional weight, Monteverdi's "Ohimè, dove'è il mio ben?" is a concentrated and deeply felt piece. Its stylistic vocabulary, too, is wider than that of any other *ottava* setting. The declamatory gesture at the beginning of the setting and the use of unprepared dissonances in bars 2 and 3 of stanza 2 betray Monteverdi's experience as an opera composer. And the harsh dissonance in bar 12 of stanza 2 that gives such a cutting edge to the bitterness of the text is certainly a legacy of the middle-period madrigals.

It is a measure of Monteverdi's technical mastery that we are not aware of the constraints placed on his madrigalian approach by the rigid framework of the *Romanesca,* though his setting conforms in every respect to the disciplines of the genre, even to the extent of introducing a little ornamentation into the setting of stanza 3. So personal, however, is his expression of the text and, indeed, the choice of Tasso's impassioned outcry "Ohimè, dov'è il mio ben?" rather than the more resigned "Vostro fui, vostro son," that we are left to wonder whether this setting was not composed much earlier than 1619 and closer in time to the death of Monteverdi's own wife.

Madrigals

In matters both of style and technique, the madrigalian duets published in monody books represent a fusion of elements drawn from Florentine monody with elements taken over directly from the sixteenth-century madrigal and canzonetta. Of the elements that can be identified as Florentine, the most obvious and most important is the use of the continuo itself. The cultivation of a rhetorical manner of vocal writing is another; and Caccini's restrained and affective style of ornamentation influenced a number of the composers of madrigalian duets. And though most of the early madrigals are ensemble works using only fairly short points of imitation, we should not overlook the importance of solo writing *per se* for the development of the duet. First, because passages for solo voice are found in several madrigals published after 1615. And secondly, because the advent of accompanied solo song made it possible to begin a composition for vocal ensemble with an extended solo melody which could then be used in whole or in part for contrapuntal elaboration.

Not all the early composers favored this type of opening. Some preferred only a short point of imitation (vol. 2, no. 4), or a declamatory gesture (vol. 2, no. 5), or a homorhythmic opening (vol. 2, no. 6). Many of those who do use extended melody at the beginning of their duets simply proceed to repeat it with two voices in parallel thirds or to use the end of the melody as the basis of *scherzando* interplay between the voices. But even at the beginning of the seventeenth century we find some madrigalists writing what amounts to a small-scale fugal exposition. In a fairly simple form, this was adopted by Francesco Dognazzi for the opening of his madrigal "O dolcissimi sguardi" (1614). He sets the first line of text in a broad arioso, answers it at the same pitch in the second voice and, at the same time, introduces his setting of the second line as a countersubject (ex. 41). After this, however, he abandons the broad style of the opening in favor of a *scherzando* elaboration of the second line. G.P. Negri went one stage further in his "Voi dite di partire" (1613) and used a regular subject and countersubject (ex. 42), repeating them in combination several times to reinforce the point of the text:

Example 41

Example 42

| Sop. I: | Subject | - | Countersubject | - | S | - | C/S - | S |
| Sop. II: | | | Subject | - | C/S - | S | - | S |

By making the voices weave in and out of one another, Negri avoids the
necessity of constructing invertible counterpoint, a technique we have noted
in connection with Monteverdi's five-part madrigal "La piaga c'ho nel core."[79]
Only one of the monodists seems to have used this technique. This was
Marc'Antonio Negri, Monteverdi's colleague for some years at St. Mark's,
who employed it in his madrigal for soprano and bass "Per far nova rapina"
(1611). He, however, did not write an opening solo at all, so that at the
beginning of his duet lines 1 and 2 of the text are set simultaneously as subject
and countersubject.

Other characteristics of early madrigalian duets derive more obviously
from sixteenth-century ensemble music. The most important of these is the
use of brief melodic motives in a *scherzando* type of imitation, a device
borrowed from the canzonetta and light madrigal and used to extend the
material generated in the course of a duet. A number of madrigals, too,
including works by Florentines like Marco and Giovanni Battista da
Gagliano, Domenico Belli, and Filippo Vitali, are cast in the bipartite form of
the canzonetta. All the madrigals in Mutis's 1613 book are tripartite
structures.

The most difficult question when it comes to identifying the antecedents
of madrigalian duets are those of style, for not all of the earliest composers are
as obviously Florentine-orientated as, for example, Giulio Romano. The
nature of the problem will become clear if we examine more closely the
madrigalian duets published during the first decade of the seventeenth
century.

We noted earlier that madrigalian duets with continuo appeared in print
only in small numbers at the beginning of the seventeenth century. Seven in all
were published up to 1610. Four of them are found in one publication,
Euterpe, by the inventive young Bolognese composer, Domenico Brunetti.
They are:

"Canta Euterpe," for soprano and tenor
"Amor, s'io non ti credo," for two sopranos
"Consumando mi vò," for soprano and bass
"Sei tu, cor mio," for two sopranos

The first of these madrigals may well have suggested the title of the
volume. Its text is a declaration of independence from the narrower confines of
Florentine thinking on the relationship between poetry and music. The first six
lines will suffice to give its flavor:

Canta EUTERPE la parte
Acuta, et io la grave:
Il canto insieme uniti è più soave.
Essa con mille fughe e mille giri
Va dolce in me scherzando.
Io scherzo, e faccio in lei mille sospiri.

Euterpe sings the high part, and I the low; singing together is even sweeter. She, with a thousand flights and turns, plays sweetly in me. I jest, and create in her a thousand sighs.

This is full of pictorial images, and Brunetti loses no opportunity to translate them into music, tickling the ear with virtuoso roulades for "giri" and "scherzando," and contrasting an ornamented line for Soprano solo at "Canta Euterpe" with the tenor's weightier, undecorated, and descending line for "Et io la grave," before bringing the two voices together in parallel tenths for "Il canto insieme." This type of approach is clearly related to the more virtuosic madrigals of a composer like Marenzio. At the same time, though, there is no doubting Brunetti's relationship to Florence, for the affective ornamentation that he uses for Euterpe's solo is borrowed from Caccini's madrigals; and the "mille sospiri" of line 6 are conveyed by means of a written-out *trillo*.

The few bars quoted by Bukofzer[80] from the opening of "Amor, s'io non ti credo" will help to illustrate the hybrid nature of Brunetti's style. The first soprano line is essentially a continuous arioso solo which is not unlike one of the more melodious of Caccini's madrigals. But here the arioso is colored by brief points of imitation and parallel writing produced by the second voice. The general conception, too, is more energetic than one would expect from Caccini. The pointed rhythms of the cadence at bars 5-6 owe something to the canzonetta, and the word "fugge" is painted in lively dotted rhythms of the kind that we find in Monteverdi's *concertato* madrigals.

Sigismondo d'India's light-hearted pastoral madrigal "Fresche erbette novelle" (1609)[81] is even more clearly related to the canzonetta. It consists simply of a series of imitative points using the close, quasi-canonic *scherzando* imitation that characterises many early madrigalian duets, though rarely as relentlessly as this. Dance-like rhythms and an airy texture are the essence of this piece and even the continuity of the text is sacrificed to the phrase structure of the music as the voices cadence at bar 3.

Ghizzolo's bipartite "Qual di nova bellezza" (1610), a "Canto di Sirene" for two sopranos with a *risposta* for solo bass (Neptune) is rather more Florentine in style. It begins, for example, with an exclamation (ex. 43). But the Florentine work which it most resembles is the duet "Ben nocchier" from Caccini's *Euridice,*[82] for it employs the same kind of quasi-canonic technique. It may, indeed, have been taken from a stage work, though Ghizzolo makes no mention of this.

Example 43

The only madrigal published before 1610 which is unequivocally Florentine in style, in fact, is Severo Bonini's setting of Petrarch's sonnet "I' vo
piangendo."[83] It is conceived mainly as a declamatory arioso and can best be
thought of as an augmented monody in which the less dominant voice at any
given moment serves merely as an added sonority. The style of the first section
of the work, in which the poet repents his past life, is appropriately restrained,
with only a little gentle ornamentation such as we can see at bars 47 and 53-54.
Bonini cannot resist madrigalian word-painting altogether, however, and this
comes to the fore at the beginning of the second section, where words like
"guerra" and "tempesta" prompt some lively interaction between the voices
leading, after a short silence in bar 67, to the antithesis, "Mora in pace."

The madrigals of the first decade, then, are a mixed group. And though all
but d'India's little canzonetta look toward Florence to some degree, the variety
of their styles should warn us to guard against easy generalizations about the
Florentine origins of the madrigalian duet. It is clear, even from the study of so
small a group of settings, that the virtuoso madrigal, the canzonetta and even,
perhaps, the canonic duo had a part to play in shaping the language of the new
genre.

All that seems to be missing is any real evidence that the more serious
sixteenth-century madrigal influenced the style of the madrigalian duet. In the
first instance, we find this evidence not in Italy but in England, in the fine
declamatory madrigals that Angelo Notari included in his *Prime Musiche
Nuove* (1613). I have transcribed one of these, his setting of Rinuccini's
"Intenerite voi," as volume 3, no. 5.

Notari (*b* Padua, 14 January 1566; *d* London, December 1663) adopted a
Florentine-style title for his collection of music for one, two, and three voices.
But if his duets are Florentine at all, then they represent Florence viewed
through the eyes of Monteverdi. I do not know when Notari made the duet
arrangements of Monteverdi's five-part madrigals that we find in *GB-Lbm,*
MS.Add. 31,440. His own madrigalian duets, however, are full of idioms

reminiscent of Monteverdi's early and middle-period madrigals. The purposeful bass line supporting a chain of dissonances that we see at bars 46-50 of "Intenerite voi" is one of these idioms; the cadential figure at bars 6-10 another. And the *échappée* figure with which the first phrase of "Occhi un tempo, mia vita" ends (ex. 44) is reminiscent of the similar device used in Monteverdi's "Ohimè, se tanto amate," one of the five-part madrigals arranged for two voices in Add. 31,440.

Example 44

During the second decade of the century, the madrigalian duets published in monody books acquired a more consistently Florentine hue. The spirit of compromise with other traditions was not, however, entirely lost, as we can see from Sigismondo d'India's setting of Guarini's "Langue al vostro languir" (1615).[84] This is the only madrigal included in d'India's *Musiche a due voci* and it shares with the ottava settings of the volume a propensity towards virtuoso ornamentation of a more elaborate kind than we find in Caccini's madrigals. By and large, however, d'India reserves his more florid ornamentation for the penultimate syllable of the line. In those cases where he does not—at bars 32-36 and 78 to the end of the setting—the florid statement is preceded by a plainer setting of the same words. This accords with Caccini's practice.

The virtuoso ornamentation is, of course, meant to be enjoyed for its own sake, but in d'India's hands it proves to be functional as well as decorative, matching both the languors of the opening line and the ardors of the final point. It is apparent from this setting, which is again an augmented monody, that d'India had absorbed all the lessons of Florentine declamatory song. And he displays an almost mannerist concern to highlight every nuance of the lover's complaint, from the dramatized direct speech of bars 10-20 to the intense chromaticism of bars 50-54. Only the sixth line of the text defeats him; and this he passes over in an embarrassed three bars of counterpoint (58-60).

In the same year that d'India published his setting of "Langue al vostro languir," Marco da Gagliano issued his *Musiche a 1, 2 e 3 voci*.[85] This book represents the first substantial contribution by a Florentine composer to the literature of the two-part madrigal. It contains a variety of madrigalian types and exemplifies very well the range of techniques employed by the early madrigalists. In the choice of texts set, however, it is not wholly representative of the madrigals found in monody books.

By the time that he published his *Musiche* of 1615, Marco da Gagliano was a man of some eminence. He was eminent, however, not only in the musical world, but also as a cleric. He was a canon of the ducal Church of San Lorenzo in Florence, where he also held the post of choirmaster. And in 1615 he was also appointed an Apostolic Prothonotary.

Gagliano's dual career as musician and cleric is reflected in the generally serious quality of the texts which he set as duets. Three of the six madrigals in his book are, in fact, settings of spiritual verse. These are "O meraviglie belle," a song for the Nativity; "Vergine chiara," a setting of part of a stanza from Petrarch's *canzone* to the Virgin; and the splendidly dark-hued penitential madrigal "O vita nostra, al fin polvere et ombra." Of the secular poems set, two are sonnets—Bembo's "Cantai un tempo", and "Mira, Fillide mia." Only the five-line madrigal "In un limpido rio," set for soprano and alto, has the concise, epigrammatic quality that we associate with most of the madrigal verse set in the early seventeenth century. Although Gagliano's choice of texts was unusually serious, his example was followed, to some extent, by other Florentine composers. Both Domenico Belli (1616) and Piero Benedetti (1617), the latter a member of Gagliano's *Accademia degli Elevati,* included hymns to the Virgin in their books. And Giovanni Battista da Gagliano paralleled his elder brother's setting "O vita nostra" with his own "Ecco, che pur s'arriva" (1623), the words of a man on the point of death, which he set in a style redolent of early Florentine monody (ex. 45).

Example 45

Of Marco da Gagliano's settings, both "In un limpido rio" and "Vergine chiara" are short ensemble madrigals of a type found in many monody books:

like many madrigals of their type they are declamatory, but only lightly ornamented. Gagliano cast them both as bipartite structures with each section repeated. The first is a slight piece, though it has some subtle touches, including the idea of setting the first line for solo voice only and the neat way in which Gagliano distinguishes between narrative and direct speech in bars 9-10 by an abrupt change of chord and a distinction between an imitative and a homophonic texture. "Vergine chiara" is more powerful in expression. Its two sections show how, by 1615, the duet had already acquired its own vocabulary of musical imagery, and each illustrates a different opening gambit. In the first section, the Virgin is addressed in two solo statements of the first line a fifth apart in pitch. The phrase is then rounded off by a homorhythmic consequent which also serves to suggest her enduring quality. The lines following are set in that type of close imitative writing which had already become a cliché of the madrigalian duet, especially in passages which suggested no distinctive musical image. Here, though, the use of a quasi-canonic technique perfectly matches the line "D'ogni fedel nocchier fidata guida." The second section of the madrigal begins with one of the types of fugal openings that we discussed earlier. The first five syllables of the line are set for tenor II and the continuation acts as a countersubject to the answer in tenor I; the musical phrase is completed by *scherzando* interplay based on the countersubject. This section of the setting also contains one of the earliest examples of a line set for solo voice and not repeated by the two voices together. The use of this technique is suggested by the sense of the line—"peccatrice, Io nol niego, Vergine"—a personal statement by the sinner, and Gagliano sets it in an arioso style as if in a solo madrigal.

The madrigal which most clearly reflects Gagliano's skill in declamatory writing is "O vita nostra," a setting which, for Gothic horror, vies with his more famous monody "Valli profonde." Instead of inventing imitative points for the opening of this madrigal, Gagliano begins with homorhythmic writing and is thus able to use a recitative-like syncopation at bar 3 to underscore the crucial word "polvere." The essence of this piece is terse, epigrammatic statement, of which the outstanding example is found in the setting of "Quanto orror già t'ingombra," where the tension created by the incantatory setting of the initial words is released on the word "già" by juxtaposition of major chords with roots a third apart neatly calculated to produce a frisson of terror in the listener.

In contrast, the two sonnet settings, "Cantai un tempo" and "Mira, Fillide mia," seem expansive and lyrical in character. Both are arioso settings in three musically unrelated sections corresponding to the two quartets and the sestet of the sonnet respectively, a technique which is clearly analogous to the simpler stylized arias used by Rontani for his setting of "Su la sponda del Tebro."[86] Both contain extended passages of solo writing, and in the third section of "Cantai un tempo," the more artificial of the two settings, Gagliano provides us

with a lesson in ornamentation. The setting is cast in an A B B' form. In the first
B section, the line beginning "e quanto è grave" is set as a plain arioso solo for
soprano I (ex. 46a); in the second B section, however, the same line is presented
in an ornamented version (ex. 46b).

Example 46

Passages of solo writing are found in a number of madrigals published
after 1615. In some cases—in Gagliano's "In un limpido rio," for example—the
solo line is taken over by the second voice and used as the basis of a passage in
imitation. This is a technique that we also encounter in a more extended form in
Monteverdi's work, as in bars 13-42 of "Non è di gentil core."[87] Several
monodists, however, Florentines in particular, employ passages of solo writing
as a distinct technical feature of their two-part madrigals. Vitali's "Come sian
dolorose" (1617), for example, begins with an extended arioso for the soprano,
in which the first three lines of the text are set (ex. 47). This line is completely
self-sufficient, and is not used as the basis of contrapuntal interplay. At the
beginning of the second section of the setting, Vitali balances the opening solo
by giving the tenor a fine solo arioso (ex. 48). The lines which he sings are then
set differently for two voices to complete the madrigal. Similar examples of
solo writing can be found in Visconti's "Cruda Amarilli" (1616), in "Quel sol de

gl'occhi miei" (1618) by the Roman composer Nicolò Borboni, and in Giovanni Battista da Gagliano's "Ecco, che pur s'arriva" (1623). But few of the solos found in early duets are quite as intense as the short recitative "Sentii dal gran dolore" (ex. 49) which Benedetti introduced into the setting of his own madrigal text "Della mia Filli lagrimar vid'io" (1617) in order to dramatize the lover's emotion on seeing Phyllis weeping. A plan of the setting (which is quite short) will show how the device is used in context:

Example 47

Example 48

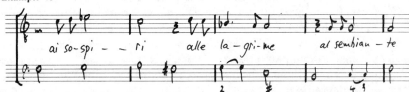

Example 49

Della mia Filli lagrimar vid'io
I bei celesti lumi.
"celesti"
E mentre io rimirava
Sparse di vaghe perle,

A 2: parallel declamation
Sop. I, then Sop. II: ornamented setting of

A 2: parallel declamation

L'impallidite guancie,	A 2: *scherzando* interplay
Sentii dal gran dolore	Sop. II: Recitative
Mancarmi l'alm'el core.	
Meraviglia d'Amore, [bis]	
oimè, quel pianto	A 2: parallel declamation
Pianto non fu,	A 2: imitative
ma foco	A 2: parallel declamation
Per cui, miser, mi struggo a poc'a poco.	A 2: parallel declamation

> I saw the celestial eyes of my Phyllis pouring forth tears. And while I gazed at her pale cheeks, bedewed with beautiful pearls, I lost my heart and soul to her great sorrow. Oh marvel of Love, alas, those tears were not tears at all, but a fire in which I am consumed little by little.

This passage is the nearest relative that I have found in monody books to the recitative style employed by Giovanni Valentini for the three large-scale madrigals for two sopranos—"Ti lascio, anima mia," "Vanne, O carta amorosa," and "Piansi, lunga stagione"—that he included in his *Musiche a doi voci* (1622), a large and pretentious volume dedicated to Ferdinando Gonzaga, duke of Mantua, on the occasion of the marriage of his sister, Eleanora, to the Emperor Ferdinand II. Valentini was, in fact, imperial court organist to Ferdinand II, whom he had followed to Vienna from Graz. He seems to have spent most of his working life outside Italy. Before his appointment at Graz in 1614, he had been organist to King Sigismund III of Poland. At Vienna, he succeded Giovanni Priuli as imperial court choirmaster in 1629.

Valentini's madrigals do not really belong to the mainstream of development of the Italian madrigalian duet. All three of the works in his 1622 book involve extended, dialogue-like exchanges between two solo voices, punctuated by passages of two-part writing. "Vanne, O carta amorosa"[88] is typical of their general manner, though the only ensemble work that it contains is found at the end of the setting.

The texts that Valentini set were not specifically designed to accommodate the alternation of voices that he employs: they are not, for example, dialogues or strophic texts, nor do they feature passages of free verse contrasted with passages of a more regular verse structure. They are, in fact, madrigalian texts, if rather long ones. As we can see from "Vanne, O carta amorosa," however, Valentini divides the text according to its sentence structure, allotting the first sentence to soprano II, the second to soprano I and so on, a technique which is actually a quite ingenious way of introducing variety into an extended setting, though it has little to do with the recitative and aria division of later baroque duets. He unifies the setting by reintroducing, at bars 34-45, the material first stated by soprano I at bars 17-22. On second hearing, the material is stated first by soprano II and then by both voices singing in parallel, leading to the final ensemble.

The beginning of "Ti lascio, anima mia," the first of the madrigals in Valentini's book, lends itself more readily to an alternation technique, for at the fifth line the mode of address changes from the direct speech, in which the poet announces that he has to leave his beloved, to a more impassioned lament which could conceivably reflect the feeling of both the poet and his beloved. This, Valentini treats by changing from solo to duet, though he still maintains a recitative style:

Sop. I:	Ti lascio, anima mia.
	Giunta è quell'hora,
	L'hora, oimè, che mi chiama a la partita.
Sop. II:	Io parto, io parto, oimè, convien ch'io mora
	Perchè convien partir da te, mia vita.
A 2:	Ah, pur troppo è'l dolor ch'entro m'accora;
	Non mi dar col tuo duol nova ferita.

I leave you, my soul. The hour has come, alas, when I must depart. I go, alas, and I must die because I go from you, my life. Ah, the sorrow which is within me afflicts me so much; do not give me a further pain with your grief.

This type of conception was not entirely new in the field of the madrigal. As early as 1615, for example, Alessandro Grandi had begun his madrigal "O Filli, O Filli" with two long solo arioso passages sung alternately by first and second tenor. But the idea of elevating it to a fixed principle of composition was new (as I am sure Valentini was well aware). The relentlessly operatic style of the solo writing (and of some passages of duet writing in "Vanne, O carta amorosa"), too, was a novelty in the madrigal, for composers working in Italy tended to work in arioso styles.

These madrigals are, then, novelties, and the air of experimentation is heightened, in "Vanne, O carta amorosa," by Valentini's use of esoteric proportions such as $\frac{9}{8}$ and $\frac{7}{9}$ (see bars 19-21) to dictate to the performer the stress patterns of the declamation. As novelties these madrigals are very interesting indeed, and we may imagine that they considerably enhanced Valentini's reputation at the Viennese court. Their influence on music in Italy is difficult to judge. Madrigals like Crivelli's "Nude figlie del cor" (1626),[89] Rovetta's "O Rubella d'Amor" (1629),[90] and Galeazzo Sabbatini's "Dove, misero me?" (1636), which is specifically designated "recitative," certainly use extended solos. But they do not follow the same extensive open-work plan of Valentini's madrigals, nor do they use a Florentine style of recitative. I would be inclined to attribute the use of solo writing in the madrigalian duets written in the 1620s and 1630s rather to the influence of Grandi and Monteverdi.

Schmitz saw in Valentini's work the first stages of development towards the late baroque chamber duet, with its alternation of solos and duets.[91] He was, however, careful to stress the unusual nature of these pieces. On balance, it would seem safer to regard the madrigals, at least, as a late flowering of a purely Florentine style and a manner of declamation that had its origins in Peri's *Euridice*.

7

Madrigal and Aria, 1615-1643

S'il Grandi allor, s'il Monteverde a gara
In vestir sacri, o lascivette carmi
Con dolce canto, e sinfonia si rara,
Stati in quella stagion fossero in armi,
Qual dalle lor discordie, illustre e cara
Consonanza nascea dentro a que' marmi,
Dove la Maga in quelle fiamme estive
S'ingegna d'allettar l'alme più schive.
      (Giulio Strozzi, *La Venetia edificata,* 1624, XIII. 74)

The year 1615 stands out as a particularly significant date in the early history of the *concertato* duet. Not only was it the year which saw the publication of the first book devoted entirely to the medium of the continuo duet (d'India's *Musiche a due voci*) and the first important collection of duets by a Florentine composer (Marco da Gagliano's *Musiche a una dua e tre voci*), but it was also the year in which Alessandro Grandi issued his *Madrigali concertati a due tre, e quattro voci,* the first book of *concertato* madrigals to include duets. From 1615 onward, and particularly from the early 1620s, we have to take account of both monody books and madrigal books as sources for duets.

Although, as I suggested earlier, it is an over-simplification to think of the monodists and the madrigalists as two mutually exclusive schools of composers, it is, nevertheless, true that the composers who issued their duets in monody books and those who preferred a madrigal-book format do, by and large, form two distinct groups. And the distinction is not merely musical but also, to a great extent, geographical.

We noted in the last chapter that Roman composers began to rival the Florentines in publishing duets after about 1620. If we study the distribution of composers who issued their duets in monody books from 1619 onward, we see that almost half of them worked at Rome or in nearby towns. Half again as many worked in an area bounded by Florence in the north and Naples in the south.

There seems to have been a good deal of interchange of personnel between Florence and Rome during the early seventeenth century. We have already seen that Rontani moved to Rome from Florence in 1616 and that Falconieri spent some years in the Holy City. Filippo Vitali seems to have been particularly mobile. After studying at Florence, he worked at Rome for a period after 1618. By 1623, however, he was back at Florence, where he seems to have remained until 1631. He sang in the Papal choir from 1631 until, in 1642, he succeeded Marco da Gagliano as choirmaster of the Ducal church of San Lorenzo at Florence. Kapsberger and Frescobaldi spent periods at the Florentine court, and it was only during his Florentine sojourn that Frescobaldi published his two books of arias (1630). Luigi Rossi was at Florence, too, between May and November 1635, and Ghislanzoni suggested that it might have been during this period that he wrote some of his duets for performance by the soprano Angelo Ferrotti and the tenor Odoardo Ceccarelli.[1]

Monody books containing duets were also published by Venetian composers during this period: by Berti (1624), Milanuzzi (1630), and Fontei (1635 and 1636). The publisher Bartolomeo Magni issued Monteverdi's *Scherzi musicali* of 1632 in this format. Other composers working at Venice who issued their duets in monody books—Sances (1633 and 1636), Manelli (1636; the book was actually seen into print by his wife), and Laurenzi (1641)— were, however, Roman by birth and training.

Madrigal books, on the other hand, were issued mainly by composers working in northern Italy. We do find, it is true, a small group of composers— G.F. Anerio, Olivieri, Bonaffino, Pasquali, Giovanni Ferrari, Tarditi, and Cremonese—working in towns and cities to the south of Florence. But by far the greater number of composers who issued their duets in madrigal books worked within an area bounded in the west by Milan and Genoa and in the east by Udine and Pesaro.

Venice, which nurtured the talents of Grandi and Monteverdi, of Biagio Marini, Turini, Pesenti, and Rovetta, was perhaps the most important center of this activity. But other cities are also worthy of note for the musicians of distinction that they produced. Ferrara, with its cathedral and twin institutions, the *Accademia della Morte* and the *Accademia dello Spirito Santo,* maintained a musical tradition, though a more modest one than it had enjoyed during the reign of the Este family. Grandi, trained at both Ferrara and Venice,[2] had worked for both Ferrarese academies and at the cathedral before returning to Venice in 1617 to work under Monteverdi. The academies also provided employment for such interesting figures as Ceresini and Crivelli; and Ignatio Donati, who became choirmaster at Milan Cathedral in 1631, was choirmaster of the *Spirito Santo* in 1616. Verona, which boasted probably the earliest of the Italian musical academies, the *Accademia filarmonica,* was the home and first working place of Stefano Bernardi, a distinguished composer and respected teacher who was later employed by the Prince-Archbishop of Salzburg. Some evidence of the respect in which Bernardi was held is found in the wording of the title page of Bellante's *Concerti accademici* of 1629, which reflects the title of Bernardi's publication of 1615-1616 and, perhaps, the role of the *Accademia filarmonica* in encouraging musicians. The strength of the Veronese musical tradition is further suggested by the relatively large number of Veronese composers who figure in the early history of the *concertato* duet.

The geographical distinction between the two groups of composers issuing duets in madrigal and monody books has two important implications. First, it means that the great flowering of madrigalian duets after the second decade of the seventeenth century was very largely a north Italian phenomenon. Second, unless we assume that Roman composers lost all interest in writing duets during the late 1620s, the decline in importance of printed monody books as sources for duets during this period suggests that more and more Roman compositions were being circulated in manuscript well before 1640.

Scoring

The part-book format in which madrigal books were printed had considerable advantages for the composer of ensemble music since it enabled him to publish a large collection of music, music sometimes conceived on an ambitious scale, in a concise, and therefore relatively cheap form. For singers, too, it had the distinct advantage that only one copy had to be bought, even for performances involving five or six people. And there is an unexpected bonus for the historian, for in order to provide the performers with a clear guide to the contents of the volume and the location of individual pieces in the various part-books, composers were forced to be far more specific about the scoring of their duets than were the monodists. Furthermore, since individual madrigal books often contain far more duets than monody books did, we can generalise with more certainty about the composers' (and their patrons') preferences in terms of scoring.

Table 2 shows the range of scorings found in a number of individual madrigal books published between 1615 and 1642. The list of publications is not exhaustive, but it includes the work of all the more important madrigalists and of those lesser figures who published ten or more duets (only books that have survived complete are included). The numbers of duets include both madrigals and strophic duets, but dialogues have been omitted since their scoring was often dictated by dramatic considerations. Duets for two trebles and for two "canti" have been subsumed under duets for two sopranos. It is possible, though, that the designation "canto" may have been intended to imply that either sopranos or tenors could perform the duet. Comparatively few duets published in madrigal books have no indication at all of the voices intended. The canzonetta "Chiome d'oro" in Monteverdi's 1619 book is one. It is marked simply "for two voices" even though all the other duets in the volume have more specific headings.

Table 2.   Table of Scorings

Book	Year	SS	AA	TT	BB	SS/TT	AA/SS	TT/SS	SA	ST	AT	SB	S/TB	TB
Accademico,	1621	4	1	4							1			
Anselmi (ed.),	1624	6		4		1			1	3				
Bernardi,	1619										3			
	1621	4	1	2					1	1	5			
Ceresini,	1627	5		3						4				3
Colombi,	1621	2		3						5				
Cremonese,	1636	5		3						1		1		
Crivelli,	1626	5		5						1				
Gio.Ferrari,	1628	5		5										
Grandi,	1615	1		3						1				
	1622	5		3						3				
Marastone,	1624	6	1	2					4	2	2			
	1628	3		4							5			2
B. Marini,	1634		1											
	1635	4		3	1		1					1		
Merula,	1633	4							4	1	1	2		
	1642	1												
Monteverdi,	1619	6	1	8										1
	1632			2										
	1638			4										
Obizzi,	1627	7		2						1		2		
Olivieri,	1617	1		12							1	2		
Pesenti,	1621	5		6		1								
	1628			9	1	2								1
	1638			2		2							1	
	1641			6		5								1
Possenti,	1623					17				2		2		
Priuli,	1625	1		2								1		
Rigatti,	1636	4		1							1			2
Rossi,	1628	10		3							2			
Rovetta,	1629	3		6								1		1
	1640	2		1										2
G.Sabbatini,	1625					5		2			1	1	1	
	1626		1	2		2			1		1		1	
	1627					1			1				1	
	1630	1				3			2			2		
	1636					2					3			
Tarditi,	1633	6	1	4								2		
	1629			1										
	1642	3							1			4		
Turini,	1621	1		3							1	1		1
	1624	1		2					1		2	1		1
Vignali,	1640	4	1	6						1				1
Vivarino,	1624	8		4								3		
Totals		123	8	130	2	41	1	2	14	26	29	26	4	16

Table 2 serves to confirm the impression gained from monody books of the overwhelming popularity of equal voice-pairs or, to be more precise, of duets written for two sopranos or two tenors. For there are remarkably few duets from this period for two altos or two basses. What is, perhaps, more surprising is that only a few composers actually suggest that their duets for two sopranos might be performed by two tenors or *vice versa*. And some of the books that do include alternative scorings also contain duets which are written specifically for two sopranos or two tenors. This suggests that we should always take the composer's stated scoring seriously, though, as in the case of duets in monody books, the absence of an indication of alternative scoring does not mean that it was never admitted.

A few composers—Bernardi, Sabbatini, and Turini, for example—offered their prospective customers quite a wide choice of scorings. And unequal voice-pairings are not infrequent in madrigal books. Merula (1633), indeed, seems to have favored them above the more usual equal voice-pairs. Of the unequal voice-pairs, soprano and tenor, alto and tenor, and soprano and bass seem to have been most favored.

Madrigals

With the advent of the madrigal book as a source for duets it becomes possible not only to observe the general characteristics of early duet writing, but also to discuss the development of the madrigalian duet in terms of the distinctive contribution made by individual composers. For while few monody books contain as many as five or six madrigals, madrigal books containing ten or more are not at all unusual. At the same time, the sheer quantity of the surviving material makes a discussion of every individual's contribution impossible within the confines of the present study. In order to focus the discussion, therefore, I have chosen to concentrate on three strands of development which can be observed generally in madrigals published between 1615 and 1643. These are: 1) the composition of relatively small-scale arioso settings, a tradition stemming from the work of Grandi and the monodists; 2) the composition of more ambitious settings belonging to the well-established tradition of madrigalian composition in which the main aim was the matching of textual and musical imagery; and 3) in both large- and smaller-scale settings, the gradual acceptance of aria styles as a distinct element of musical language in through-composed settings: an element that was sometimes employed in response to verbal imagery, but sometimes used to articulate a change of direction in the meaning of the text.

The two most important pioneers of the duet in madrigal books were Grandi and Monteverdi, the two composers linked as the twin musical champions of Venice in the text quoted at the head of this chapter. Einstein also

linked Grandi with Monteverdi, though in less complimentary terms, saying
that he

> may be regarded as having lived off Monteverdi's patrimony: untroubled by his scruples . . .
> less imposing and less interesting but at the same time more progressive and more
> versatile . . . [3]

To say this, however, is not only to misjudge Monteverdi's work, for he was
more versatile, and in some respects just as "progressive" as Grandi, but also to
place the two composers in a false perspective. As far as his duets are
concerned, Grandi cannot be considered a pupil of Monteverdi, nor were his
musical aims the same as those of his older contemporary.

Grandi was still resident at Ferrara and employed as choirmaster of the
cathedral there when his first book of madrigals was published in 1615. The
contents of the book were dedicated to the members of the Ferrarese
Accademia degli Intrepidi, for whose entertainment they had probably been
written. The names of academies, indeed, feature in a number of early
seventeenth-century dedications, suggesting that many madrigalian duets may
have had their first hearing as part of the musical entertainments provided to
round off an evening of academic debate.

In trying to assess Grandi's historical position, we must remember that his
first book of madrigals was issued, like Marco da Gagliano's *Musiche,* in what
were effectively the cradle years of the madrigalian duet. Although his concise
madrigals were published in a different format from those of the monodists,
they belong essentially to the same family as the short settings included in
monody books published during the second decade of the century, settings like
Gagliano's "In un limpido rio" and "Vergine chiara."

Three of the five madrigalian duets in Grandi's 1615 book are quite clearly
Florentine-oriented. "O Filli, O Filli," for example, begins with a very plain
nine-bar recitative sung by tenor I and then repeated to new words by tenor II.
The final section of "Non sa che sia dolore," too, is an open-work plan
consisting of a twelve-bar arioso stated once by each voice as a solo and then
repeated by the two voices singing in parallel thirds. "Udite, lagrimosi spirti
d'Averno,"[4] a setting of Mirtillo's act II lament from *Il Pastor Fido,* also has a
declamatory opening, with tenor II echoing tenor I in a phrase which ends with
a typically Florentine ornament. After the initial statement, the two voices
continue their declamation in parallel thirds, a technique that we have already
encountered in madrigals by d'India and Gagliano.

Despite its clear affinities with the Florentine madrigal, however, the
regular phrase-structure and harmonically generated arioso style of "Udite,
lagrimosi spirti" also bespeaks a relationship to the aria. The declamatory solo
phrase that we see at bars 12-15, for example, is a four-bar melody whose

rhythmic structure is dictated by the regular movement of the bass rather than by the rhythms of the text. The last, unaccented, syllable of the word "affetto" seems, indeed, to be unduly stressed by the harmonic change at the beginning of bar 14.

The melodic foundation of Grandi's arioso writing can be seen even more clearly in the solo line with which "Non sa che sia dolore" begins (ex. 1). This is an autonomous melody consisting of a two-bar antecedent written in an affective style, and a two-bar consequent that is rhythmically more lively, employing syncopation at the end of bar 3. Having stated this melody once in its entirety at the beginning of the madrigal, Grandi proceeds to divide it into its constituent parts, sharing them between the voices and building a large paragraph of twenty bars by means of repetition and sequence. The whole madrigal is built of paragraphs of this sort. The second paragraph, setting lines 3-5 of the text, lasts twelve bars, and the third, which consists of open-work writing of the type later used by Valentini, lasts for no fewer than forty-four bars. This gives us an A B C structure in which the two outer sections are extended developments of their thematic material. The similarity of this plan to the tripartite structure of many canzonettas need not be emphasised.

Example 1

The use of a melody divided into two self-sufficient parts which are then repeated in sequence, used as the basis for imitative interplay, or simply contrasted with each other is a favorite developmental device in Grandi's madrigals and one that he employed in many variations. At the beginning of "O chiome erranti,"[5] for example, he states the themes once as a solo, begins the answer in the second voice, treats the second part of the theme in parallel thirds and then uses the first part of the theme independently as an imitative point. Another example of this technique is seen at bars 23-27, where antecedent and consequent are presented as a dialogue between the voices.

"O chiome erranti" and its companion piece in the 1615 book, "Nulla più vago miro,"[6] are unashamedly tuneful. "Nulla più vago miro," in fact, begins with a six-bar melody whose constituent phrases are divided between the two voices (ex. 2). The opening theme of "O chiome erranti" exploits the paired quavers that we noted earlier in connection with strophic arias.[7] The setting is built almost entirely from short melodic phrases used as solos, or for *scherzando* interplay, or simply sung in parallel. The rhythmic pulse of the piece is skillfully interrupted by affective phrases—at bars 8-9 and 23-24, for example—and slowed for the ending of the piece by burgeoning roulades on the penultimate syllable of the last line: a Florentine device, but one to which Grandi gives a characteristic twist by repeating the last line in a new setting over a more purposeful bass.

Example 2

The madrigals of Grandi's 1622 book, published after he had succeeded to the position of assistant choirmaster of St. Mark's, Venice, do not differ in kind from the two basic types—tuneful and declamatory—that we find in the 1615 book, nor do they use fundamentally different techniques. But Grandi seems to have acquired, perhaps from his contact with Monteverdi, a taste for the more intense type of declamation that we can see at the beginning of "O come è gran martire."[8] His command of melody seems more assured in these works, as we can see from the long arch of "S'ogn'un ama il suo core," bars 33-39 of the same madrigal. This, too, employs the same "walking bass" technique as Grandi's solo cantatas.

The 1622 book contains some of Grandi's finest madrigals, among them the spacious "Di voi, ben mio" and the consistently powerful "Spine care e soavi." (The splendid opening phrases of this latter madrigal appear, with only negligible differences, as the opening bars of the madrigal "Luci belle et amati," published a year earlier by the otherwise unknown composer who styled himself Accademico Bizzarro Capriccioso, and who seems to have lived at Fano, where he had been a pupil of Massimillo Freduti, the choirmaster of Fano cathedral.)[9] And finally, the book contains the exquisite miniature setting of Marino's "Rose, rose beate."[10] Like "Spine care e soavi," this is cast in a simple A B A form. It begins with Grandi's favorite device—the contrast of an affective gesture with a livelier consequent. But here the imitative treatment of the consequent, with its imaginative rhythmic displacement, is of the finest workmanship.

In the field of the madrigalian duet Grandi was essentially a miniaturist. His work continued the tradition of the shorter settings found in monody books, though in his hands the short madrigal became less Florentine, more aria-like in style, a type of composition characterised by generally unornamented melodic lines of regular phrase-structure and by the interplay of short motives used to build longer paragraphs.

Grandi's first book of madrigals enjoyed an extraordinary success in print. It was reissued three times before 1620 and twice more, in 1622 and 1626 respectively. Its influence, and that of the second book of madrigals, which was also reprinted twice, seems to have been extensive, both directly, in providing stylistic models for other composers, and indirectly, in popularising short arioso duets.

The term *madrigaletto* has sometimes been applied to this type of setting by historians, but it is not clear whether early seventeenth-century composers used the term as an indication of the style and scale of their compositions, or whether they used it simply to distinguish publications containing music scored for a few voices from those containing larger-scale polyphonic madrigals.

Three composers—Bernardi (1621), Salamone Rossi (1628), and Biagio Marini (1635)—published duets under the title *Madrigaletti*. Of these, the works which most resemble those of Grandi are the duets of Bernardi and Rossi. Rossi, the Mantuan instrumentalist and composer who had been first in the field of the polyphonic *concertato* madrigal, shares Grandi's gift for melody, but lacks his range of invention and his ability to develop thematic material at length. His settings are generally very short, through-composed works with the last line repeated. Their texture is characterised by a short opening point of imitation followed by writing mainly in parallel thirds.[11] Only in "Volò ne' tuoi begli occhi" is an extended solo introduced during the course of the piece.

In their brevity and dependence on melody, Rossi's *Madrigaletti* resemble settings of single canzonetta stanzas. Bernardi's duets, on the other hand, though indebted to the style of the canzonetta, are more varied in texture and madrigalian in approach. His duets share some features in common with those of Grandi—the use of extended solos, *scherzando* interplay and writing in thirds—but he avoids Grandi's technique of paragraph building, preferring instead to adopt a line-by-line setting. His "Esser vorrei con cento lumi in fronte," for example, begins with an extended solo for the tenor (ex. 3) which is immediately repeated a fourth higher by the alto. Only when we reach the words "per consolar," the beginning of the third line of the text, is imitation introduced, and then only to initiate a solo setting of the remainder of the third line and the whole of the fourth. Despite such obvious madrigalisms as the painting of the word "stringermi" (ex. 4), the style of "Esser vorrei" clearly owes much to the canzonetta. And in the setting of "Ecco pur ver me si movono" the relationship between arioso madrigal and canzonetta, suggested first of all by there being no extended solos, is confirmed by the fact that the composer has chosen to make a through-composed setting of a strophic text.

Example 3

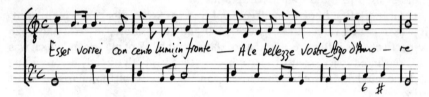

Example 4

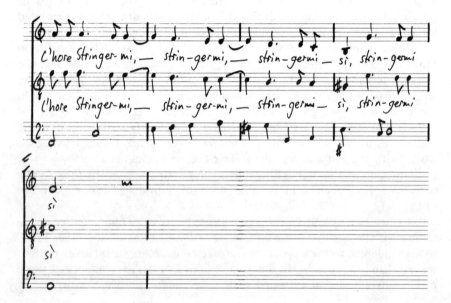

The text of "Ecco pur ver me" is in seven four-line stanzas, composed of two lines of *ottonari sdruccioli* and two of *quaternari*. The first four stanzas are given below.

Ecco pur ver me si movono
Quei bei lumi
De duo fiumi
Di dolcezz'al cor mi piovono.

Filli mia se dolce hor veggioti,
Filli cara,
Non amara,
Più vederti o provar deggioti.

Liete pur ecco sfavillano
Quelle stelle
Che non felle
Vere gioie al cor mi stillano.

Deh tornate, calde lagrime,
Giù nel centro,
Dove dentro
Vien ch'ogn'alma afflitta lagrime.

The setting alternates two passages in duple meter (stanzas 1, 4-5) with two in triple meter (stanzas 2-3, 6-7). The change from duple to triple meter at the beginning of stanza 2 seems to have been suggested both by the change from description to direct address and by the joyful tone of stanzas 2 and 3; and the return to duple meter and a more declamatory style at stanza 4 seems to be suggested by the mention of tears (ex. 5). The return to expressions of pleasure at stanza 6 then prompts the return to triple meter.

The publication of Biagio Marini's *Madrigaletti* (1635) seems to have been delayed by ten years and its contents may well belong to the period of the composer's employment at the court of the Count Palatine Wolfgang Wilhelm at Neuburg in Bavaria. Marini's settings are weightier in content than the title *Madrigaletti* might seem to imply. Three, at least, are settings of sonnets by Girolamo Preti. In terms of style, Marini's duets owe less to Grandi than to Florentine solo song, as we can see from the setting of lines 1-3 of the madrigal "Arso e ferito e porto" (ex. 6). This particular madrigal and the quasi-dialogue "Cintia, lungi da me" employ an open-work plan of solos similar to that found in Valentini's madrigals of 1622, and this may in itself argue for their having been written while Marini was working outside Italy.

Short arioso settings, occasionally with formal repetition schemes, form a distinct class of madrigalian duets published during the 1620s and 1630s, and they were by no means restricted to publications entitled *Madrigaletti*, as we can see from Rigatti's "Baccia Lidio gentile,"[12] a short madrigal included by the

young choirmaster from Udine in his *Musiche concertate* of 1636. Nor were
they restricted to sources devoted exclusively to short settings. The *Primo
Libro delli Madrigali concertati* of Giovanni Battista Crivelli, for example,
opens with the long sonnet setting transcribed as volume 2, no. 23, but it also
includes short arioso madrigals like "O stelle ardenti," which is cast in a
bipartite repetition scheme with the second section set as a triple-meter *bel
canto* duet. In this piece, Crivelli shows himself Grandi's spiritual successor as
well as being one of his actual successors as choirmaster to the *Accademia dello
Spirito Santo* of Ferrara. The text is, in fact, one that had been set by Grandi
himself and published in his 1622 book. A comparison of the opening bars of
the two settings suggests that Crivelli (ex. 7a) may have modeled his setting
quite consciously on that of his older contemporary (ex. 7b). And he uses
Grandi's developmental technique of juxtaposing antecedent and consequent
to build larger paragraphs.

Example 5

Example 6

Example 7

Giovanni Bernardo Colombi, who was working in 1621 as organist and choirmaster of the collegiate church at Novellara, near Reggio Emilia, and Giovanni Ceresini, who in 1627 was choirmaster of the *Accademia della Morte* at Ferrara, also seem to have modeled their duet writing on Grandi's. Ceresini's madrigals are remarkable for their long opening solos, often spanning three or four lines of text, as we can see in "Simulacro d'Amor" (ex. 8). Here the solo line is no fewer than ten bars long, and it is repeated in its entirety by the second soprano before the constituent phrases are treated in imitation. A similar technique, with a solo again spanning three lines of text, is employed by Colombi for the opening of his setting of Marino's "Perchè fuggi tra salci," though here the second voice repeats only the first two lines before the first passage of imitation begins. Several of Colombi's duets—"È sì dolce il penar, dolce il languire" is one—open with declamation which seems to be Florentine in manner (ex. 9). Since the solo line continues with a rhythmically more lively phrase (ex. 10), however, and this phrase is later used as the basis of imitation, it is not clear whether his model is Florentine or a madrigal like "Non sa che sia dolore" from Grandi's first book of madrigals.

Example 8

Example 9

Example 10

If the tradition of shorter arioso settings can be seen to stem from Grandi and the monodists, the parallel tradition of longer and more substantial settings seems to stem directly from Monteverdi's seventh book of madrigals. For extended madrigalian duets like d'India's "Langue al vostro languir" and the two sonnet settings in Marco da Gagliano's *Musiche* are rare in monody books.

One thing should be emphasised, however, and that is that the two traditions of arioso madrigal and longer settings were not mutually exclusive. The influence of Grandi's first book of madrigals seems to have extended beyond the ranks of its direct imitators. Far from Grandi's living off Monteverdi's patrimony, as Einstein would have it, Monteverdi may well have acquired one or two techniques from Grandi.

This, at least, seems to be evidenced by his setting of "Non è di gentil core."[13] Monteverdi constructs the setting in four large paragraphs with a coda based on the last line: A (bars 1-13)   B (13-42)   C (43-56)   A[1] (57-77)+ coda (78-91). The repeated A section, in which the two vocal lines are simply exchanged, is suggested by a repetition in the text.

The setting begins with a theme which is constructed in a very similar manner to the themes by Grandi that we have discussed: that is, it consists of a fairly slow antecedent followed by a rhythmically livelier consequent. The first paragraph is built from sequential repetition of the two parts of the theme treated as independent entities: in this case by simultaneous statements of the two parts in quasi-invertible counterpoint. The second paragraph begins with an extended solo whose constituent parts are then treated in *scherzando* imitation and in parallel writing. And the third paragraph, in which Monteverdi neatly dramatizes the lover's ardor through a series of rising phrases, makes great play with writing in parallel thirds. The coda involves virtuoso ornamentation for the word "arde." This is not Florentine ornamentation, however, for it functions within the harmonic progression.

Nothing could be more different from the sombre and intense madrigals of book VI than this frothy virtuoso piece. Some of the techniques that it uses can certainly be traced back to Monteverdi's earlier music, but there is no reason to suppose that he disdained to learn from a man like Grandi. On the contrary, the evidence not only of "Non è di gentil core," but also of the openings of other light madrigals like "Io son pur vezzosetta" and "Perchè fuggi tra salci" seems to confirm his debt to Grandi. In "Tornate, O cari baci," for the lines "Voi di quel dolce amaro / Pascete i miei famelici desiri,"[14] Monteverdi adopts one of Grandi's favorite devices, an affective declamation in one voice answered by a lively consequent in the other.[15] Throughout his career, Monteverdi had shown a Stravinsky-like aptitude for absorbing new styles and techniques and creating from them something uniquely his own. In turning to the new light-hearted duet, then, what better man to learn from than its pioneer?

Monteverdi brought to his duets two particular qualities that serve to set them apart from those of even his most able contemporaries. The first was the breadth of his musical experience. For during the course of his career he had written canzonettas, serious madrigals, operas, and ornate *concertato* madrigals. In writing his duets, then, he was able to call on a range of styles and techniques to create the exact image that he wished to convey.

The experience of Mantuan madrigals like "A un giro sol" is put to good use, for example, in such serious settings as "Interrotte speranze" (1619)[16] and the later "O sia tranquillo il mare" (1638),[17] in both of which Monteverdi uses the device of the unison line which parts to create a dissonance. This is particularly poignant in the latter setting, where it is used to underscore the lover's cry that he will *never* cease his lament for betrayed love. On the other hand, a lament like "Non vedrò mai le stelle."[18] prompts an operatic style of declamation, complete with accented dissonances in the manner of Peri such as we see in bars 5 and 8. And finally, in setting the text "O come sei gentile," in which the lover compares his state with that of the caged bird, and his song with hers, Monteverdi uses ornamentation not only for such obvious phrases as "tu canti, io canto," but also begins with a highly decorated line for the syllable "O" and concludes the first paragraph at bars 15-16 with a Florentine ornament. The theme of the text—singing—is thus encapsulated in the style chosen for the opening lines.

The other particular quality that Monteverdi brought to the duet was his ability to dramatize his setting: that is, not merely to match the imagery of the text, but also to intensify it or to create a mental picture for the listener which is not suggested by the text alone. This quality is, of course, apparent in the laments, but it can also be detected in the opening phrase of "Ah, che non si conviene,"[19] where the line sweeps up an octave to create an exaggerated avowal of the lover's fidelity, and in the concluding bars of "Ardo e scoprir" (1638),[20] in which the faint-hearted lover's words die on his lips in a series of truncated phrases. In "Vorrei baciarti, O Filli,"[21] Monteverdi first suggests the lover's shyness by means of abrupt cadences, then has his words tumbling over each other before reaching a more confident statement of his intention to kiss the nymph.

Although the majority of the texts that Monteverdi set as duets are madrigals, a substantial minority of them (and a majority of the more intense and serious texts) are sonnets.[22] It was, of course, quite possible for the composer to set a sonnet as though it were a piece of madrigal verse: that is, by following the sense and imagery of the text alone. Nevertheless, the peculiar nature of the sonnet form—its consistent pattern of eleven-syllable lines, and its possible points of articulation at the ends of the two quartets and again at the end of the first tercet—sometimes suggested a formal pattern. This is the case at the beginning of Monteverdi's setting of "O viva fiamma,"[23] where each pair of lines in the octave is set to a variation of the same theme (bars 1-13). But the outstanding example of the integration of form and imagery in Monteverdi's sonnet settings in provided by "Interrotte speranze.[24] Here, the octave and the first tercet (bars 1-38) explore images of deepest gloom. Monteverdi creates for these lines a superbly intense arch of melody in which the two voices move constantly to and from the unison. Each phrase of the melody corresponds to one line of the text and the first musical paragraph (bars 1-14) corresponds to the first quartet. The whole paragraph is then repeated for the second quartet (bars 15-28) and then the idea is inverted for the first tercet (bars 29-38). Not only does the music correspond to the poetic form, but its relentless quality provides an apt image for the ills that eternally beset the lover.

Sonnets form the basis of a number of the more serious duets found in madrigal books. I have included two in the anthology: the intense declamatory setting of "Nude figlie del cor, rime languenti," which forms the *proemio* (preface or introduction) to Crivelli's 1626 book,[25] and the setting of Marino's "Ardo, ma non ardisco il chiuso ardore" (1638) by the Venetian composer Martino Pesenti.[26]

Crivelli's setting follows the structure of the sonnet quite closely. The first quartet is set for two voices, with lines 1 and 3 of the text having matching cadences (bars 4-6, 13-14). The second quartet and first tercet are set for tenor I and tenor II respectively, and the final tercet is again set for both voices. Pesenti, on the other hand, depicts individual images in a more madrigalian fashion. Nevertheless, he shows a careful control of pacing, with the weight of the setting concentrated on the two tercets. Marino's sonnet is rather curious in structure. The first tercet appears to form the conclusion of the text, but is then capped by the second tercet. Pesenti solves the problem of this dual climax by creating a striking contrast of motives for the phrase "Così tremo et agghiaccio" (see bars 54-57) in the first tercet, but then caps this by setting the second tercet as an extended aria over a descending tetrachord ostinato (bars 83-171) which occupies half of the total length of the setting.

Pesenti, who was blind from birth, was generously described by his publisher, Alessandro Vincenti as "una delle meraviglie di questa Città" (dedication to 1638 book) and "meraviglia del nostro Secolo" (dedication to 1641 book). The assured handling of "Ardo, ma non ardisco" certainly seems to merit something of Vincenti's enthusiasm, and it also serves to illustrate the way in which madrigalists working after the late 1620s used extended passages of arioso writing as a solution to the problem of creating extended settings in the medium of the duet. Pesenti's earlier madrigals are much shorter. Some, like "Ohimè, se tanto amate" (1621),[27] are based entirely on Grandi's technique of building paragraphs (in this case bars 1-17, 28-45, 45-72) from the constituent phrases of a solo line; others, like "Al foco de doi lumi un giorno Amore" (also 1621), temper this technique with more extended declamatory openings, in this case one that seems to have been borrowed from Monteverdi's "Interrotte speranze" (ex. 11).

Example 11

Al foco de doi lumi un giorno Amo - - re Stese sue faci con la mano ardi — ta

Al foco de doi lumi un giorno Amo — re Stese sue faci con la mano ardi — ta

The use of serious, declamatory writing can also be found in the madrigal writing of Francesco Turini, a composer who began his career as organist at the court of the Emperor Rudolf II, but later (by 1620) moved to the post of organist at Brescia cathedral which he seems to have held until his death. The text of Turini's madrigal "Dove, ah dove ten vai?" (1621),[28] abstracted from the libretto to Monteverdi's *Orfeo,* has much of the serious quality of Petrarchan verse. And Turini sets it in a suitably old-fashioned style, using parallel chromaticism to create a sense of desolation at the loss of hope. A similar chromatic language is also used in his setting "Amorosetti fiori" (also 1621), where it is employed to create a contrast to the extended paragraph of writing in triple meter with which the setting opens.

Example 12

Chi vuol haver fe - lice e lieto il co-re Non segua il crudo Amore, Non segua il crudo Amo —

re, Quel lu - sin - ghier

This serious vein is, however, only one aspect of Turini's musical personality. Several of the settings in his 1621 book—"Chi vuol haver felice e lieto il core" (ex. 12) and "Luci belle e spietate,"—for example—and many of the settings in his 1624 book employ aria-like writing over basses moving mainly in crotchets, or in crotchets and quavers.

This type of bass line is a striking feature of a number of duets published in madrigal books. Monteverdi, for example, distinguishes between narration and direct speech in "Dice la mia bellissima Licori"[29] by a change from homophonic declamation to an imitative duet over a "walking bass." Antonio Marastone uses a "walking bass" throughout his attractive setting of "Armato il cor" (1624).[30] And in Tarquinio Merula's "Cogli Dori gentile" (1633; ex. 13) a "walking bass" supports melodic idioms that are virtually indistinguishable from those found in the aria "Amo l'è ver".[31]

Example 13

This type of "walking bass" may well have been popularized by the technique of Grandi's strophic bass cantatas, but in the field of the duet they can also be traced in Florentine settings like Domenico Belli's "Quasi vermiglia rosa" (1616) and Antonio Brunelli's *scherzo* "Già di paglia 'n su la riva" (1616). It may be significant that this latter piece is to be perfomed either by voices or by instruments; and Tarquinio Merula's sonnet setting "La Donna è mobil verga" (1642), which employs a bass moving consistently in quavers, is the only setting that I have encountered outside the field of the *concertato* aria that calls for a violone to double the continuo line.

The popularity of the "walking bass," may, then, be attributable to the influence of instrumental idioms, transferred to vocal writing in the arias of composers like Grandi. Certainly, in a setting like Galeazzo Sabbatini's "Udite, O selve, udite,"[32] it forms the basis of aria-like writing such as we can see at bars 39-55; and the extensive use of a "walking bass" throughout the first section of this extended setting creates a lively rhythm which acts as a foil to the sudden intrusion of recitative at bar 82.

Galeazzo Sabbatini is one of the most interesting and original of the lesser-known composers to emerge from this study. He was choirmaster of Pesaro cathedral from 1626 to 1630, choirmaster to the Duke of Mirandola from 1630 to 1639, and the author of a primer on continuo playing.[33] There is some circumstantial evidence that he may have studied Monteverdi's duet writing. The setting of "Udite, O selve, udite" (1630),[34] begins with a falling fifth motive which is reminiscent of the opening of Monteverdi's "Tornate, O cari baci" (1619); and the augmented triad that Sabbatini employs at bar 85 is also employed by Monteverdi at a similar juncture in his setting. Nevertheless, the scale of Sabbatini's madrigal sets it apart from Monteverdi's duets. The length of the text stretches the madrigalist's ability to create a coherent whole and, despite the reuse of material from bars 15-16 to create a duet at bars 95-97, our interest is sustained chiefly by the range of Sabbatini's invention.

Inventiveness is the hallmark of Sabbatini's best writing. It can be seen, for example, in the fugal exposition with which he begins the madrigal "Ohimè, misero, io canto" (1626)[35] and in the arresting gestures that he invents for the openings of madrigals like "A che tanto piagarmi" (1630; ex. 14) and "Folgori Giove pur tuoni tempesti" (1636; ex. 15), this last, incidentally, being a very similar figure to that used at the beginning of the madrigal "Fulmina da la bocca" in the first book of madrigals (1625).

Example 14

If Sabbatini's "Udite, O selve" illustrates the encroachment of duple-meter aria writing over a "walking bass," the other setting of his which is included in our anthology—"Ohimè, misero, io canto"—illustrates the parallel encroachment of aria writing in triple meter, for its last line is set as a fully fledged *bel canto* arioso of 24 bars in which individual words and phrases are repeated several times.

Example 15

The use of extended passages of triple-meter arioso, sometimes to extend what would otherwise be a short setting, becomes a regular feature in madrigalian duets from the late 1620s, and not simply for the purpose of word-painting. This is exemplified in the work of Giovanni Rovetta, who succeeded Grandi to the post of assistant choirmaster of St. Mark's, Venice, in 1627 and ultimately succeeded Monteverdi as choirmaster there in 1644. Of the ten madrigals published in Rovetta's 1629 book only three—"Ohimè, chi mi ferisce?," "È partito il mio bene," and "Portate, onde correnti"—do not contain passages in triple meter, while "Quel neo ch'appar nel viso" is in triple meter throughout.

As we can see from the two examples from Rovetta's 1629 book transcribed in the anthology,[36] the madrigalian duet had traveled a great distance in terms of style even during the fourteen years that had elapsed since the publication of Grandi's first book of madrigals. For in his madrigal writing, at least, Rovetta is Grandi's, rather than Monteverdi's pupil, as the melodic opening of both madrigals, and even the harmonically generated passage of declamatory arioso at bars 14-18 of "O Rubella d'Amor" demonstrate.[37] His madrigals are, however, generally longer and require a more virtuoso vocal technique than Grandi's; and when they employ writing in triple meter it is as a distinct facet of style unrelated to word-painting in the usual sense. In "Chi vuol haver felice e lieto il core" triple meter is introduced at bar 29 in contrast to the preceding *scherzando* in order to highlight the moral of the madrigal. And in "O Rubella d'Amor" it is used as part of a complex rondo structure which also features passages of recitative (bars 43 to 57, 88 to 110).

Rovetta's "O quante volte, O quante" (1640),[38] though still recognizably madrigalian in approach, points unmistakably to the future. Although, structurally speaking, it lies in the tradition begun by Grandi, Grandi's extended paragraphs have now become the basis of a composite form:

A (bars 1-16)	Fugal exposition. The subject is a single arch of melody, five bars long. Soprano I and soprano II each sing both subject and countersubject so that the exposition is based on double motives until bar 14.
B (bars 16-20)	Declamatory interruption à 2.
C (bars 21-39)	Refrain. Begins in triple meter and continues in duple meter. Lovers are counseled to seek pleasure only.
D (bars 39-44)	Recitative for soprano I.
C (bars 45-51)	Refrain. Triple meter only.
D (bars 51-57)	Recitative for soprano II.
C (bars 57-65)	Refrain. Triple meter and duple-meter continuation.
D (bars 65-79)	Recitative, developed into final duet.

In this madrigal we find a stylistic vocabulary appropriate to the writing of sectional cantatas. The text, however, is still cast in the single stanza form of the madrigal and written in seven- and eleven-syllable lines. The changes in style within the setting are prompted by the sense, rather than by the sense *and* the structure of the text, as one would expect to find in the later cantata. Nevertheless, the use of a refrain links this madrigal clearly to the so-called "rondo-cantatas" of the mid-century Roman school of composers.

New Directions in the Strophic Duet

With the decline in the number of monody books published after 1623 that contain duets, a discussion of strophic duets based on material from these sources alone would be meager indeed. From 1619 onward, however, madrigal books must also be taken into account as sources for strophic duets; and these often include works which rival madrigalian compositions in scale and complexity.

Many of the duets published in monody books after 1623 are the work of composers associated with Rome. At Rome itself, Kapsberger continued to publish volumes of *Villanelle* until 1640, and he was joined in print by such figures as Alessandro Capece (1625) and Pietro Paolo Sabbatini (1628 and 1631) whose strophic duets, amiable though they are, show no real advance in style and technique over music written a decade earlier. Only the work of Francesca Campana (1629) and Filippo Vitali (1632) reflect the growing interest among composers of solo songs in writing arias in triple meter.

Between 1632 and 1640 there is a gap in Roman publications. This is disappointing since the 1630s evidently saw considerable changes in taste and technique among Roman composers. This is suggested by the two strophic duets published by Lorenzo Corsini (1640) in a volume dedicated to Cardinal Antonio Barberini. Both are settings of two stanzas only (a characteristic of some of Luigi Rossi's duets) and both employ rich, languorous triple-meter *bel canto* writing of a kind which is a far cry from Roman music of the late 1620s (ex. 16).

Example 16

A full picture of the development of the strophic duet in Roman circles from the late 1620s onwards would have to take into account the large quantity of music which survives only in manusript and which lies outside the scope of the present study. Something of the change of taste that was taking place during the 1630s can, however, be glimpsed in the publications of two Roman composers working in other Italian cities during this period. The first is Girolamo Frescobaldi, who published his two books of *Arie musicali* (1630) at Florence while serving as organist to the Grand Duke of Tuscany. Frescobaldi's strophic duets are all cast in triple meter, though their mainly syllabic settings, cross-rhythms, and occasionally old-fashioned harmonic progressions link them to the earlier triple-meter canzonetta. The second is Giovanni Felice Sances, whose books of *Cantade,* only two of which survive (1633 and 1636), were published at Venice. In Sances' work, as, for example, in "Chi nel regno almo d'Amore" (1636),[39] we find evidence of a richer harmonic palette and the use of melismas against a slow-moving bass, traits which suggest the influence of the type of *bel canto* writing found in the solo arias of the Venetians Grandi and Berti.

A number of madrigal books, too, include simple strophic arias and such well-established forms as strophic variations and variations on stylized arias. Of these last, the *Romanesca* proved the most durable, with settings by Valentini (1621), Banchieri (1626), Bellante (1629), Gregori (1635), and Rigatti (1636). Gregori and Rigatti chose stanzas from Marino's *Adone* for their settings, but ottavas were not the only kind of text set. Banchieri, for example, chose a sonnet, "Io son pur vezzosetta pastorella," and Valentini a *canzone,* "O Dio quel dolce a Dio."

It is not, however, such well-established forms that are the main concern of this chapter. A number of duets published in both monody and madrigal books between 1616 and 1643 represent new directions of development.

Duets on Ostinato Basses

The first of these developments to note concerns duets founded on ostinato basses. The earliest of these are simply strophic duets in which the same music is repeated for each stanza. Falconieri's 1616 book, for example, includes an *Aria sopra la Ciaccona* for soprano and bass—"O vezzosetta dalla chioma d'oro." This setting employs a bass (ex. 17) closely akin to the so-called "chaconne" bass used later for extended variations; and it is stated twice within the setting of the stanza.

Example 17

The appearance of the designation *ciaccona* does not necessarily indicate the use of an ostinato. It can simply indicate a particular type of dance-song. Frescobaldi's "Deh vien da me pastorella" (*Secondo Libro d'Arie,* 1630), for example, consists of three sections of duet writing separated by two passages of solo recitative. The bass for the first of the duet sections begins with the same pattern as Falconieri's duet, but is then developed into a longer, more diffuse line lacking any regular repetition pattern. And Francesco Manelli's *ciaccona* "Con lieto baleno" (1636) is simply a strophic dance-song which makes no use of an ostinato and has a bass pattern which seems quite unlike the "chaconne" bass.

Manelli was, nevertheless, among the first composers to publish duets using an ostinato bass. His strophic aria "Che mi potrai tù far," published in Robletti's anthology *Le Risonanti Sfere* (1629), is written on a bass, apparently of Manelli's own invention though related to the harmonic pattern of the "chaconne" bass[40] (ex. 18), which is stated four times to form the basis of the setting.

Example 18

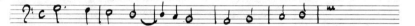

The extent to which Manelli was a pioneer of settings on ostinato basses cannot now be determined with certainty. His *Ciaccone et Arie* (1629), which survives only in an incomplete form, may have included settings on ostinati. It is possible, too, that he may be identified with the composer who called himself Il Fasolo, whose dialogue setting "O sfortunata chi mi consola?" (1628), to a text later reset by Manelli (1636), is the earliest vocal work to employ the so-called "passacaglia" (i.e. descending tetrachord) bass as an ostinato.[41]

The "passacaglia" bass, an "emblem of lament" as it has been called,[42] was little used by composers of duets. Apart from the two dialogues just mentioned and the final section of Pesenti's sonnet setting "Ardo, ma non ardisco il chiuso ardore" (1638),[43] the *ciaccona* [*sic*] "O piaggia felice albergo beato" in Spighi's 1641 book is the only other example found in published sources before 1643.

The "chaconne" bass, on the other hand, served several composers as the foundation for extended variations published during the 1630s. For the most part these are settings of strophic texts, though, as in the case of Sances's "Lagrimosa belta" (1633), the beginnings and ends of the stanzas are not always clearly delineated in the settings. In addition to Sances's setting, chaconne variations based on strophic texts were published in Gregori's *Ariosi Concenti* (1635) and in the *Madrigali et altre Musiche concertate* (1633) of Tarquinio Merula, then choirmaster of Santa Maria Maggiore, Bergamo.

Merula was one of the most able exponents of large-scale aria settings during the 1630s, as the fluent melodic lines, rhythmic subtleties, and chromatic inflections of his chaconne "Lidia ben chè m'alletti" show.[44] The strophic structure of this setting is easy to distinguish. The three stanzas of the text are set as solos for soprano (bars 1-13), alto (bars 50-66) and soprano (bars 101-117) respectively, while the refrain, which has the same number of lines as the stanza, is set as an extended duet (bars 13-46, 66-97 and 117-150), culminating each time in a duple-meter coda.

A similarly well-defined structure characterises Francesco Negri's "Ginevra, ah no, più mia ridir potrai" (1635), though here the text is a sonnet. The two quartets and first tercet are separated from each other by a single statement of the bass as though they were stanzas of a strophic text. At the last tercet, however, the setting moves directly into recitative, with a return to the chaconne bass only in line 13. The effect is dramatic, but is not clearly supported by the sense of the text, where the change in direction of diction comes at the beginning of the first tercet.

It is difficult to avoid the suspicion that Negri's choice of a sonnet rather than a strophic text may have been influenced by the publication, three years earlier, of Monteverdi's "Zefiro torna, e di soavi accenti." But Negri's setting lacks two qualities that distinguish Monteverdi's work. The first is the inventiveness and apparent spontaneity of Monteverdi's vocal writing. The second is the choice of a text which not only affords opportunities for word-painting, but also provides the basis for a convincing overall design.

It is easy enough to point to instances of melodic word-painting in Monteverdi's setting, but its inventiveness is as much rhythmic as melodic, with skilful contrasts of pacing matching contrasting images in the text. A typical example is found at the very beginning of the piece. The bass itself is measured in units of three semibreves. When the voices enter, however, their lines are measured in units of three minims, beginning one minim after the bass and producing a delightful cross-rhythm (ex. 19). This serves to throw into relief the setting of the second phrase—"e di soavi accenti—where both bass and vocal line are rhythmically in phase with each other, producing a much smoother outline to complement the sense of the text.

Example 19

As far as overall design is concerned, Monteverdi follows a scheme of contrasts similar to that which he used in setting Petrarch's "Zefiro torna e 'l bel tempo rimena" as a five-part madrigal (1614). Rinuccini's sonnet is, in fact, a reworking of Petrarch:

(Petrarch)

Zefiro torna, e 'l bel tempo rimena
E i fiori e l'erbe, sua dolce famiglia,
E garrir Progne, e pianger Filomena,
E primavera candida e vermiglia.

Ridono i prati e 'l ciel si rasserena;
Giove s'allegra di mirar sua figlia;
L'aria, e l'acqua, e la terra è d'amor piena;
Ogni animal d'amar si riconsiglia.

Ma, per me, lasso, tornano i più gravi
Sospiri, che dal cor profondo tragge
Quella ch'al ciel se ne portò le chiavi;

E cantar augelleti, e fiorir piaggie,
E 'n belle donne honeste atti soavi
Sono un deserto, e fere aspre e selvaggie.

(Rinuccini)

Zefiro torna e di soavi accenti
L'aer fa grato e 'l piè discioglie a l'onde
E, mormorando tra le verdi fronde,
Fa danzar al bel suon su 'l prato i fiori.

Inghirlandato il crin Fillide e Clori
Note temprando lor care e gioconde;
E da monti e da valli ime e profonde
Raddopian l'armonia gli antri canori.

Sorge più vaga in ciel l'aurora e 'l sole,
Sparge più luci d'or; più puro argento
Fregia di Teti il bel ceruleo manto.

Sol io, per selve abbandonate e sole,
L'ardor di due begli occhi e 'l mio tormento,
Come vuol mia ventura, hor piango hor canto.

In both sonnets the lover contrasts the joys of spring's return with his own inner desolation. Rinuccini favors a single contrast, beginning at the second tercet. Petrarch's approach is more complex. He begins the contrasts at the beginning of the first tercet, but reinforces it with another, sharper contrast between lines 13 and 14. In both musical settings Monteverdi employs triple-meter aria writing for the images of spring's return, contrasting this with more poignant duple-meter styles. His Petrarch setting treats the two quartets and lines 12-13 as though they were two and a half stanzas of a strophic aria for five voices. The plangent settings of lines 9-11 and 14 form, respectively, a subsidiary and a main climax. A parallel approach is adopted for the Rinuccini setting. Lines 1-11 are set over the "chaconne" bass, though without any division into "stanzas." Lines 12-14 are set as recitative, with the final phrase, "hor canto," set over the "chaconne" bass. Line 14 (the final phrase excepted) is then set again in recitative to produce the main climax. If the setting ended here, then the parallel with the five-part madrigal would be exact; but where the madrigal ends in deepest gloom, the chaconne ends more optimistically, with a final extended flourish for the phrase "hor canto."

The similarity between the overall designs of the two settings confirms the idea, suggested earlier, that while Monteverdi was responsive to changes in musical taste and style, his basic approach to text setting remained unaltered. Like Stravinsky, he was able to master new techniques while retaining his own individuality.

Arias for One and Two Voices

From 1618, when Rontani published his setting of "S'io miro i biondi crin," arias which include extended passages of solo writing began to appear regularly in both monody and madrigal books. In some cases—Frescobaldi's *ceccona* "Deh vien da me pastorella" (*Secondo Libro d'Arie,* 1630), for example—the use of solo writing can be explained only in terms of the response of an individual composer to a particular text. Of far greater general significance for the later development of the chamber duet, however, are those works in which the scoring is varied in reponse to the structure of the text. A text with refrain, for example, might prompt a change in scoring. At the simplest level, as in Berti's "Morir lieto e contento" (1624), the body of the first three stanzas is set as a recitative for solo voice, while the single-line refrain is set as a duet, with a good deal of word repetition.[45] Kapsberger's "Ardir alla guerra poiche 'l tamburo" (*Libro Quarto di Villanelle,* 1623) exhibits a more complex scheme. The refrain, set in triple meter, is first sung by both voices. Five stanzas, set in duple meter, are then sung by soprano I, with soprano II singing the refrain. The final stanza is again sung by soprano I, but this time the refrain is performed by both voices. In Fontei's "Scorre Amor la terra e 'l cielo" (1639), stanzas 1 and 2 are sung by sopranos I and II respectively, while stanza 3, set as a duet, is a variation over the same duple-meter bass. The refrain, set in triple meter, is performed by both voices.

In most arias for one and two voices the scoring is simply varied from one stanza, or group of stanzas, to another. Some of the settings which adopt this principle—Rontani's "S'io miro i biondi crin" (1618) and "O del carro stellato" (1620)—are sets of strophic variations, as are Possenti's lament "Tra questi sassi e luogh'aspri e selvaggi" (1623)[46] and Bellante's "Aure fresche, aure volanti" (1629),[47] which uses two bass lines, one for the duets and *sinfonie* and another for the solo stanzas.

The majority of settings are, however, what I have termed "sectional arias," that is, arias in which each stanza is set to different music without the consistent relationship of harmonic scheme which characterises sets of strophic variations. Sectional arias can be distinguished from madrigals in several sections only by their texts and, to a lesser extent, by their styles. Arias of this kind, set for two voices throughout, appeared in print as early as 1608 (Cagnazzi, *Passatempi*) and can still be found as late as 1642, in Tarditi's *Canzonette amorose*. But it was only with the publication of Anerio's *La Bella Clori armonica* of 1619 that the idea of introducing a variety of scoring becomes evident.

Sectional arias for one and two voices with continuo alone are found mainly in monody books, and thus seem to have been the province mainly of composers associated with Rome. I have included three settings of this kind in the second volume of this study. Anerio's "Apertamente, dicea la gente" (1619),[48] a setting of Chiabrera's gracious declaration of constant love, is written in a light canzonetta style, with clear-cut phrase structures. The change from duet to solo at stanza 3 is not obviously dictated by the sense of the text, but may have been suggested by the personal interjection "O meraviglia" in the second line. The scheme of Sances's much richer setting "Occhi sfere vivaci" (1633)[49] is symmetrical—stanzas 1 and 2 à 2, 2 and 3 à 1, 4 à 2, 5 and 6 à 1, 7 and 8 à 2—and has no relation to the sense of the text. Manelli's "Ti lascio empia, incostante" (1636)[50] is particularly interesting, since it demonstrates the potential of the sectional aria for contrast between solo recitative and arioso for two voices. What is lacking, as in the case of the later madrigalian duet, is any real textural distinction, in terms of sense and versification, between the two stanzas.

Concertato Arias

A number of duets for one and two voices are arias *concertate con strumenti*, that is, arias in which melody instruments play simultaneously with the voices as well as providing ritornellos between the stanzas of the setting. Duets of this type, which are generally conceived on a large scale, are found almost exclusively in madrigal books, where they are listed among the music for four- and five-part ensemble. Quagliati's *La Sfera Armoniosa* (1623) and Mila-nuzzi's *Settimo Libro delle Ariose Vaghezze* (1630) are the only monody books to include *concertato* arias.

The sole *concertato* aria in Quagliati's book—"O come dolce Amore"—is, in any case, an atypical work in that it calls for only one melody instrument.

The majority of *concertato* arias are scored for two voices, two violins, and continuo. Three of Galeazzo Sabbatini's arias (1630 and 1636), however, also require a bass instrument, Turini's "Vezzose aurette" (1621) is scored for three unspecified instruments, and all three of Bernardi's arias (1619) are scored for violin, cornetto, and trombone.

The extent to which the instruments are concerted with the voices varies a great deal between one setting and another. In a very few instances, in those arias like Sabbatini's "Io vo cercando" (1630) which are simple strophic arias, there is interplay between voices and violins throughout the setting. More usually, though, the instruments join the voices only in the final stanza, either for a few bars, to provide a final climax, as in Monteverdi's "Chiome d'oro" (1619), or to form a counterpoint to the voices during the whole stanza, as in Turini's "Fortunata pastorella" (1624).[51]

No fewer than twenty-one *concertato* arias survive in madrigal books published before 1643, even if we discount Grandi's *Arie, et Cantade* of 1626, a volume which seems to have been devoted entirely to the genre. The earliest settings were published in 1619, in the madrigal books of Monteverdi and Bernardi. Monteverdi's "Chiome d'oro," which is also the earliest duet cast in the form of a strophic-bass cantata,[52] and the first aria of Bernardi's book— "Ecco 'l mio cor tormentato"—use two voices throughout the setting, a procedure which is typical of the majority of *concertato* arias. About one third of the arias that survive complete, however, are scored for one and two voices. As in the case of arias with continuo only, they are cast either in the form of strophic variations—Rovetta's "Vivo in foco amoroso" (1629), Sabbatini's "Chiome crespe" (1630), and his "Non è ne mai sarà" (1636)—or in the form of sectional arias. Among the latter, Turini's *gagliarda* "Fortunata pastorella" (1624) and Merula's delightful "Amo, l'è ver" (1633)[53] illustrate the range of styles to be found in this type of setting.

The significance of duets in which the scoring is varied, and especially of those in which the scoring is varied from stanza to stanza, is that they represent a principle of composition that could be applied to any strophic or sectional text. Examples can be traced in Italian duet writing certainly until the beginning of the eighteenth century. Stradella's "Fulmini quanto sa" (*GB-Och,* MS 997, ff. 1-12v) and Alessandro Scarlatti's "E pur vuole il cielo e Amore" (*I-Bc,* MS DD. 43), for example, are both sectional arias for one and two voices. Stradella's setting begins with a duet; and part of this duet is then used as a refrain to the succeeding solos. Scarlatti's is a setting of six stanzas in varying meters. Stanzas 1 and 6 are extended duets, while stanzas 2 and 3, 4 and 5 form arioso-aria pairs for solo voices.

8

Duet and Dialogue

The term "dialogue" was widely used as a musical designation by composers of the sixteenth and seventeenth centuries. As far as vocal music is concerned, it was used in two general senses: first, to denote the setting of a text involving conversational exchanges between two or more characters, and second, as the title for a work that employed musical devices such as alternation, echo, or contrast in a way which is analogous to the exchanges of spoken dialogue.

During the sixteenth century, the designation came to be used for various kinds of secular composition: for echo madrigals, for madrigal pairs of the *proposta-risposta* type, and for polychoral madrigals in general. Fewer than half of the dialogues in Gardane's anthology *Dialoghi musicali* (*RISM* 1590[11]) are, in fact, settings of dialogue texts. The applicability of the term to sixteenth-century music was discussed in an important article by Kroyer,[1] who coined an elaborate vocabulary of classifications to account for the various elements of dialogue that he perceived in choral settings. His work was extended and criticised in an article by Harran, who argued for a clear distinction to be drawn in critical writings between settings of dialogue texts and music composed in a dialogue style.[2]

During the early decades of the seventeenth century, with the decline in popularity of the *a cappella* madrigal in general and the polychoral madrigal in particular, the designation "dialogue" came to be used only for settings of dialogue texts. Among the composers of the new *concertato* music for solo voice and small ensemble, Pietro Pace's use of the term *dialogo* for his echo madrigal "Sei tu, cor mio?" (1613) is wholly exceptional. It is with settings of dialogue texts only, then, that we shall be concerned in this study.

This is not, however, the end of the problem of delimitation. Like other literary genres, dialogue texts were set to music in a variety of ways, even in the seventeenth century. Not all settings differentiate between the characters of the dialogue. Some settings, for example, are for accompanied solo voice only. Fornaci's setting of Guarini's "Tirsi morir volea" (1617) is one, Barbara Strozzi's dialogue between Fear and Hope, "Timore, e che sarà godremo?" (*Cantate, Ariette e Duetti*, 1651), another. Strophic texts in particular lent themselves to settings which ignore character differentiation. Marino's popular dialogue text "Press'un fiume tranquillo," which is cast in four six-line stanzas, is a good example. Lambardi set it simply as a four-part villanella (1607); and in 1619 Anerio set it as an aria in four sections for two sopranos and bass, treating the first three stanzas as duets for soprano and bass and the last as a trio. Among the composers of duets, both Radesca and Cagnazzi wrote strophic dialogues in which each character is represented by two voices. Radesca's "Il partire, gran martire" (1610), for H[uomo] and D[ama], is a case in point.

A dialogue without character differentiation is, however, something of a contradiction in terms, and even during the heyday of the polyphonic madrigal composers had adopted various techniques to suggest the alternation of speakers. They did not always strive for complete realism, however, as we can see in Verdelot's six-part setting of "Chi bussa?," in which the words of the man are set for the two highest voices of the ensemble while those of Cupid are allotted to the four lowest.[3] But at least the composer employs his groupings consistently to convey the impression of dialogue. A similar, but more naturalistic differentiation can be seen in Baldissera Donato's "Ahi, miserelle" (1553), a seven-part dialogue for nymphs and shepherds on the subject of the rape of Proserpine.[4] In this setting, a trio of high voices (C A T) for the nymphs is contrasted with a low-voice group (A T T B) for the shepherds, the two groups joining for a final chorus in praise of Pluto.

In his setting of Petrarch's sonnet "Liete e pensose" (1559),[5] a dialogue between the poet and the friends of Laura, Willaert, too, divided his seven-part texture into groups of three high and four low voices. He did not, however, adhere mechanically to this grouping for the last five lines of the text, but gradually introduced the lower voices beneath the ladies' group to provide a musically satisfactory conclusion to the work. It is worth noting that only the highest voice of each group (canto and alto respectively) has the complete text of the exchanges and it seems probable that this dialogue was, in fact, performed by two accompanied solo voices.[6]

The third dialogue setting that Einstein included in his anthology—Andrea Gabrieli's "Tirsi morir volea" (1587)[7]—again makes use of high and low voice-groupings for the words of the nymph and shepherd. But it also introduces another problem, that of incorporating long passages of narration. Gabrieli makes much use of the low voice-group for the narrator, suggesting through its dark color the impending "death" of the lovers. But he is not consistent in this. Toward the climax of the couple's lovemaking, for example, he builds to a full seven-part texture, with close imitation at "E 'l nettare amoroso" suggesting Thyrsis's darting tongue.

The problem of distinguishing between the narrator and the characters of the dialogue proper was fully solved only in the *concertato* madrigal, as we can see in the two dialogue settings—"A Dio, Florida bella" and "Presso un fiume tranquillo"—that Monteverdi included in his sixth book of madrigals of 1614.[8] In both of these settings Monteverdi uses soprano and tenor soloists for the characters of the dialogue and an ensemble as narrator. "A Dio, Florida bella," with its memorable passage of confused sound at the words "Quinci e quindi confuso un suon s'udio di baci e parole," provides a worthy successor to the lovemaking of Gabrieli's "Tirsi morir volea" and a fitting culmination to the tradition of polyphonic dialogue settings. At the same time, however, Monteverdi's *concertato* dialogues can be seen as a link between the polyphonic tradition and such recitative-dialogues with chorus as Rovetta's *La Gelosia placata.*[9]

The adoption of the *basso continuo* as the basis of accompanied solo song provided seventeenth-century composers with the technical means to bring a greater degree of realism and expressive flexibility to their dialogue settings than had been possible in the polyphonic madrigal; and many of the volumes of monodies and *concertato* madrigals that were published in Italy during the first half of the century contain dialogue settings in which the roles are assigned to accompanied solo voices (recitative-dialogues). It was for this type of unstaged dialogue setting, which paralleled the development of opera, that the theorist Giovanni Battista Doni coined the phrase *dialoghi fuor di scena.*[10]

In the main, recitative-dialogues are scored for voices with continuo only. Some, however, like M.A. Negri's "Poich'a baciar n'invita" (1611; soprano and tenor) include instrumental movements. And a few are arias "concertate con stromenti," though they do not necessarily follow a simple strophic form. These are Bernardi's "Bellezze amat'oimè" (1619; soprano, tenor, cornetto, violin), the two dialogues "Poich'a baciar n'invita" and "Filli, cor del mio core" (both 1621; both scored for soprano, tenor, and two violins) by Accademico Bizzarro, and Arrigoni's "Se non m'aiti Amor" (1635; soprano, tenor, two violins). Accademico's dialogues, too, include instrumental *balletti* composed, not by Accademico himself, but by "Signor Massimillo [Freduti], maestro di cappella di Fano."

The earliest recitative-dialogues were published by Domenico Maria Melli, who included two—"Cara e vezzosa Filli" (Thyrsis and Phyllis) and "E quando cessarai?" (Daphnis and Eurilla)—in his *Seconde Musiche* of 1602. We should not be surprised that the first recitative-dialogues for two voices should have appeared in the same year as Caccini's *Le Nuove Musiche* while duets appeared only later and more tentatively. Melli may well have become interested in setting dialogue texts because of their similarity to the dialogue of opera. The largely syllabic style of his "E quando cessarai?" certainly seems operatic in origin, though his other dialogue settings involve elements of madrigalian ornamentation. At all events, though, his choice of two voices for his dialogues was determined by the nature of the texts and his decision to set them in the new monodic style. These decisions were quite different from the considerations of structure and sonority which led composers to write duets. The constant solo exchanges that characterize through-composed dialogue settings are quite unlike the textures of most madrigalian duets, the duets of Valentini excepted.

Eugen Schmitz recognised the distinction between duets and dialogue settings, but failed to reach the logical conclusion that recitative-dialogues should be treated as an independent genre to be studied *in toto* rather than divided arbitrarily between studies of monody, the duet, the continuo madrigal and the cantata.[12] In his article on chamber duets, for example, he started from the position that recitative-dialogues should be regarded as a special type of duet. This is, however, to work from a false premise: for while it is true that a number of duets are dialogue settings, not all recitative-dialogues are duets. A quite substantial proportion include a third character. Occasionally the third character acts as narrator, as in Grandi's "O dolcissima morte" (1615), for Venus, Adonis, and a shepherd (respectively, and surprisingly, tenor, soprano, and bass), in which the shepherd plays Peeping Tom to the others' lovemaking. But more often the third character is an active participant in the dialogue, as, for example, in the two dialogues "Amorosa Licori" (Thyrsis, Licoris, and Phyllis) and "Perchè non togli?" (Amarantha, Chloris, and Armilla), both of which are attributed to "Giuseppino" in *I-Vc*, the "Fucci" MS.[13] The second of these, in which three nymphs discourse on love before joining to sing its praises, is also attributed to Paolo Quagliati, in Costantini (ed.) *Ghirlandetta Amorosa* (1621). All four of Francesco Rasi's *Dialoghi Rappresentativi* (1620), which make up the best-known early seventeenth-century collection of secular dialogues, are for three voices.

Although two or three voices are most usual in recitative-dialogues, a few call for four. Examples include Grandi's "Horsù, pastori, sediamo sul prato" (1622; Elpino, Fileno, Mopso, Ergasto), and "Sfogava un alma accesa" (1618), a dialogue for Lover, Disdain, and Love with the "Poet" (soprano) as narrator, by Gioseffe Marini, choirmaster at Pordenone, a town located between Treviso and Udine. Since the musical outline of these settings is essentially the same as that found in recitative-dialogues for two voices, it would be a purely arbitrary decision to omit them from our discussion.

Both of the dialogues that Melli included in his *Seconde Musiche* consist of a series of alternating solos culminating in a short ensemble, a closed musical form characteristic of many early recitative-dialogues,[14] and one that was ultimately to invade the world of opera.[15] His later setting of Marino's "Poich'a baciar n'invita" (1609; Amyntas and Chloris), however, exemplifies a different type, in which there is no ensemble writing at all. Differences in musical approach of this type were often dictated by the nature of the text. The text of Melli's "E quando cessarai?," for example, concludes with the words "Let us sing the praises of Love. . . . ," which invite ensemble treatment. "Poich'a baciar n'invita," however, ends with complementary strophes which do not immediately suggest a duet. This is a poetic device rather than one of *poesia per musica.* Schmitz drew a distinction between the two types of setting, but he did so on musical grounds, viewing the first as a type of duet, the second as a monody:

> Its [the dialogue's] literature in the new style does not belong exclusively to the form of the duet: in the early history of monody there are far more dialogues which proceed as discussions between solo voices and thus lack the two-part section which characterizes a duet.[16]

Besides taking issue with Schmitz's statistics, I would suggest that the distinction that he drew is an artificial one. It implies, for example, that we should include the two dialogues of Melli's 1602 book in a study of the duet, but omit any consideration of his setting of "Poich'a baciar n'invita." There is no real justification for this, since the differences between the dialogues are textual rather than musical. Furthermore, individual texts were sometimes treated with, sometimes without, ensemble writing. Accademico Bizzarro, for example, managed to produce an ensemble in his setting of "Poich'a baciar n'invita" (1621) by telescoping the final speeches of Amyntas and Chloris into a bitextual duet.

A striking instance of the variety of musical possibilities inherent in a single dialogue text is provided by Chiabrera's "Chi nudrisce tua speme, cor mio?." This text was published as early as 1603 as a *scherzo* without named characters, in which form it appears to be an introspective dialogue between the lover and his heart. Later, however, Chiabrera incorporated the text into his libretto *Polifemo geloso* (1615), where it appears as a dialogue between Acis and Galatea.[17] None of the composers who set the text, however, used these names. In its original *scherzo* form the text appears as follows:

> Chi nudrisce tua speme,
> Cor mio, che fiamma crescea tuoi desiri?
> Due begli occhi lucenti.
> Chi raddolcisce il fiel de' tuoi martiri?
> Pur due begli occhi ardenti.
> E chi ti doppia, e chi t'inaspri i guai?
> Di due begli occhi i rai.
> Ma chi t'ancide, e chi t'avviva anciso?
> Di due begli occhi il riso.

> Who feeds your hope, my heart, what flame has increased your desire? Two beautiful shining eyes. What assuages the bitterness of your torment? Again, two beautiful, burning eyes. And what redoubles and exacerbates your woe? The rays of two beautiful eyes. And what kills and yet revives you when dead? The smile of two beautiful eyes.

As it stands, then, the text consists only of question and answer, and Piero Benedetti set it in exactly this form, as a series of alternating solos (1611). But both Marco da Gagliano (1615) and Sigismondo d'India (1615) included duet writing in their settings. D'India first of all sets the last two lines as alternating solos and then repeats them twice more as an extended duet. Gagliano, too, repeats the last two lines, but sets only the repeated final line as a short duet. Mutis (1613) adopted a different approach altogether. In his setting for three voices the questions are given to a solo tenor, and the answers are set as florid duets for two sopranos. All three voices then join to sing the last two lines as a concluding ensemble.

On a much larger scale Valentini published, in 1622, a setting for soprano and bass of part of act II, scene 6 of Guarini's *Il Pastor Fido*. This is the lively and amusing scene in which the scheming nymph Corisca is trapped by the Satyr whose affections she has slighted. He catches her by the hair and refuses to let go, despite her protestations. As the scene rises to its climax, the two roundly abuse each other and Corisca escapes by slipping off the wig that she has been wearing, leaving the Satyr, where he has fallen, to nurse his bruises. Valentini set lines 1-136 of the scene, ending with four lines of the Satyr's last speech which he abstracted as the final chorus:

> O maraviglia inusitata. O ninfe,
> O pastori, accorrete e rimirate
> Il magico stupor di chi sen fugge
> E vive senza capo.

> O marvellous. Ye Nymphs and Shepherds run,
> Flock hither to behold a wonder; one
> That runs away without her head, by skill
> In Magick.[18]

These he set for six-part chorus with two violins, though he also provided an alternative two-part version for use in more modest circumstances. Four years later, in 1626, Tarquinio Merula published a rival setting, also for soprano and bass (to which publication Valentini contributed a laudatory sonnet). He, however, set the complete dialogue of the scene, omitting only Guarini's final chorus. His setting contains no ensemble work at all.

Even these few examples will serve to show that it is not sufficient, nor even desirable, to take the limited view that recitative-dialogues are simply a special type of duet. To attempt a further classification of two-part dialogue settings into duets and monodies on the purely musical grounds of whether or not they include ensembles is to introduce a false distinction. The only satisfactory approach is to consider recitative-dialogues as a distinct genre and one which must be studied as a whole. The task is, in fact, not very great, since far fewer dialogues than duets were published between 1602 and 1643.

Most of the dialogue texts that were set to music in early seventeenth-century Italy are love lyrics of one kind or another. Many involve named or unnamed figures from pastoral mythology; and despite their apparent similarity to operatic scenes they belong to a lyric tradition which extends back to the bucolics of Theocritus and the amoebean eclogues of Virgil. Only a very few dialogues stand outside the twin worlds of the pastoral and the amatory lyric. Two of them—Monteverdi's *Combattimento di Tancredi e Clorinda*, drawn from Tasso's epic *La Gerusalemme liberata*, and Merula's *La Tognada*, which treats the subject of the judgment of Paris—are discussed in the following chapter. A third is Bartolomeo Barbarino's "Ferma, ferma Caronte" (1607), for soprano and bass, which is, surprisingly, one of only three dialogues between Charon and a soul wishing to cross the River Styx to survive in early seventeenth-century Italian sources,[19] though the subject had been popular during the sixteenth century and remained so among English composers of the seventeenth century. Barbarino's dialogue seems to have been known in England, for it survives in an ornamented version, in the manuscript of Angelo Notari (*GB-Lbm,* MS Add. 31, 440).

The pastoral dialogues that most resemble short operatic scenes (though there are none like them in the earliest operas) are those that involve an amorous encounter between a shepherd and a shepherdess. They take various forms. In some the shepherdess plays hard-to-get. In Fornaci's "Dunque, per esser bella" (1617; Lilla and Eurillo), in fact, she remains obdurate throughout, leaving no occasion for a final duet. In Melli's "E quando cessarai?"[20] she yields, though only when she is assured of the shepherd's honorable intentions. In other dialogues, however, such as the popular "Perchè piangi pastore?,"[21] she is only too willing a participant in love-making. The text of "Perchè piangi, pastore?" has all the hallmarks of Marinism, with the kiss evidently having a double meaning rooted in the erotic life-death symbolism that features in many pastoral lyrics of the period.

One of the most delightful of these brief encounters is (?) Rinuccini's "Bel pastor, dal cui bel guardo," which was set by Marco da Gagliano (in Benedetti, 1611) and Monteverdi (1651).[22] Here, the shepherdess tries to inveigle her shepherd into declaring how much he loves her. He teases by saying that he loves her as much as she loves him. There follows a series of exchanges in which he wittily refuses to be drawn into making a more poetic declaration, and these are punctuated by the refrain "Come che? Come te, pastorella, tutta bella."

The amorous encounter forms by far the most familiar subject of secular dialogue texts, but the subjects treated range more widely than this, and frequently cross the borderline between the pastoral and other types of lyric poetry and between those dialogues which are, conceivably, stageable and those whose action can only be projected on to an idealized stage. Reflective dialogues like "Chi nudrisce tua speme, cor mio?" seem to fall into this last category, and they were quite popular. Berti's "Folle mio cor" (1627) and

Costa's "Miserabil mio core" (1640) are on similar themes. This type of reflective internal debate is descended from Petrarch's sonnet "Che fai alma? che pensi?," to which Crivelli's "Che fai alma? Languisco" (1626) and Bucchianti's "Alma che fai? Gioisco al dolore" (1627) stand directly in line of succession.

Another popular subject, perhaps because of the opportunities that it provided for affective declamation, is the lament of the spurned or abandoned lover. Since lamenting is essentially a solitary activity, however, it is not the easiest of subjects to treat in dialogue form. In Barbarino's "Venite, aure soavi" (1614; Amyntas and Thyrsis), for example, Thyrsis simply acts as a sounding board for Amyntas' complaints. A more satisfactory solution is found in Visconti's "O Selve, O Fiumi, O Fonti" (1616; Clorinda and Phyllis), in which Clorinda laments her separation from Lorento. Here, Phyllis has a credible role to play in comforting Clorinda and assuring her that Lorento will soon return, at which thought Clorinda takes heart and the two sing an extended duet.

At the extreme of the emotional spectrum, the desperate lover of Grandi's "Anima disperata" (1615) is at the point of death when Cupid intervenes with the promise that the bright eyes and smiling lips of his beloved will soon quieten his anguish and restore him to life. An almost identical subject is treated at greater length, and more operatically, in Orlandi's three-part dialogue "Hor già che 'l cielo" (1616; the Lover, a Friend, Cupid) to a text by another native of Verona, Alessandro Becelli. Here, Cupid is given his full stature as a god who commands the actions of the lover; and the poetic apparatus includes the use of echo effects which overawe the lover and his friend.

This text was clearly written for musical setting, but not all dialogue texts were, not even those which apparently end with an ensemble. A case in point is furnished by the dialogue "Che fai, Tirsi gentile?," which was set by d'India (1609) and the Roman-trained choirmaster of Viterbo Cathedral, Francesco Pasquali (1627). The text of their settings consists, in fact, of excerpts drawn by the composers from Marino's long dialogue-canzone *La Rosa* in which Thyrsis sings in praise of the rose, the favorite flower of lovers. The focal point of both settings is the stanza beginning "Rose, rose beate," which Grandi also set as an independent madrigal (1622).[23] But the two composers lead towards this stanza with a slightly different choice of lines: and their choice reveals their different imaginative skills as composers. I give, below, a composite of the two texts, with the line numbers of Marino's original *canzone*:

8	MOPSO:	Che fai, Tirsi gentile?
		Perchè non canti i fregi
		Perchè non canti i pregi
11		Del Giovinetto Aprile?

12		Canta con dolce stile	⎤ Set by
		Di tutti i fiori il fiore	⎥ Pasquali
14		Della stagion novell'eterno onore.	⎦ only
15	TIRSI:	Da qual fior il mio canto	
		Prenderò, Mopso mio?	
		Cantar forse degg'io	
		Del flessuoso acanto?	
		L'immortal amaranto?	
		O pur la bionda calta,	
21		Che d'aurato color le piagge smalta?	
36	MOPSO:	Canta, Tirsi, di quella	
		Ch'è più cara a gli amanti,	
		Canta gli onori e i vanti	
39		Della rosa novella.	
169	TIRSI:	Rose, rose beate,	
		Lascivette figliuole	
		Della terra e del sole,	
		Le dolcezze odorate,	
		Che dal grembo spirate,	
		Ponno quel tutto in noi	
175		Che il sol, che l'aura e che la pioggia in voi.	
113		Non ha la bionda Aurora,	⎤
		Allor che 'l ciel fa chiaro,	⎥
		Ornamento più caro;	⎥ Set by
		Di rose il crin s'infiora,	⎥ d'India
		Di rose il sen s'onora	⎥ only
		Anzi invidia ne prende	⎥
119		E vergognosa di rossor s'accende.	⎥
169-175	DUO:	Rose, rose	⎦

Pasquali contents himself with a straightforward arioso setting of the two complete stanzas (lines 8-14, 15-21) which form the first exchange between Mopsus (bass) and Thyrsis (tenor). He follows this with Mopsus' request to Thyrsis that he should sing of the rose (36-39); but he allows Thyrsis to sing only the single line "Rose, rose beate" before allotting the whole stanza (169-175) to the four-part ensemble which is really the core of the setting.

D'India took greater liberties with Marino's poem for his setting.[24] For the most part, the changes that he made occur towards the end of the dialogue, though he also reduced Mopsus' opening speech to a minimal four lines (8-11). This deprives the text of its full meaning, but it has the merit of shortening the opening exchanges in order to focus attention on the stanzas in praise of the rose. Unlike Pasquali, d'India was not content simply to set the stanza "Rose, rose beate," but also grafted on a second stanza, "Non ha la bionda Aurora," which he drew from a earlier part of the poem. The object of this rearrangement of the original becomes clear when we see that the dialogue is conceived as a series of recitatives leading to an extended strophic aria. The opening exchanges are set in a declamatory Florentine-style arioso, but the two stanzas in praise of the rose are set as a measured duple-meter aria sung by Thyrsis (the second stanza is not underlaid in Mompellio's edition). Following this, the first stanza is then repeated, with the same melodic line serving as the upper part of a sonorous duet.

The musical forms of recitative-dialogues parallel those of early seventeenth-century solo song. Most are through-composed, madrigalian settings, but there is also quite a large body of strophic dialogues; and not all madrigalian settings have madrigalian texts. Marino's poems "Presso un fiume tranquillo" and "Poich'a baciar n'invita," for example, are strophic, and the anonymous text of Melli's "E quando cessarai?" is written in *terza rima*.

The simplest type of strophic setting consists of a single aria sung alternately by the two characters of the dialogue, as in Radesca's "Il partire, gran martire" (1610). More often, however, composers sought to differentiate musically between their characters. Brunelli's "Bella Licori, i tuoi dolori" (1616; Drusilla and Licoris), for example, consists of two arias—one in triple meter for Drusilla, the other in duple meter for Licoris—which are sung in alternation before the two singers join in a final duet. Other composers, like the Roman Pietro Paolo Sabbatini, used exactly the same technique for their settings (see his "Vorrai, Laurilla mia," 1628 and *Quarto de Villanelle,* 1631); and Martino Pesenti's "Qui dove un seggio appresta" (1638; Eurino and Dorina), though more complex, is basically a development of the same idea. The first four sections comprise two alternating arias, while sections 7-10 inclusive involve a single triple-meter aria sung alternately by the two characters.

In other strophic dialogues the exchanges take place within the strophe itself. In Berti's "Folle mio cor" (1627) which comprises three stanzas of strophic variation, the two voices sing alternate lines of the text, the divisions being indicated in the musical setting by means of a vertical line between the staves. Visconti's "Chi m'asconde il mio bel Sole?" (1616) is a little more complex. In each eight-line stanza, Chloris is allotted two lines, Phyllis four, Chloris one more, and then the final line—"Canterò/Piangerò sempre d'Amore"—which forms a refrain to all the stanzas, is divided between the two singers. This is an amusing little scene, in which Chloris bewails the loss of her lover, while Phyllis, who has stolen him away, sings joyfully.

The most interesting of these strophic settings from an historical point of view, however, is the dialogue "O sfortunata, chi mi consola?" (Lucia and Cola), of which settings were published in 1628 by "Il Fasolo"[25] and in 1636 by Francesco Manelli. This is unusual, in that it is the only text involving *Commedia dell'arte* characters to have been set outside the context of madrigal comedies; and Fasolo's setting is the earliest example of an aria using the so-called "passacaglia" bass—the descending tetrachord ostinato which became popular in songbooks of the 1630s.

Fasolo's setting for soprano, tenor, and bass, published under the imposing title *Il Carro di Madama Lucia,* employs the ostinato G-F-E flat-D. It consists of two alternating arias (exx. 1a and 1b) and a final trio over the same bass in which the third (unnamed) singer is required to fit the text to the notes of the continuo part. Manelli's setting, entitled *La Luciata,* also employs the "passacaglia" bass, though in the major form F-E-D-C (ex. 2); and he wrote out the final trio in full, making the third singer, a soprano, join in the imitative interplay of the other two voices.

Example 1

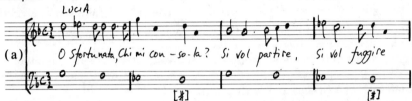

(a) O sfortunata, Chi mi con-so-la? Si vol partire, Si vol fuggire

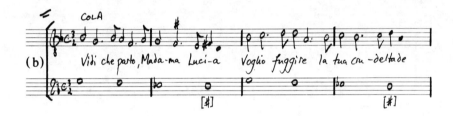

(b) Vidi che parto, Mada-ma Luci-a Voglio fuggire la tua cru-deltade

Example 2

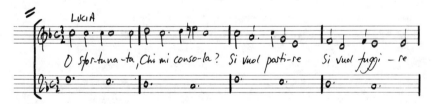

O sfor-tuna-ta, Chi mi conso-la? Si vuol parti-re Si vuol fuggi — re

In a note to the readers printed at the end of his 1636 book, Manelli made the following statement:

My *Luciata* has already appeared in print under the title of Carro Trionfale and under an academic name. This now seems too presumptuous to me and, what is worse, the third voice has to be accommodated to the notes of the Basso Continuo. I have, therefore, resolved to publish the piece as it should be sung, with the third voice matching its motives to those of the other two.[26]

This, of course, gives rise to the interesting, but unprovable speculation that the earlier setting by "Il Fasolo," who styled himself "Il Retirato" (the retired one) in the Academy of the Capricciosi, is actually by Manelli and that the two books of music attributed to Fasolo (1627 and 1628) are Manelli's op. 1 and op. 2, previously thought to be lost. It should, however, be said against this view that the two settings of "O sfortunata, chi mi consola?" differ in many respects, not least in the different forms of the ostinato that they use. Furthermore, both Manelli and Fasolo are represented in Robletti's 1629 anthology as though they were quite different people.[27]

Although strophic dialogues in general are quite numerous, comparatively few employ the techniques of strophic variation. Visconti's "O Selve, O Fiumi, O Fonti" (1616) is an interesting example, and one which combines madrigalian and strophic composition. Only the aria with which the dialogue begins is cast in the form of strophic variations. Its style, however, and the use of a "walking bass" clearly anticipates the Venetian strophic-bass cantatas of composers like Grandi and Berti (ex. 3).

Example 3

Grandi himself figures as a quite important composer of dialogue settings. His 1615 book includes four dialogues and his 1622 book two more. Only three of these are through-composed. The others employ various aria-like elements. "Horsù, pastori, sediamo sul prato" (1622) is, in fact, a set of strophic variations punctuated by a refrain for four voices. It is not a dialogue in the usual sense, for the only element of interchange comes in the final ensemble (ex. 4). Instead, each of the four shepherds involved sings the praises of his shepherdess. The four stanzas that they sing as solos and the final ensemble are all founded on the same bass, which resembles that of a cantata even though it does not move entirely in crotchets.

Example 4

The use of a refrain was anticipated in Grandi's 1615 book by the dialogue "Già vincitor del Verno" (soprano, tenor, bass). This is essentially a song in praise of spring. Like "Horsù, pastori" it can be considered a dialogue only by virtue of a single conversational exchange in which the soprano (Nisa) who complains that she is unable to enjoy spring because she lives in a winter of tears, bereft of love, is rebuked by the bass (Shepherd). Although the solo and duet sections of the dialogue are through-composed, they are punctuated by a three-part refrain, "Felice Primavera," which also forms the final ensemble. This refrain was part of the original poetic conception and not an invention of Grandi's (the text is by Marcello Macedonio).

One other work in Grandi's 1615 book, "Mira fuggir le stelle" (soprano, tenor, bass), though called an *aria* by Grandi himself, may be considered a dialogue of the same type as "Horsù, pastori." That is, it consists of a series of solos in which three shepherds call on their shepherdesses, this time to accompany them in welcoming the dawn. And like "Horsù, pastori," the setting is based on strophic variation technique, though in this case we find a much more ambitious double set of variations:

	"Mira fuggir le stelle"	(Tenor)	bass (a)
	"O di concento adorno"	(Soprano)	bass (a)
	"E vaga l'Alba"	(Bass)	bass (a)
Refrain:	"Lingua non è"	(à 3)	bass (a)
	"Et ecco spunta il Sole"	(Soprano)	bass (b)
	"L'amoroso pianeta"	(Bass)	bass (b)
	"Il raggio luminoso"	(Tenor)	bass (b)
Refrain:	"Lingua non è"	(à 3)	bass (a)
	"Quel che lingu'o pensier"	(à 3)	bass (b)

Despite the apparent similarity of through-composed dialogues to the medium of opera, it must be remembered that dialogues were essentially a lyric form. Comparatively few composers chose an unadorned recitative style for their settings. I suggested earlier that the syllabic setting of Melli's "E quando cessarai?" seems to be derived from opera. It would, however, be equally accurate to describe it as an unornamented, though harmonically more adventurous version of the arioso style found in Caccini's madrigals, for it lacks the consistently slow-moving bass which characterizes Peri's operatic style and makes comparatively little use of unprepared dissonance. Indeed, when he set the shorter text "Cara e vezzosa Filli," Melli wrote phrase endings which blossom out into ornamentation not unlike that found in Florentine madrigals (ex. 5). The majority of early seventeenth-century dialogues are, like Melli's, written in styles that can best be described as "arioso," though the term must be understood to embrace styles as distinct as the rather plain, often diatonic style used by Romans like Quagliati and Fabio Constantini, affective declamation in the Florentine manner and the more colorful style employed by madrigalists like Grandi and Turini.[28]

Example 5

Genuine operatic recitative is found in only a few dialogues, chiefly in those which are settings of longer texts. Camillo Orlandi, for example, seems to have attempted a conscious imitation of the early operatic styles in his "Hor già che 'l cielo" (1616), and although much of his setting is rather undistinguished, it does contain one striking passage which uses harmonic anticipation and abrupt changes of chord in a manner which is very reminiscent of Peri (ex. 6).

Example 6

The most important of the early dialogues written in a recitative style are, however, the settings of act II, scene 6 of Guarini's *Il Pastor Fido* by Valentini and Merula. And it may be significant that, at the time of making these quasi-operatic settings, both composers were working outside Italy in centers of Italianate culture: Valentini at the Imperial court of Vienna and Merula in the service of King Sigismund III of Poland.

It is clear from his dialogue setting that Valentini had absorbed at least some of the lessons of the earliest operas. When Corisca attempts to charm the Satyr into releasing her, for example, her music begins with a poignant accented dissonance and most of her speech is placed on the sixth above the bass, an interval which Peri also found expressive (ex. 7). At the beginning of the setting, Valentini uses the same juxtaposition of E major and G minor harmonies between the end of one phrase and the beginning of the next that both Peri and Monteverdi had employed so effectively in the messenger scenes of *Euridice* and *Orfeo* (ex. 8). On the whole, though, his setting lacks color and rhythmic flexibility, and its humor is verbal rather than musical.

Example 7

Example 8

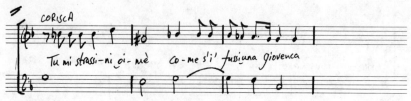

Certainly it pales in comparison with Merula's setting, for Merula displays far greater skill in pacing the recitative to match the changing emotional situation. This can be demonstrated in a single example. When Corisca fails to secure her release by exercising her charm, she rounds on the Satyr, heaping abuse on him. His surprise and mounting anger are captured neatly in Merula's setting by the use of short phrases and declamation in semiquavers (ex. 9), a rhythm scarcely used at all by Valentini. If we then compare the two settings of the Satyr's exclamations as he falls over with Corisca's wig in his hand, we can see how much more effectively Merula's exaggerated rhetoric matches the humor of the moment than does Valentini's more restrained setting (exx. 10a and 10b).

Example 9

Example 10

(a)

Merula's was not the first dialogue setting to make use of semiquaver declamation, though it was the first to do so with dramatic intent. A type of parlando recitative in semiquavers had earlier been used by Grandi in "O dolcissima morte" (1615) though purely for the purpose of word-painting (ex. 11). "O dolcissima morte" is the most extended of Grandi's settings, but it is typical of most early seventeenth-century through-composed dialogues in that its style is a mixture of the operatic and the madrigalian. The same speech for Adonis in which we find semiquaver declamation used opens with a melting madrigalian phrase (ex. 12) and ends with a cascade of roulades which could easily have graced one of Caccini's songs (ex. 13).

Example 11

Example 12

Example 13

Example 14

The use of both declamatory and arioso styles within a single setting occasionally leads to an incipient recitative-aria relationship such as that which we observed in d'India's "Che fai, Tirsi gentile?." And relationships of this kind are particularly striking when the passage of arioso is in triple meter. Prior to the late 1620s, extended passages of triple-meter arioso are rare, but two of the speeches in Barbarino's "Venite, aure soavi" (1614) end with passages that are, to all intents and purposes, miniature arias, complete with text repetition; and the style of the first of these has all the qualities of a Venetian *bel canto* aria. (ex. 14).

The use of contrasting recitative and arioso styles is explored quite extensively in the first three of Francesco Rasi's *Dialoghi Rappresentativi* of 1620. Rasi was a veteran of the early Florentine and Mantuan operas. He was a virtuoso singer who had taken leading roles in Peri's *Euridice* and Gagliano's *Dafne* and is thought to have sung the title role in Monteverdi's *Orfeo*. He was a composer of some substance, as the dialogue settings of this collection show. There are four of them in all: "Tu c'hai l'alba ne lumi" (Phyllis, a Dryad, Niso), "Tu che dolce apprendesti" (Dori, Neera, Filenus), "O ciel che volgi intorno" (Altea, Galatea, Amyntas) and "Prendi la cetra homai" (Phyllis, Chloris, Sirenus). All are scored for two sopranos and tenor (perhaps for Rasi himself), and all are to texts by the composer.

Rasi's Florentine background is certainly evident in the style of his dialogues. But for him the "representative style" did not simply mean declamatory recitative. His settings are varied by the introduction of duet writing into the main body of the dialogue (dialogues 2 and 4) and by passages of measured arioso writing. Moreover, in each of the first three settings, the opening exchanges are linked by an arioso refrain. It is interesting to note, in passing, that Rasi's text for the refrain of the third dialogue—"Deh pietose a nostri pianti / Sospirate O selve, O fronde, / Lacrimate, O selve, O campi"— bears a strong resemblance to that of the choral refrain which ends the messenger scene of Peri's *Euridice*.

The first dialogue will serve to illustrate the sort of ground plan that Rasi used.[29] The setting is carefully paced so that the longest speeches are heard first, while briefer exchanges lead to the final ensemble. Note, too, that the texts of the recitatives have a different line-length from those of the arioso refrains.

Niso:	"Tu c'hai l'alba ne lumi"	(recit.)	
Dryad:	"Dolce amor ch'unisc'i cori"	(arioso)	REFRAIN
Dryad:	"Sann'homai queste selve"	(recit.)	
	"Dolce amor..."	(arioso)	REFRAIN
Phyllis:	"Io che non habbi al sen"	(recit.)	
	"Alma Dea tanto adorata"	(arioso)	REFRAIN with same music as "Dolce amor..."
Niso:	"E così dolce il duolo"	(recit.)	
Dryad:	"Alma ch'andarno pregha"	(recit.)	

Niso:	"Si pur la donna mia"	(recit.)
Dryad:	"Hor frena 'l duolo"	(recit.)
	"Ecco pur lassa me"	(aria, 3 stanzas)
Phyllis, Dryad, Niso and Phyllis in turn:	"Per chi veloce"	(*arietta* in triple meter, 4 stanzas)
Dryad and Phyllis:	"O del arco degli strali"	(*aria alla francese,* 4 stanzas)

The *aria alla francese* has the cryptic heading: "Si può cantare all'unisono da due, il primo soprano alla francese. E si può a due voci." But it leaves unsolved the mystery of just what singing "alla francese" might be.

Rasi's *Dialoghi Rappresentativi,* with their arioso refrains and strophic arias, may be taken to mark a watershed in the stylistic development of Italian recitative-dialogues, for while dialogues in a mainly declamatory style certainly continued to appear during the 1620s and 1630s, most of the settings dating from these years also include extended passages of arioso writing. In printed sources, this new stylistic departure was the work of Venetian composers, and their dialogue settings form a new chapter in the history of the genre.

Venetian Dialogue Settings, 1624 to 1642

Between 1624 and 1642 a small number of through-composed dialogue settings, some thirteen in all, appeared in publications issued by composers working in, or near, the city of Venice. These are among the most interesting of the settings discussed in this study: interesting not only for their intrinsic musical value, but also because the composers concerned were among those who contributed to the early history of commercial opera at Venice. In the dialogue settings by these composers we can trace the evolution, in a quasi-dramatic context, of the musical styles which were to characterize early Venetian opera.

Prior to the opening, in 1637, of the Teatro San Cassiano, the first of the commercial opera houses, there had been little opportunity for Venetian composers to write operas. Monteverdi continued to produce dramatic works after his appointment to St. Mark's, but only one of them was performed at Venice. This was the opera *Proserpina rapita,* written in 1630 to a libretto by Giulio Strozzi and performed to celebrate the marriage of Giustianiana Mocenigo and Lorenzo Giustinian.[1] An earlier opera, *La finta pazza Licori,* which was Monteverdi's first collaboration with Giulio Strozzi, was written in 1627 for performance at Mantua. This opera, Monteverdi's only comedy, is known solely from the composer's letters, which detail the various stages in the preparation of libretto and score and reveal Monteverdi's evident pleasure in working with his new librettist.[2]

The pioneers of Venetian commercial opera were, paradoxically, not Venetians, but two Roman-trained musicians, Francesco Manelli and Benedetto Ferrari. We know something of the early careers of these men, but little of their activities during the decade which preceded their arrival at Venice. We do know, however, that Manelli's wife, Maddalena, who was a singer, took part in the performance at Padua in 1636 of *Ermiona,* an 'introduction to a tournament' with libretto by Pio Enea degli Obizzi and music by the Roman composer Giovanni Felice Sances.[3] The success of *Ermiona* seems to have prompted certain Venetian nobleman to encourage Manelli and Ferrari in an operatic venture at Venice during the following year. Their first collaboration,

Andromeda, with a libretto modelled on *Ermiona* by Ferrari,[4] and music by Manelli, was staged at the Teatro San Cassiano, Venice, during the carnival season of 1637-8[5] and was the first opera to which the paying public was admitted.

The success of *Andromeda* encouraged Manelli and Ferrari to collaborate again during the following carnival season in writing the opera *La maga fulminata.* It also encouraged other theatrical entrepreneurs to open rival opera houses. In 1639, the Grimani family opened the Teatro SS. Giovanni e Paolo and lured Manelli away from S. Cassiano to write the inaugural opera, *La Delia, o sia la Sera sposa del Sole,* to a libretto by Giulio Strozzi. The libretto of this opera, rather than that of *Andromeda,* was considered by Wolfgang Osthoff to be the "prototype of Venetian opera."[6] Two further opera houses were opened in quick succession, the Teatro S. Moisè in 1639-40, with a revival of Monteverdi's *Arianna,* and the Teatro Novissimo in 1641, with a production of Sacrati's *La finta pazza,* to a libretto again by Giulio Strozzi.[7]

The composers whose dialogue settings are discussed in this chapter all contributed to this growing literature. The contributions of Sances and Ferrari have already been mentioned, though it should be noted that Ferrari was active as a composer as well as librettist. The operas *Armida, Il pastor regio, La ninfa avara,* and *Il principe giardiniero,* for which he wrote both libretto and music, were performed at Venice in c. 1639, 1640, 1641 or 42, and 1644 respectively and *Il pastor regio* was revived, with a revised libretto, at Bologna in 1641. The Bolognese libretto of *Il pastor regio* had, for its concluding duet, the lines "Pur to miro, pur ti godo," which were later incorporated (perhaps with Ferrari's music) into the Venice and Naples manuscripts of Moneteverdi's *Poppea.*[8]

Monteverdi himself wrote three new operas for the Venetian commercial theatres. *Il ritorno d'Ulisse in patria,* with libretto by Giacomo Badoaro, was first given probably in 1640;[9] this was followed by *Le nozze d'Enea con Lavinia* (libretto by Badoaro) in 1640-41 and by *L'incoronazione di Poppea* (libretto by Giovanni Francesco Busenello) in 1642. Nicolò Fontei, who had been working at Venice probably since the early 1630s, had his opera *Sidonio e Dorisbe* (libretto by Francesco Melosio) given at the Teatro S. Moisè in 1642.[10] Filippo Laurenzi, who had come to Venice from Rome in 1640, together with his pupil, the singer Anna Renzi,[11] contributed, together with Tarquinio Merula, to the composite opera *La finta savia* (libretto by Giulio Strozzi; performed Teatro Novissimo, 1643); Giovanni Rovetta, by now choirmaster at St. Mark's, wrote one opera, *Ercole in Lidia* (libretto by Maiolino Bisaccioni), which was performed at the Teatro Novissimo in 1645. The English diarist John Evelyn was present at one of the performances of Rovetta's opera and wrote about it with enthusiasm, though he noted chiefly the attractions of the scenery and the charms of the singer Anna Renzi.[12]

The libretti of all these operas survive and provide one of the main sources for our knowledge of early Venetian opera. With the exception of the scores of Monteverdi's *Ulisse* and *Poppea* and the arias which Laurenzi contributed to *La finta savia*,[13] however, the music of the operas is lost. The dialogue settings published by Sances, Ferrari, Fontei, and Rovetta are, thus, doubly important since they allow us to glimpse the potential operatic styles of these composers. It is important, though, to remember that their dialogues were not written for stage performance and that the nature of the subject matter of the dialogues and its treatment in verse and music were dependent on artistic considerations different from those which would have obtained in the creation of stage music.

The earliest of the works to be discussed in this chapter—Monteverdi's *Combattimento di Tancredi et Clorinda*—has not previously been considered as a secular dialogue and some justification for describing it as such is clearly necessary. In many respects the *Combattimento* was and remains *sui generis*. First performed at the Palazzo Mocenigo, Venice, during the carnival season of 1624, it was an experimental work, the first in which Monteverdi employed his new musical concept, the *stile concitato*—the "agitated," "excited," or "warlike" style. At its first performance the *Combattimento* was given in costume, with a stylized stage performance in which Tancredi entered on a "Cavallo Mariano"[14] (which I take to mean a hobby horse) and the combatants "marched and gestured in a manner suggested by the narration."[15] Although Monteverdi, by implication at least, called his work a *madrigale con gesto*, he made quite clear in his introduction to the work that stage performance was optional: the action of the combat was, in any case, conveyed by the instrumental writing and by the musical style in which the narration was set.

The problem of placing the *Combattimento* within the framework of seventeenth-century chamber music has caused historians considerable difficulty. Recognizing its unique qualities, Schrade called the work a "scenic cantata."[16] but this description itself begs the question since it implies that *cantata* was a recognizable concept in 1638, the year in which Monteverdi published the *Combattimento*. Perhaps the best description of the work in current use is that of "secular oratorio," applied by Bukofzer.[17] This is, however, tantamount to calling the work a dialogue, since *dialogo* was a term frequently used by early and mid-seventeenth-century composers and commentators to describe the sacred works that we would now call oratorios.[18]

The designation *Testo* (text), which Monteverdi employed for the narrator of the *Combattimento* has proved another stumbling block to recognizing the work as a secular dialogue. The designation seems to link the *Combattimento* inextricably with the history of sacred dialogues, in which it was used for the Biblical narrative text. The unusual usage of the designation in a secular context derived, however, from the nature of the verse that Monteverdi was setting. The text of the *Combattimento* was adapted from Torquato Tasso's epic *La Gerusalemme Liberata* (canto XII, stanzas, 52-62.

64-68). Clearly, in the context of epic verse Monteverdi could hardly have called his narrator by the name of a shepherd, as Sances did in "Tirsi morir volea" (1633), and to set the narrative for the two singers who also took the roles of Tancredi and Clorinda was not part of Monteverdi's concept in the *Combattimento.* The neutral designation *Testo,* long sanctioned in the composition of Biblical dialogues, was thus an obvious possibility in this case.

Monteverdi was not the only composer to set epic verse in dialogue form during the early seventeenth century. In his *Dialoghi e Sonetti* of 1638, Domenico Mazzocchi published a long setting "sopra l'aria dè' sonetti" which begins "Poichè il crudo Alandin." The text was, like that of the *Combatti-mento,* drawn from Tasso's *La Gerusalemme Liberata* (canto II, stanzas 11-38, 43-49, 51-53). For the most part Mazzocchi avoided the problem of narrative by omitting it altogether. Where this was impossible, however, he employed the character *Tasso* as his narrator. Eleven years later, Giovanni Felice Sances published a dialogue setting of epic verse, "Già dell'horrido mostro" (Angelica and Ruggiero) in his *Capricci poetici* (Venice, 1649).[19] The figure *Testo* was again employed as narrator; and Sances called his setting quite unequivocally, *dialogo.* If it is not to be regarded as a stage work, then, Monteverdi's *Combattimento* must be defined as secular dialogue.

Monteverdi looked to Tasso's epic for a text in which he could exploit to the full his newly invented *stile concitato.* He found, in the story of Tancred and Clorinda, a text in which war and love were set side by side, thus affording opportunities for the musical expression of both extremes. His setting, taken as a whole, is perhaps too long for its material. It is enriched, however, by some of the composer's finest invention. His setting of Clorinda's dying words, to the accompaniment of strings and continuo, is on a par with the Ingrate's lament in the *Ballo delle Ingrate.* The simple change of harmony from C major to B flat (bars 441-2),[20] a cliché of late Renaissance music, here provides a mystical other-worldliness. Such older elements of style, combined with the freshness and vigor of the new *stile concitato* go to make up one of Monteverdi's most vital works.

The *stile concitato* was, of course, the main focus of the *Combattimento* and its raison d'être. Its invention was Monteverdi's bid for recognition as an intellectual as well as an outstanding musician. In the preface to his eighth book of madrigals (1638), he justified and explained his invention in terms uncannily like those used by the Florentine theorists Bardi and Galilei:

I have recognized that among our passions or affections *(affettioni del animo)* there are three principal ones: wrath *(Ira),* temperance (*Temperanza),* and humility or prayer *(Humiltà* or *supplicatione),* as our best philosophers affirm and even the very nature of our voice with its high, middle and low range verifies; and the art of music substantiates them as well, in the terms *concitato,* the excited, *molle,* the soft, and *temperato,* the temperate. In all the works of composers of the past I could not find an example of the excited genre, though of the soft and the temperate there were many. Yet Plato has described this type in the third book of the *Republic* in these words: "Take that harmony which in tone and accent imitates those men who bravely go to battle." Since I was aware that it is contrasts more than anything else that move our souls, and that the end of all good music is to affect the soul, as Boethius affirmed when he said that music, naturally inborn in our being, ennobles man or depraves his morals, therefore with no little study and endeavour I set about the rediscovery of this music. I took into consideration that, according to all the best philosophers, it was the fast pyrrhic metre that was used for bellicose and excited dances, while the slow spondaic metre served for the opposite expression; consequently I began to see that one semibreve in its full value corresponded to one spondaic beat, that, however, the semibreve divided into sixteen successive semicromes [semiquavers], beaten one after the other, and connected with a text that contained wrath and indignation, could well resemble the affection of which I was in search, although the text might not be able to follow the fast tempo of the instruments.[21]

The essential feature of the *stile concitato* was, then, the use of semiquaver rhythms to portray excitement and the *Combattimento* affords abundant examples of rushing scales and passages involving repeated semiquavers. In composing the work, however, Monteverdi pressed into service other musical devices to imitate the sounds and actions of war. Thus one finds, in bars 18 to 30,[22] the sounds produced by the hoofs of a galloping horse; in bars 31 to 37[23] triadic trumpet fanfares; in bars 139 to 144[24] the sound of swords clashing; and in bars 156 to 158[25] simple dominant-tonic progressions as the two warriors circle each other. Two, at least, of these extra elements, the trumpet fanfares and the dominant-tonic progressions, became so associated in Monteverdi's mind with the *stile concitato* that they appeared as independent entities in some of his later works which employ the style.[26]

In tracing the background to the invention of the *stile concitato,* Denis Arnold suggested that Monteverdi's interest in the art of war had been stimulated by his presence on Vincenzo Gonzaga's military campaign in Hungary in 1595.[27] He also instanced a number of examples in Monteverdi's earlier work and in the work of other composers which prefigured some of the elements of the *stile concitato*. To these may be added, in passing, Sigismondo d'India's strophic duet "Alla guerra d'amore" (1615), which employs triadic motives over a repeated bass note (ex. 1).

Example 1

One further factor must, however, be taken into consideration, and that is Monteverdi's own experience in writing operatic recitative. The recitative of his opera *Orfeo* contains several examples of passages in which the characters of the opera become excited or angry. In depicting these heightened states of emotion, Monteverdi imitated the acceleration in speech appropriate to them and produced, in doing so, passages in semiquaver rhythm such as those shown in example 2, which is taken from Proserpina's plea to Pluto for the release of Eurydice (act IV), and example 3, which marks the culmination of Orpheus' inner struggle and his decision to look back at Eurydice (act IV).

It may, thus, be argued that Monteverdi's *stile concitato* was, in part, a rationalization of a natural musico-dramatic process. This rationalization produced an artificial, rather than a natural style. The semiquaver passages of *Orfeo* grew out of the rhythms of the verse being set. The text of the *Combattimento,* however, was conceived neither for stage performance nor for musical setting and the semiquaver rhythms of the *stile concitato* often appear to have been imposed upon the rhythm of the verse, as may be seen from the following examples:

(a) bars 164-65

l'onta irrita   lo sdegno alla   vendetta alla   vendetta

(b) bars 231-33:

Vede   Tancredi   in maggior copia il sangue del suo nemico,

The question of speech rhythm *vis a vis* musical rhythm is not fundamental to a critical judgment of the success or failure of Monteverdi's *Combattimento.* It is, however, important in considering the relationship to Monteverdi's work of a dialogue setting published five years after the first performance of the *Combattimento* by a younger composer, Giovanni Rovetta. The work in question is the large-scale pastoral dialogue "Rattenete le destre" *(La Gelosia placata)* which Rovetta included in his first book of *Madrigali Concertati* (Venice, 1629).[28]

In *La Gelosia placata,* Rovetta employs such obvious devices of the *stile concitato* as the semiquaver rhythms and tonic-dominant progressions which characterize the introductory *sinfonia.* Elsewhere in the dialogue, however, the use of semiquaver rhythms seems to be dictated as much by the unusually energetic quality of the verse and by the anger of the two characters Licoris and Tityrus, who are engaged in a furious argument.

Example 2

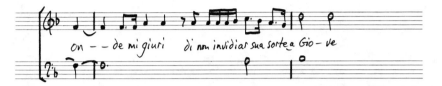

on - - de mi giuri   di non invidias sua sorte a Gio - ve

Example 3

Ohimè las - - - - so.   S'arman for-sea miei dan-ni   con

tal fuor le furie innamorate per rapirmi il mio ben   ed io'l consen - to?

Like so many of his contemporaries, Rovetta omitted to acknowledge his poet when publishing *La Gelosia placata* and he tells us nothing of the circumstances surrounding its composition. The source of the text can be traced, however, to the comedy *Il natal di Amore: anacronismo,* written by the Venetian poet and librettist Giulio Strozzi. Strozzi's importance in the early history of Venetian opera has been noted above. His comedy *Il natal di Amore* was first published in Venice in 1621 and reprinted there in 1621, 1622, 1629, and 1644.[29] The scene from which Rovetta's dialogue text was adapted appeared for the first time in the fourth, revised and enlarged edition of the play published in 1629. In this edition it appeared as act III, scene 1. Strozzi offered no explanation for his revisions nor for the new scenes that he had written; indeed, the dedication of the fourth edition was signed by the publisher Evangelista Deuchino. One can only surmise that the play was probably reworked for a performance in Venice, especially since the original prologue, in which Venus addressed the gentlemen of Rome, was omitted from the fourth edition.

Act III, scene 1 of *Il natal di Amore,* as it appears in the 1629 edition, is reproduced on the pages following for comparison with the text of Rovetta's dialogue. The original scene involves two characters from mythology: the centaur, Nessus, and Deianira, the wife of Hercules.

La Gelosia placata[30]

Chorus (C), Licori (L), Titiro (T)

1 C. Rattenete le destre,

   Sospendete l'offese,
   Amanti troppo queruli e gelosi.
   Non corran sì veloci
5 O'l dente invelenito
   O l'unghia discortese
   Al graffio, al morso, alle punture atroci.
   Chè dell'ingiurie d'iracondi amanti
   È tardo il pentimento e vani i pianti.

10 L. Lasciate ch'io l'uccida
   Chè se mio non sarà, d'altrui non sia;
   E della pena mia
   Non vo' che l'empio mancator si rida;
   Lasciate ch'io l'uccida.

15 T. Ch'io sia vostro? Ch'io v'ami?
   O Stelle, O Cieli,
   Per una perfidissima bugiarda
   Ch'io più sospiri et arda?
   Io sono il mancator? Voi la fedele?
20 Voi la bella pietosa?
   Io quel brutto crudele?
   Così dir si conviene.
   O ria menzogna, O mia tradita spene.
   Io sarò d'Amarillide; O pur voi,
25 Vi giungerete al sospirato Aminta.

Il natal di Amore: anacronismo
4th edn., 1629, act III, scene 1

Nesso (N), Deianira (D)

1 D. Lasciate ch'io l'uccida.

  N. Rattenete la destra,
   Raffrenate lo sdegno,
   Sospendete l'offese.

5 D. Lasciate ch'io l'uccida,
   Che se mio non sarà, d'altrui non sia;
   Ne della pena mia
   Voglio, che l'empio mancator si rida;
   Lasciate ch'io l'uccida.

Occhi, voi pur mirate in braccio altrui,
L'idolo ch'adorate?

30   Fuggirò sì lontan, mostro funesto,
    Che questo Sol, che questa luce appena
    A noi sarà commune.
    Io da te parto
    Col pensier, e col piede;
    O Cieli spergiurato, O rotta fede.
L. Armatevi di sdegno
35   Furie d'Averno; uscite
    Fuor dell'antro di Dite
    A tormentar il disleale indegno.
    Serpi, facelle, e strali,
    Pene, travagli, e mali
40   Assalite l'ingrato
    Indegnamente amato.

    Terra, chè non l'inghiotti?
    Chè non fulmini, ò Cielo?
    Giorno, chè non ti annotti?
    O ferro, O foco, O gielo,
45   O rabbia, ò crudeltade, O furor cieco,
    Vostro invitto valor,
           perchè si cessa?

10   Occhi voi pur mirate in braccio altrui
    L'Ercole, che adorate?
    Che più tardo? ah spergiuro
    Sia di scorno palese
    Pubblica la vendetta:
15   Misera, che presumo
    Con questa destra imbelle
    Privar di vita 'Alcide?

[45] [Lascia l'antica moglie, e da lei parte
    Col pensiero, e col piede
    Ò Cieli spergiurati, ò rotta fede.][31]

    Armatevi di sdegno
20   Furie d'Averno, uscite
    Voi dall'antro di Dite
    A tormentar il disleale indegno:
    Serpi, facelle, e strali,
    Doglie, travagli, e mali
25   Assalite l'ingrato
    Indegnamente amato.
    Fumo, che non l'acciechi?
    Foco, che non lo struggi?
    Terra, che non l'inghiotti?
30   Che non fulmini, ò Cielo?
    Giorno, che non t'annotti?
    Ò ferro, ò fiamme, ò gielo,
    Ò rabbia, ò crudeltade, ò furor cieco
    Vostro invitto valore
    Hoggi non è qui meco?

35 Ire, sdegni, e rancori
    Odij, vendette, e pene
    Danni, crucci, e martori
    Chi v'arresta? ove sete? anco si cessa?
    Mentra la fè promessa
40 Rompe a sua voglia il crudo,
    Cosi lento è il gastigo
    Cosi zoppi i tormenti?
    Segue la serva Alcide,
    Lascia l'antica moglie, e da lei parte
45 Col pensiero, e col piede
    Ò Cieli spergiurati, ò rotta fede.

N. Ah ben hà rotte Astrea
    Le bilancie, e la spada,
    Se giustitia non trovi.
50 D. Seguila, traditore.
    Vendetta huomini, e Dei, vendetta Amore.
    Mà se stà la vendetta
    Posta nelle mie mani,
    Perche la cerco, e la procuro altronde?
55 Abbandonami, lasciami, spergiuro,
    Più di te non mi curo.
    Volgi, quanto ti piace
    Servo della tua serva
    Hoggi al fuso gli stami,
60 Adattati meschin la rocca al fianco
    Per la tua bella Iole,
    Che vendetta felice,
    Mi somministra il femminile ingegno
    Contro un marito indegno.

Cosi la fè promessa
Rompe a sua voglia il crudo;

50 Cosi schernisce Amore,
    Perfido ingannatore.

Abbandonami, lasciami, spergiuro,
Più di te non mi curo.

65   Hoggi ogni moglie impari
     Da Deianira il modo
     Di vendicar'i torti
     De' malvagi consorti:

70   Io tutta lieta al fine
     Vagheggiata, e festosa,
     S'un consorte mi lascia,
     A novello amator mi farò sposa,
     Tal di gran crudeltà sia la mercede,
     Schernirò rotta fè, con rotta fede.

[50] [Seguila, traditore.
     Vendetta, huomini, e Dei, vendetta Amore][32]

     Partiti, fuggimi, affrettati, O quanto
55   Lungi da questo seno
     Hai da stillarti in pianto.
     Lungi da quell'ardor che ti da vita,
     Languirai, verrai meno.
     Io, con gioia infinita,
60   Riderò, goderò del tuo gran male,
     Brillerò, gioirò della tua **pena;**
     E tutta lieta al fine,
     Vagheggiata e festosa,

     Altrui mi farò sposa.
65   Tal, d'ingrato amator, sia la mercede,
     Schernirò rotta fè con rotta fede.

T.   Io so che non bramate,
     O mentitrice, O finta,
     Che donarvi ad Aminta.

70 L. Io so che non aspetti
     Ch'un *Zeffiro* cortese
     Ai rubati diletti.
     Vuoi seguir Amarillide che fugge?
     Seguila, traditore.
75   Vendetta, O Cielo, O Dei, vendetta Amore.

T.   Io non seguo Amarillide, ma fuggo
     Da voi che mi lasciate
     E ad altrui vi donate.

80 L. Io non ti lascio, O mentitor ingrato,
     Ma quel sen ch'adorasti
     È ben da te lasciato.

T.   E s'io no 'l lascio?

L.   Dunque non sei tu d'altra donna amante?

T.   Non amo altra Amarillide che voi,
85   D'ogni amara mia pena
     Durissima cagione; e tolto, O Dio,
     Son tanto amaramente
     Dal ben ch'io più desio?

L.   E chi ti togli, O Stolto,
90   Dal mio sen, dal mio volto?
90   Dal mio sen, dal mio volto?

T.   La vostra crudeltà.

L.   L'amore altrui.

T.   Non amo altra che voi.

L.   Perchè mi fuggi?

T.   Perchè voi mi lasciate.

95 L.   Io non ti lascio;

T.   Et io non t'abbandono.

L.   Perdonami, mio ben, ch'io ti perdono.

T.   Donati a me, ben mio, ch'a te mi dono.

L/T: Intrecciamo le destre
100 E fugga via da noi la gelosia:
     Io son tua, tu sei mia.

C.   O fortunati amanti,
     Aura d'Amor cortese
     Delle vostr'ire ha dileguato il nembo,
105 V'ha serenato i pianti;
     La Concordia vi rese.
     Titiro è di Licori
     E Licori è di Titiro;
     Nè scioglia mai più gielo
110 Importuno quest'amor, questa doglia.

Since Rovetta did not acknowledge his poet, we cannot be certain that Strozzi was himself responsible for adapting the scene of his play for musical setting. The extensive nature of the adaptation, however, the number of lines added, and the stylistic consistency of the finished product seem to argue that he did. Moreover, since Rovetta's setting was published in the same year as the scene in the original play, it seems unlikely that any other poet would have had access to the material. It also seems extremely unlikely that Rovetta would have made the adaptation himself.

Why, then, should a poet of established reputation undertake work of this kind for a relatively unknown composer?[33] It seems possible that Monteverdi's patronage was involved here. We know that Monteverdi first worked with Strozzi in 1627, the year in which Rovetta was appointed assistant choirmaster of St. Mark's. My guess would be that Rovetta came into contact with Strozzi through Monteverdi and that the text of *La Gelosia placata* was prepared soon after the completion of the opera *La finta pazza Licori;* the use of the name *Licori* for the shepherdess of the dialogue may have been no mere coincidence.

One further factor seems to argue that the text of *La Gelosia placata* was prepared after 1624 and that is its subject matter. Although Strozzi changed the characters of the original scene to the more conventional shepherd and shepherdess of the pastoral dialogue, he also turned the imprecations uttered against a character offstage into a direct confrontation—a lovers' quarrel—sharing Deianira's orginal lines between the two combatants, Licoris and Tityrus. The "warlike" nature of the resulting text would seem to be a direct reflection of the thinking which prompted Monteverdi's *Combattimento di Tancredi et Clorinda* and we know from the composer's letter of 7 May 1627[34] that the libretto of *La finta pazza Licori* had also provided opportunities for employing the *stile concitato.*

The original scene from *Il natal di Amore* is some 74 lines in length, of which 37 survive virtually unchanged in *La Gelosia placata.* In adapting the scene for musical setting, Strozzi lengthened some of the original speeches, cut others, and transposed lines where necessary to create a finished, self-contained dialogue text of 110 lines. The sort of process involved is illustrated at the beginning of the work, where the opening chorus of nine lines was expanded from only three lines of the original play. Licoris's opening speech was transferred intact from the original, but that given to Tityrus, a speech of nineteen lines, was developed from five lines of the play and three of these (lines 31 to 33 of the dialogue) were taken out of their original order. The ending of the original scene, too, had to be changed. In the play, the resolution of Deianira's predicament was deferred until a later scene. The reconciliation of Licoris and Tityrus and the chorus which rounds off the dialogue had, therefore, to be newly invented.

Although two other texts for music by Strozzi, the libretto of *La finta pazza Licori* and the sonnets *I cinque fratelli* (1628),[35] predate *La Gelosia placata,* the dialogue is the earliest of his texts which actually survives in a musical setting. The poet had clearly taken some trouble in adapting the dialogue from his original stage play[36] and produced a text that, even in terms of his own output of dialogues, contains a number of unique and unconventional elements. Perhaps the most striking of these is its energetic quality. This derives, in part, from its origins in spoken drama, but it also underlies Rovetta's use of semiquaver rhythms in the recitative sections of his setting.

The musical setting of *La Gelosia placata* is conceived on quite a large scale, lasting some twelve minutes in performance, and is itself unusual among through-composed dialogues in calling for an ensemble of two violins and a trio of voices (alto, tenor, and bass) in addition to the two characters (soprano and tenor) of the dialogue proper.[37] The dramatic situation concerns the resolution of a quarrel between two lovers, the shepherdess Licoris and the shepherd Tityrus, each of whom accuses the other, in no uncertain terms, of infidelity. The work consists of three vocal sections, chorus-dialogue-chorus, sung without a break and introduced by a *sinfonia* for two violins and continuo, a "call-to-arms" employing the fanfare motives and tonic-dominant progressions of the *stile concitato.* The trio of voices acts as the chorus, who first call on the two lovers to cease their quarrel. This sets the scene and allows the dialogue itself to begin in the thick of the conflict, without further preliminaries or narration. The terms in which the chorus's warnings are couched serve to depict the dispute as a battle, and this is reflected, in Rovetta's setting, by a hint of the *stile concitato* at bar 34. At the conclusion of the quarrel, chorus and instruments join in celebrating the return of peaceful relations.

The dialogue section itself is through-composed and contains only one closed musical form. This occurs in Licoris's opening speech, where her first line, "Lasciate ch'io l'uccida" (bars 53 to 54) is repeated at bars 60 to 63 to form a ternary structure. It may be seen, however, that this structure simply reflects a repetition of the line in the text and its original (lines 5 and 9 of the scene from *Il natal di Amore*).

The musical line consists of a mixture of declamatory recitative and passages of a more measured, lyrical arioso, a mixture flexible enough to reflect each nuance of the text and even momentary changes of mood on the part of the characters. Although the arioso passages are well developed and well defined in comparison with those of earlier monody, and though much use is made of sequential patterns, the division between "recitative" and "aria" is by no means distinct and the basis of Rovetta's technique remains that of the madrigalist.

The stylistic sources of the arioso passages in *La Gelosia placata* are to be found in the Venetian songbooks of the early 1620s. Bars 72 to 77 and 137 to

144, which have bass lines moving in crotchets, are similar in style to the strophic-bass cantatas written by Grandi and Berti,[38] two of Rovetta's contemporaries at St. Mark's. In bars 158 to 171, prompted by the words "Io, con gioia infinita," Rovetta brings into play the style of the Venetian triple-meter *bel canto* aria of which Grandi and Berti were also masters. The use of duple- and triple-meter arioso in *La Gelosia placata* is generally suggested by portions of the text which imply a moment of introspection rather than direct speech.

The recitative of the dialogue displays a much greater rhythmic variety than is usually found in dialogue settings. The languishing chromatism of bars 149 to 152 and 154 to 157, and the virtuosic word-painting of bar 93 can be numbered among the stock-in-trade of the writer of solo madrigals, but passages in the text of a more agitated mood are expressed by semiquaver movement and reveal, no doubt, Rovetta's knowledge of Monteverdi's *stile concitato*. The younger composer tends, however, to employ the style in a less limited harmonic context than Monteverdi, as may be seen in the sequential pattern of bars 111 to 116. The rhythm of the text at this point, as well as its meaning, makes the use of semiquavers seem inevitable. This less artificial use of the *stile concitato* is particularly effective in portraying a character's growing anger, as may be seen in bars 127 to 136. Here, as Licoris' anger mounts, so the vocal line rises and the climax of her outburst is marked by the semiquaver rhythms of bar 132.

The text of *La Gelosia placata* is so constructed that, after Licoris' opening lines, each of the characters states his position in an extended speech. As an understanding is gradually reached the number of lines allotted to each character in their exchanges is gradually reduced until the two lovers, finally on amicable terms, meet in short duet. The poet paves the way to the point of reconciliation by employing the device of complementary strophes characteristic of the amoebean eclogue. Thus, immediately before they are reconciled, Licoris and Tityrus appear from the similarity of their verses to be taunting each other (lines 67 to 72) and then, later, to be moving toward an understanding (lines 76 to 81). The idea is matched, in Rovetta's setting, by the use of nearly identical melodic lines for each complementary pair of tercets (bars 188 to 194 and 201 to 210).

Nevertheless, after such a lengthy and forceful argument, the reconciliation of the lovers seems, at least in the text, somewhat hasty and contrived. Rovetta overcomes this problem by slowing the pace of the music and making dramatic use of silence. In bars 210 to 211, Tityrus poses the question "E s'io no 'l lascio?." In the musical setting this question, itself characterized by a Phrygian cadence, is followed by a minim rest as its implications are borne in upon Licoris. She then replies, with a hint of coquettish submission, "Dunque, non sei tu d'altra donna amante?." The mode of address in the text has changed from "voi" to "tu" and Rovetta sets the vocal line low in the singer's tessitura. The effect is masterly, though, like the *stile concitato,* the idea of using silence for dramatic effect was probably learned from Monteverdi, who had used it in *Orfeo,* to express Orpheus' horror at the announcement of Eurydice's death,[39] and in the *Combattimento,* to express Tancred's shock on recognising Clorinda.[40]

Rovetta's contribution as dramatist, then, lies mainly in his ability to match the dramatic pacing of the text and to portray the varying states of mind of his characters. This he does with great assurance. It must be admitted, however, that much of the credit for the structure and the vivid quality of *La Gelosia placata,* its lively diction and refreshing lack of Marinist conceits, should go to the poet who furnished Rovetta with his text—Giulio Strozzi.

Strozzi was never again to write a dialogue text quite like *La Gelosia placata,* though something of its liveliness can be seen in his operatic libretti.[41] Although he provided non-operatic texts for at least three other composers— Fontei, Laurenzi,[42] and his daughter, the singer-composer Barbara Strozzi— only two further dialogue texts can be attributed to him with any degree of certainty. These are the strophic dialogue "Uccellatori, deh correte" *(L'Uccellatrice)* set by Fontei in his 1635 book, and "Anima del mio core," a *dialogo in partenza* set by Barbara Strozzi in her first book of madrigals (Venice, 1644).[43] It is possible, however, that Strozzi was also the author of six further dialogue texts set by Fontei and published in his 1636 and 1639 books.

The only post which Nicolò Fontei is known to have held in Venice was that of organist "in aede Sancte Mariae Cruciferorum" (presumably Santa Maria de' Crocicchieri), where he was working in 1638-39.[44] Gaspari suggested that he left Venice in 1640 to work in Verona,[45] but although Fontei mentioned in the dedication to his *Compieta e Letanie,* op. 5 (Venice, 1640), that his music had been favorably received at Verona, the wording of the dedication does not imply that he was then living there.[46] He certainly intended to continue his career as an organist in Venice, for on 22 January 1640 he competed against Cavalli, Giacomo Arrigoni, and Natale Monferrato for the vacant post of second organist at St. Mark's.[47] Although he was unsuccessful (the post went to Cavalli), it seems likely that he continued to live in Venice, where his only known opera, *Sidonio e Dorisbe,* was performed in 1642. It was only in 1645 that he moved to Verona where, on 13 May, he succeeded to the post of choirmaster of the cathedral.[48]

Fontei had settled in Venice probably in the early 1630s for, by 13 September 1634, the date of the dedication to his first book of *Bizzarrie Poetiche poste in musica* (1635), he was already closely associated with Giulio and Barbara Strozzi. According to the dedications of Fontei's 1635 and 1636 books, Giulio Strozzi provided all the texts for the first book and most of those for the second; the music of both books was written for Barbara Strozzi's use.

There is no evidence of Fontei's relationship with the Strozzis after 1636, though he may well have been one of the musicians who performed at the *Accademia de gli Unisoni,* founded by Giulio Strozzi at Venice in 1637. Bearing in mind his earlier relationship with the Strozzis, it may be more than coincidence that the subject matter of his dialogue "Lilla, se Amor non fugga" *(Canto di Bella focile d'Amor),* published in 1639,[49] closely resembles that of the so-called *Contesa del Canto e delle Lagrime,* two discourses read before the *Accademia de gli Unisoni* and published in 1638.[50] Moreover, considering the prominence given in the dialogue to the female character Lilla (soprano), who is characterized as a singer, we may speculate that the role was written for Barbara Strozzi, who was "queen" of the *Accademia de gli Unisoni* and to whom its other published papers were dedicated.[51]

The academic discourses which make up the *Contesa del Canto e delle Lagrime* were delivered by two founding members of the *Accademia de gli Unisoni,* Giovanni Francesco Loredano and Matteo Dandolo. The subject at issue was which of the two, tears or song, was more powerful in awakening the emotion of love. Dandolo argued the case of the former, while Loredano replied on the part of song. Loredano concluded his discourse by saying:

> But let me not, in speaking of the glories of song, prejudice you in its favor. We shall be much better able to judge, from the mouths of these musicians, the pre-eminence of song over tears in producing Love.[52]

This falls tantalizingly short of giving us any concrete information concerning either the musicians who performed on this occasion or the music that they sang. The other published papers of the academy contain equally tantalizing references to musical performances which took place at its meetings. Only Barbara Strozzi's contribution was singled out for praise.

On the basis of internal evidence, however, Fontei's "Lilla, se Amor non fugga" is a work which we might well associate with the *Contesa del Canto e delle Lagrime.* The central theme of the dialogue is the power of Lilla's singing to produce pangs of love in the admiring Lidio (tenor). In the opening section of the work, Lidio begs Lilla to "sing, fill me with love" (bars 14ff.) and speaks of the tears which her "muse" has drawn from his eyes. She declines to sing of his tears, saying that this would be beyond her powers. The three associated ideas of the dialogue are thus established as love, song, and tears, and these were the basic themes of the *Contesa del Canto e delle Lagrime.*

In the dialogue, these three ideas are further developed in the two strophic canzonettas, sung by Lilla, which form its focal points. In the first (bars 127ff.), song itself becomes an image to be explored: "Love is hidden in song . . . song is encircled with wrappers, the road holds spaces and song sends the safety of lines." In the second (bars 214ff.), the central image is grief, with tears as an associated image: "Love hides itself in grief; Love is a fire amidst the waves."

After hearing the two canzonettas, Lidio confesses himself conquered by love and the three ideas of love, song, and grief are united in the line that he sings at bars 240 to 244 and again in the final duet: "Long live grief, long live song, and long live Love which, in such tender suffering, animates the heart."

Fontei's musical setting is both ambitious and complex. Like Rovetta, he employs the style of the Venetian *bel canto* aria as the basis of extended arioso passages. Unlike Rovetta, however, he uses arioso, both in "Lilla, se Amor non fugga" and in the other large-scale dialogue of his 1639 book, "O Dio Tirsi" (Lilla and Thyrsis) to create closed musical forms and to unify sections of the settings by means of a refrain, or rondo structure. Fontei was, indeed, a pioneer of rondo structures in secular solo song. His settings of "Hor tra l'aure" and "Beltà non hò" (both published 1635) seem to be the earliest published examples of "rondo cantatas." The first of these comprises an opening section in triple meter followed by three stanzas set as a strophic-bass cantata; between the stanzas a refrain in two sections and a ritornello are to be performed.[53]

In "O Dio Tirsi," Lilla and Thyrsis each sing an extended triple-meter arioso, of which the opening bars are given as examples 4a and 4b. These arioso passages remain associated with the two characters and reappear during the work as a unifying factor. In "Lilla, se Amor non fugga" the element of rondo is used less extensively. The first section of the work (bars 1 to 84) is unified by the repetition of Lidio's arioso "Canta, Lilla," which is first heard at bars 14 to 26 and again at bars 41 to 53. At the end of the section (bars 71-74) Lilla sings a passage of arioso which, although quite different from that given to Lidio, is clearly intended to balance his earlier statements and to round off the section.

Example 4

The section which follows (bars 85 to 126) is cast in an A B A¹ form, the B section being a solo recitative (bars 97 to 100), while the outer, duet sections, marked "allegro," are written in duple-meter arioso. In these outer sections, which employ a bass line moving in crotchets and quavers, Fontei displays a surprising assurance in his handling of the harmonic problems inherent in a fast-moving bass line. The style in which he writes here, and which was to become a commonplace of later baroque music, sounds very advanced for 1639, especially since it is contrasted, at bars 113 to 115, with progressions more reminiscent of the sixteenth century.

Following the first of Lilla's two canzonettas, bars 152 to 190 are also cast in an A B A form. The B section is, again, a recitative, but the two outer sections are this time mainly characterized by the more familiar triple-meter arioso.

The whole work is unified not by a musical, but by a verbal refrain. Variants of the phrase "Il mio amor, la tua musa," which appears first at bars 9 to 11, are heard at bars 36 to 37, 64 to 65, and 250 to 252. On each occasion, however, the words are set to a different musical phrase.

The two canzonettas sung by Lilla are also worthy of note. Both are introduced by a quite lengthy ritornello for which no particular instrument is specified, and both exhibit a well-developed sense of key structure. The first canzonetta opens with a vocal phrase which cadences on C at bar 137. The second phrase, beginning on C, modulates to the dominant G (bar 141). There follow excursions to A minor (bar 144), D major (bar 146), and G major (bar 148) before the final return to C at bar 151. The second canzonetta, though less clearly organized, also exhibits the same sort of bipartite key structure. Beginning in B flat (bar 222), it modulates to F (bar 227) and back to B flat (bar 230). After a brief excursion to the dominant of G minor (bar 232), the key of B flat is once more established at the conclusion.

One further, curious element of Fontei's setting remains to be mentioned. This is his use of cadences in which an anticipatory tonic is sung in the vocal line against a dominant chord in the accompaniment. Examples can be seen at bars 40, 75, 154, 179, and 187. At first sight, this type of cadence appears to be a misprint for the more usual "Venetian cadence," examples of which can be seen at bars 116, 171, and 250. The fact that Fontei uses his own variant of this cadence regularly throughout the piece, however, coupled with the fact that more usual cadences are used at other points, suggests that the harmonic acerbities were intentional. This seems to be further supported by the fact that Fontei associates this cadence with expressions of grief. It is interesting to note, too, that Barbara Strozzi used a similar cadence in her solo cantata "Udite, amanti" (*Cantate, Ariette e Duetti*, Venice, 1651) at the words "e sotterrimi" (ex. 5).

In its exploration of two contrasted ideas—song and grief—Fontei's "Lilla, se Amor non fugga" foreshadows Carissimi's better-known dialogue *I due filosofi*[54] (text by Domenico Benigni), in which the contrast of major and minor modes was exploited to depict the contrasting philosophies of Democritus (the so-called "laughing philosopher") and Heraclitus (the "weeping philosopher"). Another feature of Carissimi's dialogue, the use of the two singers both as narrators and as individual characters, was also foreshadowed in Fontei's work, in "Dicea Clori a Fileno," one of the smaller-scale dialogues the composer included in his 1636 book. In both Carissimi's and Fontei's settings, the action of the dialogue is introduced by a passage of narration too short to warrant the introduction of a third singer. The solutions to the problem adopted by the two composers are very similar in character. In both cases the narration is set in a passage of homophonic writing with the merest hint of imitation before the final cadence (exx. 6a and 6b). Whereas Carissimi then begins the dialogue section with the chord on which the narration ended, however, Fontei employs the ingenious device of making a chromatic change in the bass line, thus effectively dividing the narrative function of the two voices from their role as the characters of the dialogue.

Example 5

Example 6

(b)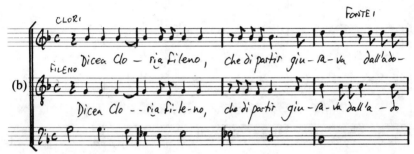

"Dicea Clori a Fileno" is, perhaps, the most attractive of the four dialogues in Fontei's 1636 book. The situation presented is simple: the shepherd Filenus (tenor) swears that he will abandon his nymph Chloris (soprano); she implores him to look at her again; he does so, is overcome by the power of her gaze, and realizes that he cannot leave her. In his setting, Fontei displays the same concern for formal design found in "Lilla, se Amor non fugga." There is no hint of rondo structure, certainly, but the final section of the setting is shaped into an A B A form: the two A sections, which consist of short exchanges in duple meter, with some use of a "walking bass," surround a central *bel canto* duet of considerable beauty (ex. 7).

Example 7

Of the three other settings in the 1636 book, "Spesso mutano stanza i nostri cori" (Chloris and Thyrsis) qualifies for the designation *dialogo* only by virtue of a short exchange between the two singers in its opening section. Like "Dicea Clori a Fileno," it contains some of Fontei's most attractive music, and it again shows the composer's ability to shape large musical paragraphs. The opening section of the work is most interesting in this respect. After an extended duet in triple meter and the short exchanges between the two characters already mentioned, the musical line with which the setting began (ex. 8) is reintroduced as the basis of an imitative duet.

Example 8

"Dio ti salvi, pastor" is more clearly dialogue-like in nature. The work opens as Nymph and Shepherd (soprano and tenor) greet each other:

Ninfa:	Dio ti salvi, pastor.
Pastore:	Ninfa, buon dì.
Ninfa:	Come stai?
Pastore:	Come sto.
Ninfa:	Che mal hai?
Pastore:	Che mal ho
	tu sai, crudel.

Rather than set these exchanges as recitative, Fontei links them together by employing a sequential walking bass as the basis of a musical paragraph before breaking into recitative as the Nymph asks "Io crudel?." Following the recitative, in which the Nymph tells the shepherd that he expected too much progress in one day, the two characters join in a long duet in two sections, the first in duple, the second in triple meter, in which they swear mutual fidelity.

"Fortunato Cantore" is conceived on a rather larger scale than the other dialogues of Fontei's 1636 book and anticipates "Lilla, se Amor non fugga" in that its subject is singing. The two characters of the dialogue are given pastoral names—Phyllis (soprano) and Thyrsis (also soprano)—but the imagery of the text avoids commonplace pastoral love-play, taking instead the image of the singer as Jove's eagle, soaring above the heads of mortals. In setting the dialogue to music, Fontei was clearly writing to display the vocal talents of Barbara Strozzi and lost no opportunity afforded by the text to indulge in virtuoso passage-work (ex. 9). Since the *passaggi* are written over a relatively static bass, the resulting style seems old-fashioned by comparison with the other dialogues in the book and the piece is almost wholly dependent for its effect on the skill of the performers.

Example 9

The text of "Fortunato Cantore" is written, for the most part, in a mixture of seven- and eleven-syllable lines and in stanzas of varying length. In Fontei's setting this is reflected by the predominance of duple meter. After the opening exchange between Phyllis and Thyrsis, however, in which their identity as singers is established, the poet pursues the image of the flight of eagles as Phyllis encourages Thyrsis to "fly that I might follow you" (vola pur ch'io ti seguo). Their "flight" and "pursuit" take the form of two four-line stanzas of regular *ottonari,* which Fontei sets in triple meter, the same suave melody being sung first by Thyrsis and then by Phyllis. For the only time in the setting Fontei here abandons passage-work for its own sake and subordinates it to the demands of melody (ex. 10). After this excursion into triple-meter arioso, duple meter is re-established. Phyllis sings that she is falling to the ground, beaten down by the wind, and calls to Thyrsis for help. Fontei captures the idea in his music by moving suddenly away from the cadence center of D minor to that of

F major and completing Phyllis' cry for help with a perfect cadence in the continuo (ex. 11). As Thyrsis offers words of encouragement, D minor is again established and Phyllis takes heart as the two singers join in a concluding duet in which virtuoso passage-work is given full rein (ex. 12).

Example 10

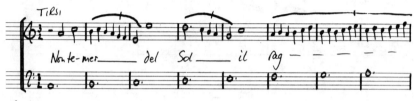

Example 11

Example 12

The involvement of Roman-trained musicians in the creation of Venetian opera has already been mentioned. Three of the composers who came to northern Italy from Rome during the decade 1630-1640—Sances, Ferrari, and Laurenzi—and who worked as composers of dramatic music, also included through-composed dialogue settings in the song books that they published at Venice. Like Rovetta and Fontei, they introduced a broader vocabulary of styles into a form which had hitherto been dominated by recitative and chose, for the most part, texts which would justify contrasts between recitative and arioso.

In this respect it is, perhaps, significant that the only setting of Guarini's pastoral "Tirsi morir volea" as a recitative-dialogue should survive from the 1630s.[55] The setting was one of two dialogues published by Sances in his *Cantade... Libro Secondo, Parte Seconda* in 1633.[56]

Guarini's text has achieved a good deal of notoriety from Einstein's heartfelt condemnation of it as:

> more obscene than the coarsest *mascherata*, the most suggestive *canto carnascialesco*, or the most impertinent chanson. It could not be further removed from true poetry, and yet is the madrigal text most frequently composed during the so-called Golden Age of the genre.[57]

Viewed against the background of the achievements of such poets as Bembo and Della Casa, Einstein's judgment of Guarini's text may well seem valid:

viewed in the context of seventeenth-century poetry, however, it seems too harsh. In "Tirsi morir volea" Guarini stretched erotic ambiguity to the point where it was no longer ambiguous. In doing this, however, he imbued his text with a humorous quality which Einstein overlooked, but which composers took to their hearts.

From the structural viewpoint, Guarini's text consists of three passages of narration each followed by a short passage of direct speech, the whole being concluded by three lines which make the "point" of the text. The extensive nature of the narration may well have been one factor that discouraged earlier monodists from setting the text as a dialogue.

In his setting, which includes some of his most seductive music, Sances overcame the problem of narration by introducing a third character, Festaurus, as narrator. In setting the passages of direct speech, he treated the first two, sung by Phyllis (also unnamed in the original text) in duple-meter arioso (bars 16 to 29 and 70 to 74) and then combined Phyllis' second speech with the only one allotted to Thyrsis to form a duet (bars 77 to 92). The style of these passages does not differ essentially from the arioso writing of the narration sections, though more use is made of sequential writing.

The largest role, Festaurus, is given to a bass voice and Sances makes some use of its range and agility, writing, for example, a leap of a tenth at bar 8 and a scale passage spanning the same interval at bars 35 to 36. Unlike many of his contemporaries, however, he does not restrict the bass voice to the role of doubling and decorating the continuo line. In all but the shortest passage of narration (bars 75 to 76) the voice sometimes doubles the cotinuo, sometimes becomes independent from it. The change from one type of writing to the other, as at bars 5 to 6 and 38 to 40 provides an effective method both of offering musical variety and of articulating different sections of the text.

Sances's arioso writing derives its expressive power from the use of harmonic color. At the beginning of Phyllis' first speech the composer employs his favorite dissonance, the major ninth, to portray the shepherdess's amorous anguish and the effect is thrown into relief by the use of a walking bass and a more active vocal line for the remainder of the speech. Festaurus, too, is given music of some power. At bars 39 to 40 an old madrigalian cliché is given new life in the expressive chord change from F to D for the words "E sentia morte;" and at the physical and emotional climax of the work a Phrygian cadence is employed twice, at bars 65 to 66 and 68 to 69 with increasing degrees of dissonance to depict not so much the action of Phyllis's "languid and trembling eyes" as the strength of the emotion which lies behind them. The pleasure of the lovers' "death" is given further emphasis in the suave triple meter of the concluding trio by the harmonic clashes in bars 98 and 102; clashes reminiscent of Monteverdi's Mantuan madrigals.

The characteristics which make Sances's setting of "Tirsi morir volea" so successful—harmonic color and graceful melodic line—characteristics rather of the writer of arias than of the musical dramatist, seem most successful when the text is capable of division into short paragraphs. The other dialogue of Sances's 1633 book "Lilla bell'e crudele" is, however, more conventional in outline and the individual speeches are longer than in Guarini's text.

In "Lilla bell'e crudele" the two characters Lilla (soprano) and Filenus (tenor) each sing in turn before joining in a final duet. The content of their conversation is Marinist in flavor. Filenus asks Lilla if she cannot read in his eyes that he is dying of love for her. She replies that his love is reciprocated and that he has written this in her eyes with Love's arrow. For the next pair of exchanges the imagery explored is that of the mouth and the tongue and the couple finally join in a kiss. The duet points the moral: "Let us take pleasure while we may, for the heart's gaiety flies away with time and beauty dies."

Sances sets all but Lilla's last statement in duple meter with a line halfway between recitative and arioso and punctuated by frequent and extended cadences. The musical phrases are generally longer than those of "Tirsi morir volea" and Sances shows himself less successful in setting a text which does not lend itself to short, rounded arches of melody. At the end of each speech the last line is repeated, generally in sequence, to provide a musical as well as a verbal conclusion. Only in Lilla's last speech do we find a minature recitative and aria. The speech begins with the words "Ecco, Filen, ti bacio; prendi questo e quest'altro e quest'ancora," which are set in duple meter; at the words "vita dell'alma è bacio...," however, which conclude the speech, the line blossoms into the sensuous triple-meter arioso of which Sances was a master (ex. 13).

Example 13

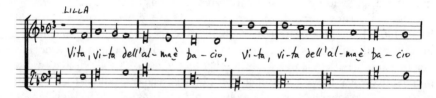

Unlike Sances, who was both born and trained in Rome, Benedetto Ferrari sprang from northern Italian stock. He was born in Reggio Emilia, probably in 1603 or '04, but seems to have served his musical apprenticeship as a choirboy at the German College in Rome, where his activities are documented for the years 1617-18.[58] By 17 July 1618, he had left the choir of the German College and, from 1 January 1619 until 31 March 1623 was employed as a musician at the Farnese court at Parma.[59] The course of his career between 1623 and 1637, the year in which he collaborated with Manelli to produce

Andromeda at Venice, is uncertain, though he seems to have been known at the Modenese court. On 8 August 1623 he wrote from the home of his uncle, the governor of Sestola, near Lucca, to Alfonso d'Este, enclosing examples of his compositions for two and five voices (now lost)[60] and, ten years later, he dedicated his first book of *Musiche Varie* to Duke Francesco I d'Este. It is possible that Ferrari was known in Venice and was perhaps living there prior to 1637, for in that year he dedicated his second book of *Musiche Varie* to Viscount Basil Feilding, English ambassador to Venice.

Ferrari is represented in this study by one work only, the dialogue "Amar, io ti consiglio" (Lydia and Filenus) which he included in his 1637 book. The text of the dialogue, by an unknown poet, is unusual in that the situation presented remains unresolved at the end of the work. Filenus counsels Lydia to love (with himself in mind). She rejects his counsel with the pert rejoinder that "offering advice to others is a false kind of help" and remains obdurate to the end. The closing duet, set by Ferrari as a recitative (ex. 14), is highly individual, even eccentric in character. As Lydia steadfastly refuses to take any notice of Filenus' cajoling, his frustration rises to a climax as he pictures the vengeance that Love will take; but Lydia has the final word, a scornful, deflating question "e come?."

From the structural viewpoint, Ferrari's dialogue stands on the borderline between a through-composed and a strophic setting. The text itself consists of nine five-line stanzas of regular rhyme-scheme (a b b c c) and syllable content (7 11 7 11 11). Ferrari treats the first four stanzas in a mixture of recitative and arioso, but sets stanzas five to eight as strophic variations. There is no absolute distinction in meaning or content between the two groups of stanzas which would suggest a difference in musical treatment, though the first four stanzas involve rather more direct question and answer than stanzas five to eight, which form a more generalized exchange on the nature of beauty.

The style of the strophic variations is an elegant triple-meter arioso. The bass line, which is identical for each of the four stanzas, is freely invented, but the pattern of the so-called "chaconne bass" appears as an instrumental ritornello (ex. 15). In the setting of each stanza, the "chaconne bass" is heard twice as an introduction, twice after the first three lines of text, and once more under the sustained final note of the vocal line. Ferrari writes longer, more irregular phrases than Sances and his vocal line, in consequence, seems less suave and rounded. It is, however, no less expansive. The more poignant moments of the text are expressed by chromatic inflection (A flats when the cadence center is F, D flats when the cadence center is B flat) which, at the end of the fifth stanza, gives rise to the chord of the diminished seventh (ex. 16). Example 16 also shows one of Ferrari's most characteristic cadences, a variation of the "Venetian cadence" in which the anticipatory note is the supertonic rather than the leading note.

Example 14

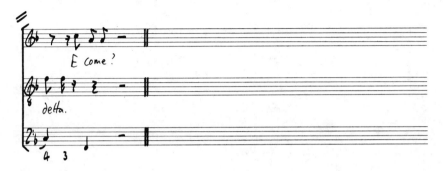

Example 15

Example 16

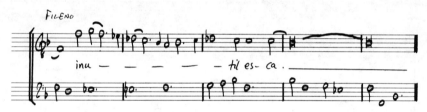

The musical setting of the first four stanzas, like that of the final duet, is highly individual. The first four lines of each stanza are set as a series of short musical gestures, with a new idea for virtually every line (ex. 17). The technique lacks a clear sense of musical continuity and seems to require some physical movement on the part of the singers to bridge the changes in style. The last line of each stanza is set in a more expansive, continuous arioso, stanzas one and two being in triple meter, stanzas three and four in duple meter. The four stanzas are unified, musically, by Ferrari's use of written-out appoggiaturas such as may be seen in example 17 and again, in two different rhythms, in example 18, the opening of the second stanza.[61]

Ferrari's dialogue is curiously hybrid in style and it would be of the greatest interest to know whether the histrionic manner in which he set the first four stanzas of this work was carried over into his own operatic music. Unfortunately, like the final question of the dialogue itself, this question must remain unanswered since none of Ferrari's operatic music has survived.

Example 17

Example 18

Two more settings only remain to be discussed in this chapter. The first of these—Vincenzo Providali's text "O cara genitrice," set to music by Filiberto Laurenzi and published in 1641—is also the one which seems most like a operatic scene taken out of context. Although the action of the dialogue is self-contained, the words which the characters speak imply the possibility of subsequent events. In setting the text to music, Laurenzi, like Rovetta before him, followed perceptible divisions in the text, employing recitative and arioso to distinguish between passages of direct speech and passages that are more reflective in character or involve a statement of resolution to act.

The scene involves the two deities Venus (soprano) and Cupid (soprano) who conspire to capture the heart of an unnamed maiden. At the beginning of the dialogue, Cupid greets his mother and asks her why she has descended from the heavens (recitative). She replies that she has come to enlist his aid in softening the hard heart of a beautiful nymph and asks him to employ his arrows in firing her heart with love (recitative). In the most extended section of the dialogue, Cupid then replies that he will do this in the twinkling of an eye (ex. 19) for he is always at Venus' disposal (triple-meter arioso). He then addresses the audience, warning "maidens and warriors" alike that they are all subject to the mother of Love (recitative, with a semiquaver roulade at the word "guerrieri") and sings of the glories of love (triple-meter arioso). He concludes by saying that he always carries with him fire and arrows and that everyone is subject to him (recitative). Venus urges him to depart and finally resolves to go with him (recitative), concluding her speech with the words "Andiam...di compagnia" which are taken up in the concluding, triple-meter duet "Let us go, singing together...to victory."

Like Ferrari, Laurenzi had begun his musical career as a choirboy in Rome. In 1633 he was a soprano at the church of San Luigi dei Francesi,[62] where Luigi Rossi was organist. In Rome he had become the teacher of the soprano Anna Renzi, in whose company he journeyed to Venice in 1640[63] and with whom he remained associated until at least 1644, when Giulio Strozzi dedicated to him his *Le glorie della signora Anna Renzi romana.* The evidence of his dialogue setting shows that by 1641 he had absorbed the style of *bel canto* writing fashionable in Venice. Little remains to indicate his Roman background except the tendency, in recitative passages, to paint words like "alta" and "volo" by means of florid passage-work and, perhaps, the *cambiata* figure in the fourth bar of example 19.

The last of the dialogue settings to be considered here is Tarquinio Merula's "Paride, voglio il pomo" *(La Tognada),* which was issued in the new edition of his *Primo Libro de Madrigaletti a 3 voci* published at Venice in 1642. When this volume was published, Merula was, of course, resident at Bergamo. For the purposes of this chapter, however, he can be considered Venetian by adoption since he contributed, together with Ferrari, Laurenzi, and three other composers, to the composite opera *La finta savia* (libretto by Giulio Strozzi) which was staged at the Teatro Novissimo in Carnival, 1643.

Example 19

Like his earlier essay in dialogue form, Merula's *La Tognada* is a comic scene, this time a parody of the Judgment of Paris in which the hopeful candidate for the award of the golden apple is not a goddess at all, but Togna (alto), an Arnalta-like figure of low birth and less beauty.[64] Her ceaseless importuning for the golden apple leads Paris (bass) to call her a "shapeless, slobbering, repellent, toothless, smelly old woman" (ex. 20) and he advises her to look at her reflection in the fountain before imagining that she qualifies as a beauty. She retorts that the waters of the fountain always offer back a distorted image and appeals to Cupid (soprano) to give judgment in her favor. He, however, reserves the golden apple for Venus and awards Togna a cream cheese (riccota) with which to fill her stomach and whiten her cheeks. The dialogue ends with hoots of derision from the chorus, whose music is characterized by the use of "clumsy" false relations (ex. 21). The setting, though lively, lacks variety. Most of the speeches conform to the same pattern: a call to attention followed by a series of short melodic phrases repeated sequentially over relentless crotchet and quaver basses. This type of pattern can be traced in the comic scenes of Venetian opera,[65] but it is here carried to extremes.

Viewed as a group, the Venetian dialogue settings surveyed in this chapter display a fascinating diversity of literary and musical invention. They are important as the stylistic precursors of Venetian opera, and in many cases they are all that survives to show what their composers' operatic music might have been like.

Example 20

Example 21

The similarity between dialogue settings and early Venetian opera is not, however, confined to matters of style. Venetian librettists from Ferrari onward subdivided the acts of their operas into individual scenes on the model of spoken theatre; and they included scenes in dialogue which are similar in scale and outline to many of the independent dialogues published in books of songs and madrigals. The delightful encounter between a valet and a serving maid which constitutes act II, scene 5 of Monteverdi's *Poppea*[66] is a case in point, and it includes one of Monteverdi's most attractive arioso duets and a scene such as the one in which Ulysses' true identity is revealed to his son Telemachus (*Il ritorno d'Ulisse*, act II, scene 3),[67] which also consists of conversational exchanges culminating in a duet, differs in form from an independent dialogue setting only by virtue of a speech for Ulysses which comes after the duet and serves to link the scene to the later action of the opera.

The most important work of our group of Venetian settings is undoubtedly Monteverdi's *Combattimento di Tancredi et Clorinda*. It is particularly important as the source of a new style—the *stile concitato*. However, while the influence of the *stile concitato* can be detected quite clearly in a work like Rovetta's *La Gelosia placata*, few composers of secular music other than Monteverdi seem to have used it extensively. In dealing with the dialogue settings of the late 1620s and the 1630s, we become aware, instead, of the growing importance of aria styles in through-composed musical structures, and particularly of the tendency to build composite structures from shorter units of recitative and arioso. It was this concept of stylistic contrast, rather than the artificial *stile concitato*, that was to prove significant for the early development of Venetian opera; and in the realms of chamber music it marked a new stage on the path that was ultimately to lead to the separation of recitative and aria in the late baroque cantata.

10

Conclusion

We must now draw together the main ideas that have emerged in the course of this study and consider the relationship between the secular duets and dialogues surviving in printed sources and the duets and dialogues of composers such as Luigi Rossi, Giacomo Carissimi, and Antonio Cesti whose work, surviving mainly in manuscript, carries us forward to the early 1670s.

In deference to the well-established tradition that considers the recitative-dialogue to be a type of duet, we have discussed the two genres together in this study. As we have seen, however, duet and dialogue spring from quite different backgrounds in sixteenth-century music and must be considered as quite distinct even in the early seventeenth century. For while the *concertato* duet can be defined in purely musical terms as a work for two voices and continuo, the recitative-dialogue must be defined as the setting of a dialogue text which employs the new song styles of the early seventeenth century. Indeed, a substantial number of recitative-dialogues involve three characters and, hence, three singers.

Dialogue texts had been set regularly as polyphonic madrigals during the sixteenth century using a variety of techniques to suggest character differentiation. The evolution of Florentine monody, however, provided composers with the technical means to bring a greater degree of realism and expressive flexibility to their dialogue settings and recitative-dialogues began to appear in monody books from as early as 1602, when Domenico Maria Melli included two in his *Le Seconde Musiche.*

Although fewer dialogue settings than duets were published during the early seventeenth century, many books of monodies and *concertato* madrigals include at least one setting. The texts set were mainly pastoral love lyrics, but they also embraced subjects as diverse as reflective debates between the poet and his soul and the parody of the Judgment of Paris included in Merula's 1642 book. The dialogue "O sfortunata, chi mi consola?," set by Il Fasolo (1628) and Manelli (1636), seems to be unique among early recitative-dialogues in involving characters from the *Commedia dell'arte.*

The musical forms of recitative-dialogues parallel those of early seventeenth-century solo song. Thus, we find simple strophic dialogues and, more rarely, sets of strophic variations as well as the more usual through-composed settings. Although the through-composed settings resemble short operatic scenes, few composers working in the early years of the century attempted Peri's operatic style of recitative. Most preferred to work in arioso styles descended from those of *Le Nuove Musiche* and contemporary polyphonic madrigals. It is only when we come to the important group of dialogue settings found in Venetian song and madrigal books of the 1620s and 1630s that we find a perceptible relationship to operatic style, for these settings anticipate many of the stylistic features of early Venetian commercial opera.

The recitative-dialogue emerged, then, as a new solution to the old problem of setting dialogue texts. The emergence of the *concertato* duet, on the other hand, was prompted by purely musical considerations, ranging from the desire to provide simple music for a few performers to a desire to experiment with the new styles of Florentine solo song while preserving the techniques of imitation and textural contrast that were fundamental to building extended musical structures. Nor were these considerations restricted to secular music. The sacred duet was created to answer a need for simple music to be sung to the organ; the problem of building a cohesive structure, though important for the vocal duet, was crucial in the case of the instrumental duo with continuo, for here there was no text to support the structure. The possibilities for contrapuntal development and textural contrast offered by the medium of the duet serve to explain why the so-called "trio" texture remained the most characteristic scoring of instrumental ensemble music during the seventeenth century.

There are numerous cross-influences and similarities between vocal and instrumental music in the early seventeenth century and, indeed, a number of purely instrumental works were actually published in song and madrigal books. We have already noted that the so-called "walking" bass found in madrigals and arias of the 1620s and 1630s may have been borrowed from instrumental music. Conversely, in early seventeenth-century instrumental music, we can find examples of the affective gestures and restrained ornamentation that were features of the Florentine solo madrigal.[1] The similarities between duet and instrumental "trio" extend even to matters of form, for variations on melodies like the *Romanesca* and *Ruggiero* are found in both literatures. Salamone Rossi, for example, who had been the first composer to publish a trio sonata, in 1607, included sonatas on both the *Romanesca* and the *Ruggiero* in his *Terzo Libro de varie Sonate* of 1613. It is in matters of form, however, that the parallels between vocal duet and instrumental "trio" begin to break down, for the clear-cut sectional divisions and extended development of individual musical ideas that characterize instrumental forms like the sonata and canzona do not become characteristic of vocal music until rather later in the century.

In one respect, though, there is a striking similarity between the two genres in the early seventeenth century, and that is in the matter of scoring. For during these years the popularity of the instrumental "trio" for two "Canti" and continuo was closely rivaled by the popularity of "trios" for "Canto," "Basso," and continuo.[2] Similarly, two distinct types of secular *concertato* duet are found in early seventeenth-century sources. The first is scored for high voice and bass, with the lower part also serving for a *basso seguente*. This type of duet fills the duet books published during the first decade of the century. Its texture clearly owes much to solo song, and in a number of madrigal settings we can detect idioms derived from the Florentine solo madrigal. In madrigalian and strophic settings alike, however, the most important stylistic source for this type of duet is the sixteenth-century canzonetta. The second type of *concertato* duet involves the more familiar texture of two voices and independent *basso continuo*. This texture, too, seems to have been derived from the three-part canzonetta; and the most popular scoring found in early seventeenth-century duets—for two high voices—was also much favored in the late sixteenth century.

The sources in which early seventeenth-century secular duets are found are, for the most part, printed. The earliest published continuo duets are found, often together with duets for high voice and bass/*basso seguente,* in monody books. Strophic duets predominate in monody books, again suggesting a relationship between the duet and the canzonetta. After 1610, however, the madrigal gained in importance, particularly through the work of Florentine composers like Marco da Gagliano and Piero Benedetti. It is in the work of these composers that the style of the madrigalian duet most nearly approached that of the solo madrigal. In the monody books published during the second decade of the century, too, we find most of the sets of variations on stylized "arias" like the *Romanesca* and *Ruggiero.*

Few madrigals were published in monody books after 1623; and printed monody books themselves become less important as sources for duets from the mid 1620s. From the historian's point of view this is regrettable, since the work of Roman composers begins to come into focus with the monody books of the early 1620s and it is clear that the stylistic distinction between recitative and triple-meter arioso that we associate with the strophic "cantatas" of Luigi Rossi was already beginning to emerge as early as 1621 in the work of minor figures like Francesco Cerasolo.

The first book of *concertato* madrigals to include duets was Alessandro Grandi's *Madrigali concertati a 2, 3, e 4 voci* of 1615. Certain of Grandi's madrigalian duets can be shown to have stylistic affinities with the Florentine madrigal. Generally, though, they are lighter and more lyrical in style. Grandi's use of repetition and sequence to build musical paragraphs may well have influenced Monteverdi in the lighter of his madrigalian duets.

Madrigal books, which were very largely a north Italian phenomenon, become an important source for duets after 1619, the year in which Monteverdi published his *Concerto: Settimo Libro de Madrigali a 1. 2. 3. 4. et 6 voci.* As we might expect, the duets included in these books are mainly madrigal settings. Some books, however, include strophic duets; and madrigal books are the main sources for strophic duets in which melody instruments play with the voices as distinct from simply providing ritornelli between the stanzas of the aria. Some of these *concertato* arias, like a few duets found in monody books, are what I have termed "sectional arias," a type of setting that is important for the later development of the chamber duet since it can involve an alternation of scoring between one and two voices.

The madrigalian duets found in madrigal books range from short, lyrical settings to extended, serious and virtuoso pieces of the kind found in the publications of Monteverdi, Pesenti, Turini, Galeazzo Sabbatini, and Rovetta. Spanning as they do the 1620s and 1630s, the duets published by these composers exhibit some of the stylistic and technical innovations found in monodies of the same period. Two stand out in particular. These are the use of "walking" basses: basses moving regularly in crotchets. These are found in madrigalian duets by Turini and become a feature of both aria and madrigal writing in the output of Tarquinio Merula, so that an aria like "Amo, l'è ver"[3] and a madrigal like "Cogli Dori gentile," both from Merula's 1633 book, are virtually indistinguishable in style. The introduction of faster-moving bass lines also changed the nature of virtuoso writing in the madrigal: instead of roulades over a fairly static bass, such as we can see in bars 77 to 87 of d'India's "Langue al vostro languir,"[4] we now find passage-work geared to a rapid harmonic progression such as that in bars 25 to 28 of Rovetta's "Chi vuol haver felice e lieto il core."[5]

The second new stylistic characteristic introduced into madrigal settings, particularly after the mid 1620s, is the use of passages of arioso written in the suave triple-meter styles of the Venetian *bel canto* aria. Passages of this kind are found in settings by Galeazzo Sabbatini and Giovanni Rovetta and in the later books of Martino Pesenti. They can be quite extended, as in bars 29-63 of Rovetta's "Chi vuol haver felice e lieto il core."[6] Here, two lines of text are repeated several times to form a large structural unit. Nevertheless, this passage of aria writing is still being used in a "madrigalian" fashion: that is, it is being used to highlight the meaning of a particular portion of text; it is not yet being used in response to a structural change in the text of the kind that we find in cantatas.

Although a study of the *concertato* duet after 1643 would still have to take account of duets appearing in printed sources, the apparent decline of the printed book as a source for vocal music during the 1640s means that manuscripts become correspondingly more important as source material. Since the majority of mid-century manuscripts represent the work of Roman-trained composers, it is to Rome that we have to look as the main center of duet writing during this period.

A number of the manuscripts can be dated, but the material that they contain is much less easy to date. In the case of a few of Carissimi's cantatas, a *terminus* can be established by means of references found in letters and theoretical treatises: for the majority of Roman cantatas, however, the only *terminus* is the date of the composer's death. Nevertheless, given the birth dates of Rossi (c. 1597) and Carissimi (1605) and the knowledge that we have of their careers it seems probable that their earliest cantatas belong to the 1620s. We know from the small number of Roman prints of the 1620s that duets were being written at Rome and it may well be that the printed sources form only the tip of the iceberg.

The evidence of the printed sources suggests that Roman composers were particularly interested in writing strophic duets. This bias is also reflected in the output of Luigi Rossi. A study of his work, together with that of Carissimi and Cesti, suggests that the composite duet cantata of the late seventeenth century evolved from the aria rather than the madrigal. Of the sixty-five duets attributed to Rossi by Caluori,[7] more than two thirds are strophic arias and the majority of the remainder betray their relationship to strophic arias by their clear-cut repetition patterns.

Most of Rossi's cantatas belong to the group that Caluori terms *ariette corte* and divides into four formal categories:

1. *Binary cantatas.* Forty-six duets fall into this category and all are strophic arias. They have the same bipartite structure (A:B, with or without repetition of the second section) that characterizes many of the strophic duets discussed earlier in this study.
2. *Rounded binary cantatas.* These have the design Ax:Bx (repeated), in which x is a refrain. Only two of Rossi's duets—"Ho perso il mio core" and "Risolvetevi, o martiri"—fall into this category. Both have two stanzas.
3. *Ternary cantatas.* These have the design A:B:A. Four of Rossi's duets fall into this category and all have only one stanza in the surviving sources.
4. *Rondo cantatas.* These have the design A:b:A:b:A, where A is a unit whose text and music is repeated, and b a unit whose music is repeated with a new text. Some cantatas of this kind have the unique combination of ariette, recitatives, recitative-aria pairs, and strophes of octosyllables or hexasyllables "in aria," or combinations of all, or any three or two. There is no a priori formal design.[8]

None of Rossi's own *arie di più parti* is available to me, and Venables does not discuss them in detail. We can, however, study two stages in the development of this type of cantata in the work of Carissimi and his younger, though shorter-lived, contemporary, Antonio Cesti.

Whereas Rossi's duets form almost a quarter of his output of cantatas, Carissimi's eighteen duets constitute only about one sixth of the total. Of these eighteen, only half are simple strophic arias. The remainder are more complex structures, though some, like "Peregrin d'ignote sponde," correspond to Caluori's "rounded binary" form, and others, like "Il mio core è un mar di pianti,"[9] have a rondo design—xAx:Bx:C:xAx. "Ahi, non torna"[10] seems to conform, broadly speaking, to Caluori's description of an *aria di più parti*. The structure of the verse which it sets is particularly interesting since it demonstrates Chiabrera's legacy to the later seventeenth century. It is apparently constructed in three irregular stanzas. The first two are variants of Chiabrera's own rhythmic designs:

Stanza 1—8:4:8:8:8:8
Stanza 2—8:4:8:4:8:8

The third is a much more complex metric structure. Stanza 1 is set for soprano in the form A (triple-meter arioso): B (three bars of recitative):A[1]. Stanza 2 is set for soprano II in a duple-meter arioso. And the third stanza is set as a triple-meter duet. The introduction of recitative is in no way related to the structure of the text. It is used simply to highlight the change from statement to question in the fourth line of the first stanza:

[arioso]	Ahi, non torna, ed io mi moro,
	Quel tesoro,
	Che stancato ha i miei sospiri.
[recit.]	Quando fia, ch'io più ti miri,
[arioso]	Fuggitivo mio ristoro?
	Ahi, non torna, ed io mi moro.

Carissimi's cantata is, in essence, a sectional aria, and this is emphasized by the predominantly arioso style of the musical setting. As in settings of Chiabrera's poetry, the irregular line lengths of Carissimi's text provided him with interesting rhythmic patterns which he could either match or disguise in the phrase structure of the setting. There is no question of differences in line length suggesting musical contrasts.

If, however, we turn to Cesti's "Pria ch'adori,"[11] one of the composer's seven surviving duets, we can see the decisive change which transforms the *aria di più parti* into the composite cantata of the late seventeenth century, for here the text itself provides clear opportunities for the contrast of recitative and aria.

The poet is Giovanni Lotti and the text of "Pria ch'adori" was later published in his *Poesie latine e toscane*[12] where its origins as *poesia per musica* are demonstrated by the rubric "aria" which heads certain passages of the poem. The text is some seventy-six lines long—much longer than "Ahi, non torna"— and it is quite obviously divided, in terms of sense and structure, into recitatives, which are cast in *endecasillabi* and *settenari,* and arias, which are cast in *versi parisillabi,* usually *ottonari.* The cantata (or "canzonetta" as Lotti called it) begins, in fact, with four stanzas in regular *ottonari,* unified by a one-line refrain.

Cesti follows these recitative-aria divisions faithfully in his musical setting and deviates from the plan suggested by the poet only in setting as arioso the occasional *endecasillabo* occurring at the end of a paragraph of recitative. He sets the recitatives, and some of the arias, for solo voice, thus anticipating the structural methods of a composer like Agostino Steffani. In this work we reach the end of a line of development which began with the canzonettas of Chiabrera: for here the canzonetta has become the cantata.

Given Carissimi's penchant for writing oratorios, it is not, perhaps, surprising to find that he was also interested in setting secular dialogue texts. Nine such settings survive. One of them—"Alma, che fai?" (Alma, Corpo)— which was written before 1642, is spiritual rather than secular in content and is unusual in Carissimi's output in being scored for soprano and bass, while all his other dialogue settings are scored for two sopranos. Of the other settings, only two depart from the usual pastoral idiom. These are "Per mille colpe" (Pietà, Amor) of 1662, to a text by Domenico Benigni, and the most famous of the secular dialogues, "A piè d'un verde alloro," a dialogue between the two philosophers Democritus and Heraclitus in which the contrast of major and minor modes is used to represent love as a matter for "laughter" and "weeping." Carissimi's secular dialogues do not differ substantially in form or style from the Venetian dialogues of the late 1630s as represented in the work of Fontei. In terms of style, they are characterized by the alternation of recitative and passages of triple-meter arioso. In terms of form, they vary from a simple alternation of voices, as in "Io corro alle sventure" (Tirsi, Filli) of 1646, through the use of alternating passages of dialogue and duet, as in "Stelle, chi fu" (Silvio, Fileno), to more complex structures in which composite solos alternate with duet sections of narration and commentary, as in "A piè d'un verde alloro."

In comparison with this large corpus of dialogues, Antonio Cesti apparently wrote only one—"L'amoroso veleno"—and even the prolific Luigi Rossi can boast only three surviving dialogues—"Infelice pensier" (Pensiero and Amante; two sopranos), the serenata "Horche notte guerriera" (Fortuna, Amore, Amante; two sopranos and tenor), which includes a *sinfonia* for two violins, and "Rugge, quasi Leon" (Testo, Mustafà, Baiazet; three sopranos).

This last, however, is of particular interest since it appears to deal with an historical event—the murder, in 1635, of Orchan and Baiazet, the brothers of Amurath IV of Turkey.

The dialogues of Carissimi seem to be among the last settings of Italian texts to be designated *dialogo* in musical sources, for by the late seventeenth century the term had been largely displaced by the all-embracing designation *cantata*. Nevertheless, a continuing tradition of Italian dialogue settings can be traced during the late seventeenth and early eighteenth centuries in the work of composers like Stradella and Alessandro Scarlatti, and it includes Handel's pastoral and mythological dialogue-cantatas, of which "La terra è liberata" *(Apollo e Dafne)* is perhaps the finest example.

Notes

Chapter 1

1. The term *concertato* is used here, and throughout this study, in the sense in which it was understood and employed in early seventeenth-century Italy: that is, to indicate a type of music in which voices and instruments played together. The *concertato* instrument might be simply the one employed to realize the continuo line, but the term also embraced violins or other melody instruments employed in addition to the continuo. The use of the term by later composers, theorists, and historians, to denote music in which different forces opposed each other (from the Latin "concertare", to fight, to dispute) was certainly sanctioned in the early seventeenth century by Michael Praetorius (*Syntagma Musicum,* iii, Wolfenbüttel, 1619, sig. A2v)—"CANTIO, CONCENTUS, seu Symphonia, est diversarum vocum modulatio. Italis vocatur Concetto vel Concerto, quod Latinis est Concertatio, qua Variae Voces aut Instrumenta Musica ad concertum faciendum committuntur: Suavitas enim non tàm in artificio, quàm in ipsa variatione consistit: Germanicé *ein Concert*"—but he may well have been misled by the word-play in Ercole Bottrigari's *Il Desiderio,* Venice, 1594 (see C.V. Palisca, *Baroque Music,* Englewood Cliffs, 1968, pp. 63-65). Italian composers of the early seventeenth century, as of the late sixteenth, followed the meaning of their own native verb "concertare", to concert, to agree, i.e. to sound together.

2. This designation is used to indicate dialogue settings in which the roles of the dialogue are sung by solo voices with continuo accompaniment, or with continuo and *concertato* instruments.

3. Se nel cantare alcuni di questi miei Madrigali incontrarete alcune spaccature, sappiate, che ciò s'e fatto obedire alli giusti ordini de Superiori, quali per ogni buon rispetto, non permettono in stampa alcune parole, che alle volte hanno alquanto del sensuale: come bacio, Dio applicato all'amore mondano, & simili; il che dalla conseguenza del testo potrete facilmente raccogliere.

4. For a discussion of the term "cantata" and a survey of its use during the seventeenth century see Gloria Rose, "The Cantatas of Carissimi," diss., Yale U., 1960, pp. 22-25. Rose's conclusion, that "cantata" should be used as a general designation for Italian (or Italianate) vocal music for solo voice or small ensemble and continuo written during the baroque period has, more recently, been confirmed in Eleanor Caluori Venables, "The Cantatas of Luigi Rossi," Ann Arbor, 1972. For a fuller discussion of the development of the cantata, see Gloria Rose, "The Italian Cantata of the Baroque Period," *Gattungen der Musik in Einzeldarstellungen: Gedenkschrift Leo Schrade,* ed. W. Aarlt, E. Lichtenhahn, H. Oesch, M. Haas, 2 vols., Bern, 1973, i, pp. 655-77.

5. See O. Cametti, "Orazio Michi 'dell'Arpa,' virtuoso e compositore della prima metà del seicento," *RMI*, xxi (1914), pp. 203-77. The secular duet "Ho perso il mio core" reprinted in *L'Arte Musicale in Italia*, v. 113-116 is, in fact, a *contrafactum* of the spiritual trio "Afflitto mio core" (see Cametti, op. cit., p. 232).

6. G. Rose, op. cit.; E. Caluori Venables, op. cit.; I. Eisley, "The Secular Cantatas of Mario Savioni (1608-1685)," diss., U. of California at Los Angeles, 1964.

7. *G.F. Händel*, 2 vols., Leipzig, 1858, i., pp. 326-36. The designation "chamber duet" seems to have been first employed on the title page of Maurizio Cazzati's *Duetti per Camera*, Bologna, 1677; and, indeed, the term "duet" seems to have come into use only with the *Cantate Ariette, a Duetti*, Venice, 1651, of the Venetian singer-composer Barbara Strozzi. Eitner, *Quellen-Lexikon*, cited a volume by Corradini—*Arie, Duetti, Terzetti*, Venice, 1616—but I have been unable to locate the work. It may, in fact, be none other than Flamminio Corradi's *Le Stravaganze d'Amore* (1616). The late genesis of the designation "chamber duet" does not, of course, preclude its use with regard to early seventeenth-century duets, but the designation "secular *concertato* duet" has been preferred here as a more precise indication of the field covered.

8. A. Steffani, *Ausgewählte Werke . . . Erste Teil*, ed. A. Einstein and A. Sandberger (*DTB*, 6:ii), Leipzig, 1905.

9. E. Schmitz, "Zur Geschichte des italienischen Kammerduetts im 17. Jahrhundert," *JMP*, xxiii (1916), pp. 43-60.

10. A.W. Ambros, *Geschichte der Musik*, iv, 3rd edn, rev. H. Leichtentritt, Leipzig, 1909, pp. 789, 804-5, 874-75, 868, and 848 respectively.

11. H. Riemann, *Handbuch der Musikgeschichte*, ii, 2, Leipzig, 1912, pp. 33 and 299-304 respectively.

12. E. Schmitz, "Kammerduetts," particularly pp. 47-48.

13. E. Schmitz, "Zur Frühgeschichte des lyrischen Monodie Italiens im 17. Jahrhundert," *JMP*, xviii (1911), particularly pp. 45ff.

14. E. Schmitz, *Geschichte der weltlichen Solokantate*, 2nd edn, Leipzig, 1955, particularly pp. 64-65.

15. E. Schmitz, "Zur Geschichte des italienischen Continuo-Madrigals im 17. Jahrhundert," *SIMG*, xi (1909-1910), pp. 509-28.

16. J. Racek, *Stilprobleme der italienischen Monodie*, Prague, 1965.

17. W. Witzenmann, "Domenico Mazzocchi, 1592-1665: Dokumente und Interpretationen," *An Mus*, viii (1970), particularly pp. 144-56.

18. C. Gallico, "Musicalità di Domenico Mazzocchi: 'Olindo e Sofronia' dal Tasso," *Chigiana*, xxii (1965), pp. 59-74.

19. E. Ferrari Barassi, "Tarquinio Merula e il dialogo di 'Satiro e Corisca,' " *Anuario musical*, xxvii (1972), pp. 131-46, and " 'La Luciata' di Francesco Manelli . . . e un componimento del 'Fasolo,' " *Secondo incontro con la musica italiana e polacca (Miscellanee saggi convegni*, viii), ed. G. Vecchi, Bologna, 1974, pp. 211-42.

Chapter 2

1. Printed in A. Solerti, *Le origini del melodramma*, Turin, 1903, pp. 103-28. The translation of

the passage quoted is adapted from C. MacClintock, "Giustiniani's *Discorso sopra la musica," MD,* xv (1961), p. 216.

2. *Lettera a G.B. Doni,* trans. in O. Strunk, *Source Readings in Music History,* New York, 1950, pp. 363-66.

3. See L. Bianconi & T. Walker, "Dalla *Finta pazza* alla *Veremonda:* storie di Febiarmonici," *RIM,* x (1975), pp. 379-454.

4. Volume 2, no. 40.

5. Ibid., no. 13.

6. *Tutte le Opere,* ed. G.F. Malipiero, ix, p. 32.

7. See, for example, "Cantai un tempo," bars 2-3, "Alma mia, dove ten vai?," bars 2 and 4 , "O vita nostra," bars 1 and 3, in Marco da Gagliano, *Music for One, Two and Three Voices,* ed. P. Aldrich, i, pp. 2, 9, 20. In his edition, Professor Aldrich treats these and other similar dissonances as notes requiring a change of harmony over a pedal. This is not, I think, what the composer intended. The $6/4$-$5/3$ seems to have been the only progression of this type used in the early seventeenth century.

8. Solerti, *Origini,* p. 110.

9. See H. Mayer Brown, "The Geography of Florentine Monody: Caccini at home and abroad," *Early Music,* ix (1981), pp. 147-68.

10. Ibid.; but see also H. Wiley Hitchcock, "Vocal Ornamentation in Caccini's *Nuove Musiche," MQ,* lvi (1970), pp. 389-404; idem, "Caccini's 'Other' *Nuove Musiche,"JAMS,* xxvii (1974), pp. 438-60; and Professor Hitchcock's editions of Caccini's *Le Nuove Musiche,* Madison, 1970, and *Nuove Musiche e nuova maniera di scriverle (1614),* Madison, 1978. For Caccini's visits to Ferrara, where he instructed the Ferrarese singing ladies in his new manner of ornamentation, see A. Newcomb, *The Madrigal at Ferrara,* 2 vols., Princeton, 1980, i, pp. 51, 58, 202.

11. See W.V. Porter, "The Origins of the Baroque Solo Song: a study of Italian manuscripts and prints from 1590-1610," 2 vols., diss., Yale U., 1962.

12. See the list published in N. Fortune, "A Handlist of Printed Italian Secular Monody Books, 1602-1635," *R.M.A. Research Chronicle,* iii (1963), pp. 27-50.

13. For a recent discussion of the use of the *basso continuo* in sacred music in the early seventeenth century, see I. Horsley, "Full and Short Scores in the Accompaniment of Italian Church Music in the Early Baroque," *JAMS,* xxx (1977), pp. 466-99.

14. See J. Roche, "The Duet in Early Seventeenth-Century Italian Church Music," *PRMA,* xciii (1966-67), p. 33.

15. G. Dixon, "Progressive Tendencies in the Roman Motet during the Early Seventeenth Century," *Acta,* liii (1981), pp. 109, 111.

16. Roche, "Duet," pp. 44-46.

17. In Sigismondo d'India, *Il Primo Libro di Musiche da cantar solo,* ed. F. Mompellio (*Athenaeum cremonese,* ser. 1, 4), Cremona, 1970, pp. 142-49.

18. Rossi's first book of five-part madrigals (Venice, 1600) also contains madrigals to be sung to the accompaniment of a chitarrone, though the instrumental part is written in tablature. See E. Vogel, *Bibliothek,* rev. Einstein, ii, pp. 161-62.

19.   G. Rose, "Polyphonic Italian Madrigals of the Seventeenth Century," *ML,* xlvii (1966), pp. 153-59.

20.   For Nenna, see Vogel, *Bibliothek,* rev. Einstein, ii, pp. 18-19; for Monteverdi, see ibid., i, pp. 504, 506. The so-called *basso continuo* added to Monteverdi's books is what we would now term a *basso seguente.*

21.   A notable early exception is G.F. Anerio's *Recreatione armonica* of 1611, which contains music for only one and two voices, but was published in part-books.

22.   On the continued cultivation of the polyphonic madrigal at Florence during the early seventeenth century, see D.S. Butchart, "The Madrigal in Florence, 1560-1630," 2 vols., diss., U. of Oxford, 1979, and E. Strainchamps, "New Light on the Accademia degli Elevati of Florence," *MQ,* lxii (1976), pp. 507-35.

23.   The few ensemble pieces formerly attributed to Caccini were included in the *Fuggilotio Musicale* (Venice, 1613) of "Giulio Romano." These are no longer thought to be by Caccini; see Hitchcock, "Depriving Caccini of a Musical Pastime," *JAMS,* xxv (1972), pp. 58-78, in which the case against attributing the volume to Caccini is convincingly argued. Nevertheless, Caccini's contemporary Antonio Brunelli credited him with having written music for more than one voice (see Hitchcock, "A New Biographical Source," p. 146); and since, according to Newcomb (*Madrigal,* i, pp. 90-91) Caccini was in charge of a Florentine *concerto delle donne* based on the Ferrarese model, he would certainly have had ample opportunity for composing ensemble music. All that survive, however, are the ensembles of Caccini's *Euridice* and *Il Rapimento di Cefalo* and a manuscript collection of three-part *villanelle* of doubtful authenticity (see Hitchcock, "A New Biographical Source," p. 146).

24.   Of the monodists represented in Fortune, "Handlist," only Capello, Francesco Costa, Francesco Gonzaga, Miniscalchi, Puliaschi, and Puliti published solo songs only. Benedetti, Landi, and Saracini, however, published very few ensemble pieces.

25.   The choice of format between score (monody book) and part-books (madrigal book) seems to have been determined mainly by the relative numbers of solo songs and ensemble pieces included in each collection, and hence by considerations of cost and convenience as far as the performers were concerned. In several instances when solo songs were issued as part of a madrigal collection—in Franzoni's *Fioretti Musicali... Libro Terzo* (1617), Rovetta's *Madrigali concertati... Libro Primo* (1629), and Merula's *Madrigali... Libro Secondo* (1633), for example—they were also printed in score in one of the part-books.

26.   *Pace* Fortune, "Handlist," p. 36, the *Concerti... Op. 2* (1617) of the Ferrarese composer Milleville contains only sacred settings in Latin. Following Andrea Gabrieli's *Concerti* of 1587 and Viadana's *Cento Concerti ecclesiastici* of 1602, the term *concerto* had been used as a title only for volumes of sacred music. Following the publication of Bernardi's *Concerti academici* (1615/16) and Monteverdi's seventh book of madrigals, however, it also became a commonplace on the title page of secular publications: Robletti (ed.), *Raccolta de varii Concerti* (1621); Giovanni Steffani (ed.), *Concerti amorosi* (1623); Marastone (1624); Bellante (1629); Vitali (1629); Arrigoni (1635); Laurenzi (1641); Spighi (1641); Bettino (1643). The phrase *madrigali in concerto* also enjoyed a limited vogue. Derived, perhaps, from the title page of Salamone Rossi's second book of madrigals, it was also used by Milleville for his *Il Primo Libro de Madrigali in Concerto,* op. 3 (1617), a semi-dramatic entertainment for the marriage of Count Vincenzo Cantalmai, and by Pasta (1626) and Tarditi (1633).

27.   Trans. Strunk, *Source Readings,* pp. 311-12.

28.   Ed. Fano. The two madrigals cited are found on pp. 113-16 and 154-56 respectively.

29. The 1610 book also includes one piece for solo voice and one for four voices.

30. It is possible that Floriano de' Magri's *Canzonette, Villanelle et Arie... Libro Primo* (1611) should be included in this list; It was, however, issued in part-books, of which only the bass survives. I have been unable to consult this volume and thus cannot be certain of what it contains.

31. The claim that the lawyer [and possibly professional singer: see G. Casali, "La cappella musicale della Cattedrale di Reggio Emilia all'epoca di Aurelio Signoretti (1567-1631)," *RIM*, viii (1973), p. 197] Domenico Maria Melli was the first composer to publish duets rests on the two recitative-dialogues for two voices that he published in his *Seconde Musiche* (1602). The 1603 and 1609 reprints of his first book of *Musiche* (also 1602) advertise: "...Nelle quali si contengono Madrigali, et Arie a una & due voci." Neither they, nor the original printing, however, contain anything but music for solo voice and continuo. *Le Seconde Musiche*, which has the same wording on its title page, contains, in addition to solo songs, only the two dialogues. Schmitz's assertion that the volume included music for two *and more* voices [my italics] ("Kammerduetts," p. 43) is, therefore, unfounded.

32. See above, n. 24.

33. ...per comodità alcuna volta de pochi cantori.

34. For a discussion of these duets, see pp. 97-98.

35. Volume 2, no. 4; for the use of borrowed material in this duet, see p. 77.

36. See appendix, volume 2, nos. 314, 313, 315, 316.

37. *I-Fl*, Buonarotti, 46, n. 686; transcribed in T. Carter, "Jacopo Peri (1561-1623): his life and works," 2 vols., diss., U. of Birmingham, 1980, i, p. 330: Gia credevo essere in Fiorenza dove avrei potuto servire i miei patroni conforme all'obligho mio, ma poi, che queste Altezze si sono compiaciute ch'io le serva in queste nozze e no[n] è valsuto addurre scusa nessuna no[n] o volsuto mancare di darli conto del tutto e come l'Ill[ustrissi]mo S[ignor] Car[dina]le a scritto al S[ignor] Jacopo Peri con pregarlo che voglia per me esercitare le mie Musiche p[er] una voce per due e per tre....

38. See p. 100.

39. N. Fortune, "Italian Secular Monody from 1600 to 1635: an introductory survey," *MQ*, xxxix (1953), p. 175.

40. See below, pp. 178-80.

41. *Prima parte de' discorsi e regole sovra la musica*, trans. G. Rose, "Polyphonic Italian Madrigals," p. 153.

Chapter 3

1. For the texts whose poet I have managed to identify see the appendix, volume 2, from which it will be apparent that much work still remains to be done in this area. It is, however, a worthwhile task, and one that can sometimes throw new light on the work of individual composers or groups of composers. See, for example, S. Leopold, "Madrigali sulle egloghe sdrucciole di Iacopo Sannazaro. Struttura poetica e forma musicale," *RIM*, xiv (1979), pp. 75-127, and J. Chater, "Castelletti's 'Stravaganze d'Amore'(1585): a comedy with interludes," *Studi musicali*, viii (1979), pp. 85-148.

2. Francesco Rasi, *La cetra di sette corde*, Venice, 1619; Benedetto Ferrari, *Poesie*, Piacenza, 1651.

3. See A. Einstein, "Italian Madrigal Verse," *PRMA,* lxiii (1936/7), pp. 79-95.

4. J.V. Mirollo, *The Poet of the Marvelous: Giambattista Marino,* New York, 1963, p. 103.

5. A. Einstein, "Italian Madrigal Verse," p. 82.

6. Much of the technical information given in this section is derived from W. Theodor Elwert, *Italienische Metrik,* Munich, 1968; 2nd edn as *Versificazione italiana dalle origini ai giorni nostri,* Florence, 1973, reprinted 1976.

7. Elwert, op. cit., p. 29.

8. *Versificazione,* pp. 8-18. *Dieresi* is, of course, never used when the letter *i* is employed simply as a diacritical sign indicating the softening of the preceding consonant, as in the words *cielo, giardino.*

9. For a fuller exposition of this rule, see Elwert, op cit., p. 15.

10. Elwert, op. cit., p. 35.

11. Ibid., p. 39.

12. See Elwert, op. cit., pp. 79-81.

13. Dante, *De Vulgari Eloquentia,* trans. A.G. Ferrers Howell, London, 1904, pp. 81-83: ... sed nullum adhuc invenimus in carmen sillabicando endecadem transcendisse, nec a trisillabo descendisse. Et licet trisillabo carmine atque endecasillabo et omnibus intermediis cantores Latii usi sint, pentasillabum, eptasillabum et endecasillabum in usu frequentiori habentur; et post hec trisillabum ante alia. Quorum omnium endecasillabum videtur esse superbius, tam temporis occupatione, quam capacitate sententie, constructionis et vocabularum;... Et dicimus eptasillabum sequi illud quod maximum est in celebritate. Post hoc pentasillabum et deinde trisillabum ordinamus. Neasillabum vero, quia triplicatum trisillabum videbatur, vel nunquam in honore fuit, vel propter fastidium absolevit. Parisillaba vero propter sui ruditatem non utimur nisi raro;....

14. Examples from Elwert, *Versificazione,* pp. 60-61. The accents are indicated by showing the number of the syllable on which they fall.

15. The *capitolo,* the form in which Petrarch's *Trionfi* are written, consists of a sequence of *terzine* rounded off by a single line rhyming with the middle line of the last *terzina.*

16. E. Williamson, *Bernardo Tasso,* Rome, 1951, pp. 46-49.

17. Trans. Einstein, *The Italian Madrigal,* i, pp. 209-210: grandissimo artificio, affine che soddisfacciano al mondo, perche etiando, ch'io non habbia giudizio di musica, ho almeno giudizio di conoscer quali debbiano esser le composizioni che si fanno per cantare. Elle son piene di purità, d'affetti amorosi, di colori, et di figure accomodate a l'armonia.

18. Ibid., i, pp. 97-104.

19. Ibid., i, p. 103.

20. E. Hatch Wilkins, *A History of Italian Literature,* rev. T.G. Bergin, Cambridge Mass., 1974, p. 179.

21. See Elwert, *Versificazione,* p. 136.

22. Wilkins, op. cit., p. 181.

23. A. Einstein, *Italian Madrigal,* i, p. 174.

24. See the examples quoted in R. Spongano, *Nozioni ed Esempi di Metrica Italiana*, Bologna, 1966, pp. 193-95.

25. See, for example, the *villanella* written in regular *ottonari* quoted in Einstein, *The Italian Madrigal*, ii, pp. 582-83.

26. For a *villanella* employing *quinari*, see ibid., ii, pp. 588-89.

27. Ibid., iii, pp. 56-58.

28. See the list of settings in S. Leopold, "Madrigali," p. 103.

29. Volume 2, no. 21.

30. A. Adami, *Osservazioni, per ben regolare il coro della cappella pontificia*, Rome, 1711, pp. 191-92.

31. In the earlier of these two publications, the first pair of texts were described, incorrectly, as sonnets.

32. Mentioned in the dedication to *Euridice* and the preface to *Le Nuove Musiche*.

33. *Jerusalem Delivered*, trans. Edward Fairfax, ed. H. Morley, London, 1890, p. 94.

34. See volume 2, no. 32.

35. Volume 2, no. 33.

36. Reprinted in *La Flora*, iii, pp. 86-87.

37. Ottavas apart, I have found only one text by Guarini, the *canzone* "Vivo in foco amoroso" (Rovetta, 1629) and two by Marino, "Silenzio, o Fauni" (Valentini, 1621) and "Beviam tutti, io, beo, tu bei" (Valentini, 1622) from the mythological idyll *Arianna*, which were set as arias during the period.

38. Volume 2, no. 8. A similar theme, less powerfully expressed and more diffuse, may be seen in Galeazzo Sabbatini's madrigal "Udite, O selve" (volume 2, no 18). In view of its length, the text of Sabbatini's setting may well have been taken from a pastoral play, though its authorship is unknown to me. It was not taken from the plays of Tasso or Guarini, nor from Guidobaldo de' Bonarellis *La Filli di Sciro*, Venice, 1607.

39. See Volume 2, no. 9.

40. Ibid., no. 6.

41. Ibid., no. 11.

42. Ibid., no. 16.

43. Cassola's madrigal is quoted above, p. 27.

44. Volume 2, no. 11.

45. Ibid., no. 12.

46. Mirollo, *The Poet of the Marvelous*, p. 86.

47. Ibid., p. 25.

48. The first part of *La Lira* was devoted entirely to sonnets, the second part to madrigals and *canzoni*. The third part, which included all three verse types, was published in 1614 after Marino's release from prison in Turin.

49. Trans. Mirollo, *The Poet of the Marvelous,* p. 127.

50. Volume 2, no. 13.

51. Ibid., no. 23.

52. Adapted from the translation in Mirollo, op. cit., p. 145.

53. Volume 2, no. 22. The sonnets "La vè quel monte" (Biagio Marini, 1635) and "Un rio qui gorgogliando" (Priuli, 1622; B. Marini, 1635) by the Marinist poet Girolamo Preti (1582-1626) are in a similarly graceful, pastoral vein, and the latter contains many pictorial images of the kind that one generally associates with the madrigal verse of the late sixteenth century.

54. Volume 2, no. 12.

55. Mirollo, *The Poet of the Marvelous,* p. 23.

56. Possenti clearly borrowed the title of his publication from that of Marino's collection. Apart from Arianna's lament, he also included in the same book a setting for accompanied solo voice of stanzas 4-10 and 80 of the pastoral idyll *I Sospiri d'Ergasto.* None of the duets in the volume, however, seem to have been drawn from *La Sampogna,* though there is a two-part setting of an anonymous *Lamento di Leandro Pastore.*

57. Volume 2, no. 19.

58. Adapted from the translation in Mirollo, *The Poet of the Marvelous,* p. 80.

59. Volume 2, no. 38.

60. Ibid., no. 5.

61. First stanza only.

62. Translated in *La Flora,* ed. Jeppesen, iii, p. 24.

63. Volume 2, no. 29.

64. Ibid., no. 27.

65. F.L. Mannucci, *La Lirica di Gabriello Chiabrera: storia e caratteri,* Naples, 1925, p. 122.

66. F. Neri, *Il Chiabrera e la Pleiade francese,* Turin, 1920, p. 51.

67. Strophic texts using Chiabrera's new metric schemes were called *scherzi* as early as 1601 by Isabella Andreini (*Rime,* Milan, 1601). In all probability Monteverdi (or his brother Giulio Cesare, who collected the *Scherzi musicali* for publication) simply borrowed the term from current poetic usage.

68. For a complete list of these schemes see Elwert, *Versificazione,* pp. 158-59.

69. Neri, *Chiabrera,* pp. 53-57.

70. Volume 2, no. 30.

71. Cf. Fortune, "Solo Song," p. 167.

72. The composers Ghizzolo (1610) and Capece (1625) began their settings of this canzonetta with the second stanza, "Vaghe faville."

73. See volume 2, no. 35.

74. Reprinted in *La Flora,* ed. Jeppesen, pp. 91-93. Jeppesen printed only two of the six stanzas that Sances set.

75.　See volume 2, nos. 4 and 5.

76.　Ibid., no. 31.

77.　This text seems to have been imitated by the Florentine courtier Ferdinando Saracinelli in his canzonetta "Alma mia, deh che farai?," which was set as a duet by Brunelli (1614) and Calestani (1617).

78.　Volume 2, no. 26.

79.　Ibid., no. 10.

80.　A. Einstein, "Italian Madrigal Verse," p. 93.

Chapter 4

1.　I have omitted from this list one publication issued outside Italy—the *Bicinia, sive cantiones suavissime duarum vocum*, printed in 1590 by the Flemish publisher Phalèse—which includes madrigals reprinted from the volumes of Gero and Asola as well as Italian settings by Andrè Pevernage and Cornelius Verdonch. Also omitted is the manuscript collection of *Madrigali a due voci di Pomponio Nenna di Bari Primo Libro*, 1630 (*I-Vnm*, Cod. It. IV. 723), dedicated to Martio Colonna, Duke of Zazarolo. I have been unable to consult this volume and cannot be sure whether it contains only unaccompanied duos. Since Nenna died before 22 October 1613, 1630 must be the date of compilation of the manuscript. Phalèse included a textless duo by Nenna in his *Bicinia* (it is reprinted in *Invitation to Madrigals*, iv, ed. Thurston Dart, London, n.d., pp. 52-53), but I can trace no sixteenth-century source for any of his two-part madrigals; nor have I been able to find any further information relating to them.

2.　The first extant printing of this volume, dating from 1526, was not known to Einstein when he revised Vogel's *Bibliothek;* the earliest printing that he listed dates from 1531. The 1526 printing may itself, however, have been reprinted from a lost first edition of 1523: see *Eustachio Romano, Musica Duorum*, Rome, 1521, ed. H.T. David, H. Mayer Brown, E. Lowinsky (*Monuments of Renaissance Music*, vi), Chicago, 1975, p. 7.

3.　Festa's madrigal is transcribed in *L'Arte Musicale in Italia*, ed. L. Torchi, 7 vols., Milan, 1897-1908, i, pp. 53-54.

4.　There is an apparent contradiction here. The printing issued by Gardane in 1541 advertises Gero's madrigals as newly composed, but it contains a dedication signed by another Venetian publisher, Girolamo Scotto, who stated that Gero's duos had been composed at his (Scotto's) request. Bianconi, in "Weitere Ergänzungen zu Emil Vogels 'Bibliothek der gedruckten weltlichen Vocalmusik Italiens, aus den Jahren 1500-1700' II. Folge," *An Mus*, xii (1973), p. 162, mentioned a copy of a single part-book of Gero's duos in Palermo, Biblioteca Nazionale, whose title page bears neither date nor printer's name. He argued that since this was bound with two Gardane prints of 1539 it probably represented an edition dating from before 1541. Carapezza, in *Musiche Strumentali Didattiche (Musiche Rinascimentali Siciliane*, ii), Rome, 1971, p. xxxiii, went one stage further and suggested that this printing was issued by Scotto himself in 1539/40. Doubt has recently been cast on this early dating in Ihan Gero, *Il Primo Libro de' Madrigali italiani et Canzoni francese a due voci*, ed. L.F. Bernstein and J. Haar, New York, 1980, pp. xxv-xxvi. Bernstein and Haar suggest that the Palermo copy was published between 1541 and 1543.

5.　Not a new setting by Gero as Vogel thought (*Bibliothek*, i. 285).

6. Two madrigals edited by R. Bartoli in *Composizioni Vocali Polifoniche a due, tre e quattro voci sole dei secoli XVI e XVII,* Milan, 1917, pp. 38-42.

7. Present location unknown; formerly in Celle, Kirchen- und Ministerialbibliothek.

8. Copy formerly in Berlin, Staatsbibliothek, but destroyed during the Second World War: see D. Kämper, "Das Lehr- und Instrumentalduo um 1500 in Italien," *Mf,* xviii (1965), p. 249. Four of the madrigals are transcribed in Einstein, transcriptions, vol. lviii.

9. Two madrigals edited by R. Bartoli in *Composizioni Vocali Polifoniche,* pp. 34-37.

10. E. Vogel, *Bibliothek,* i, p. 45. Fourteen madrigals from Asola's volume are edited by R. Bartoli, op. cit., pp. 2-29.

11. Two madrigals edited by R. Bartoli, op. cit., pp. 30-33.

12. Einstein, *The Italian Madrigal,* i, pp. 140-43.

13. See the example printed in K. Jeppesen, *Die mehrstimmige italienische Laude um 1500,* Leipzig, 1935, p. xxii. Two-part *laudi* were also written during the sixteenth century: several were printed in Animuccia's *Secondo Libro delle Laudi,* Rome, 1570 and in the collection listed in Vogel, *Bibliothek,* rev. Einstein, as 1563[3]. Kämper, in "Das Lehr- und Instrumentalduo," p. 242, listed two duos with Italian incipits for titles—"O fonte de bellezze" and "Biancho ligiadro"—which form an appendix to the first book of *Musica Disciplina* by Ugolino de Orvieto. These are, however, textless duos.

14. L.F. Bernstein, "Cantus Firmus in the French Chanson for Two and Three Voices 1500-1550," diss., U. of New York, 1969, p. 147. See also Ihan Gero, *Il Primo Libro,* ed. Bernstein & Haar, pp. xxxv ff.

15. Edited in *Eustachio Romano.*

16. The text is printed in Einstein, *Italian Madrigal,* i, p. 143.

17. Ibid., i, p. 144.

18. *Le Istituzioni Armoniche,* 1558, bk. iii; see Strunk, *Source Readings,* p. 245.

19. See *Eustachio Romano,* p. 37.

20. *Thoscanello de la Musica,* 1523.

21. Dodecachordon, 1547.

22. Another is illustrated by Willaert's famous duo "Quid non ebrietas designat," written c. 1520, an exercise in chromaticism which apparently ends on the harmonic interval of a seventh; (see Kroyer, *Die Anfänge der Chromatik im italienischen Madrigal des XVI. Jahrhunderts,* Leipzig, 1902, pp. 29-35). As Lowinsky has shown, however, in "Adrian Willaert's Chromatic 'Duo' reexamined," *Tijdschrift voor Muziekwetenschap,* xviii (1956), pp. 1-36, the duo was, in fact, a reduction for illustrative purposes of a composition originally conceived for four voices.

23. For a fairly complete list of textless and instrumental duos of the sixteenth and seventeenth centuries see *Musiche Strumentali Didattiche,* pp. xxix-xxxii.

24. The term *bicinium* seems not, however, to have been used in Italy where, if more specific designations were not used, "musica" or "duo" were preferred. The north European penchant for the term led to its also being used for *concertato* music as, for example, on the title page of Giovanni Rovetta's *Bicinia Sacra,* issued by Phalèse in 1648.

25.   A. Einstein, "Vincenzo Galilei and the Instructive Duo," *ML,* xviii (1937), p. 367.

26.   Ibid., p. 363.

27.   *Eustachio Romano,* p. 31.

28.   *Pace* Einstein, "Vincenzo Galilei," pp. 363-64, both of Licino's books were originally issued with a separate "Resolutio," though that for the first book is now lost; see C. Sartori, *Bibliografia della Musica Strumentale Italiana Stampata in Italia fino al 1700 (Biblioteca di Bibliografia Italiana,* xxiii & lvi), 2 vols., Florence, 1952 & 1968, i, p. 12. The fourth canon of Licino's second book is reprinted in *Invitation to Madrigals,* iv, pp. 6-7.

29.   *Musica Strumentale Didattiche,* p. xxiii..

30.   Sartori, *Bibliografia,* i, p. 99.

31.   *Eustachio Romano,* p. 5.

32.   Idem.

33.   Trans. J. Haar, "*Pace non trovo:* A study in literary and musical parody," *MD,* xx (1966), p. 122.

34.   The long life of Gero's collection links it to three other duo publications first issued during the sixteenth century, all of which are more clearly didactic in intention. One of these was Gardane's *Canzoni francese a due voci* (Venice, 1539), which was reprinted until 1635 as well as being excerpted in Rhau's *Bicinia* and copied almost in its entirety into a German manuscript; see *Sixteenth-Century Bicinia: A Complete Edition of Munich, Bayerische Staatsbibliothek Mus. Ms. 260 (Recent Researches in the Music of the Renaissance,* xvi & xvii), ed. B. Bellingham and E.G. Evans Jr., Madison, 1974. The other two were both collections of textless duos. Grammatio Metallo's *Ricercari,* first published in 1591, were reprinted up to 1685; but the longest lived of all duo collections was the *Primo Libro a due voci* of Bernardino Lupacchino and Joan Maria Tasso, first printed in 1559 and subsequently reprinted no fewer than 22 times until 1701. Two works from this collection, one each by Tasso and Lupacchino, are edited in *Invitation to Madrigals,* iv, pp. 1 and 11 respectively.

35.   This is the earliest printing to survive, but it was itself a reprint of an earlier first edition of which the publisher and date are unknown.

36.   L.F. Bernstein, "Cantus Firmus", pp. 155-56 (Moderne, *Parangon,* Bk. iv), pp. 166-67 (Gardane), pp. 176-77 (Gero). For Gero, see also Ihan Gero, *Il Primo Libro,* ed. Bernstein & Haar.

37.   Bernstein, "Cantus Firmus", pp. 171-73.

38.   Ibid., pp. 165-71.

39.   J. Haar, "A Diatonic Duo by Willaert," *Tijdschrift van de Vereniging voor Nederlandse Musiekgeschiedenis,* xxi (1969), pp. 68-80.

40.   Ibid., p. 74.

41.   Ibid., p. 70.

42.   See Ihan Gero, *Il Primo Libro,* ed. Bernstein & Haar, p. xxxii.

43.   The texted duos in the 1565 reprint of Lupacchino & Tasso, *Il Primo Libro* are also based on madrigals from Arcadelt's first book: see T.W. Bridges, "Bernardo Lupacchino," *The New Grove,* xi, p. 334.

44. The duo has "pensassi," Berchem's setting "potessi." Berchem's setting may be found in Arcadelt, *Opera Omnia,* ed. A. Seay (*Corpus Mensurabilis Musicae,* xxxi), ii, pp. 84-86.

45. Arcadelt, *Opera Omnia,* vii, pp. 185-86.

46. Willaert, *Opera Omnia,* ed. H. Zenck, W. Gerstenberg, B. & H. Maier (*Corpus Mensurabilis Musicae,* iii), xiv, pp. 20-26.

47. In the section of his *Indice di tutte le Opere di Musica che si trovano nella stampa della Pigna,* Venice, 1621 devoted to music for two voices, Alessandro Vincenti included the following entry: "Di *Hippolito Sabino,* sopra i madrigali di Cipriano." This volume does not, however, seem to have survived, and is not mentioned in the article on Sabino by P.A. Myers in *The New Grove,* xvi, pp. 367-68.

48. Einstein, *Italian Madrigal,* ii, pp. 547-48.

49. The musical settings are not, however, related to those in Gabrieli's *Libro Primo de Madrigali a tre voci.*

50. *Pace* Fortune, "Solo Song and Cantata," p. 181, who implies that two-part canzonettas were written in the mid-sixteenth century.

51. The majority of the Petrarch settings are, however, textually incomplete. Several are settings of the octave of a sonnet only, others of the octave and first tercet.

52. As far as new collections are concerned, Gabriello Puliti's *Scherzi...a 2 voci* (1605), cited in Schmitz, "Kammerduetts," n. 2, is a collection of textless duos, though it is omitted from Carapezza's list in *Musiche Strumentale Didattiche.*

53. See *Musiche Strumentale Didattiche,* p. xxxi.

Chapter 5

1. N. Fortune, "Solo Song and Cantata," p. 181.

2. See H. Mayer Brown, *Sixteenth-Century Instrumentation: the music for the Florentine Intermedii* (*Musicological Studies and Documents,* xxx), [Rome], 1973, particularly pp. 11 and 81-82.

3. See G.L. Anderson, "The Canzonetta Publications of Simone Verovio, 1586-1595," diss., U. of Illinois, 1976.

4. Einstein, *Italian Madrigal,* ii, p. 780.

5. Ibid., ii, pp. 822-23.

6. See Emanuel Adriaenssen, *Pratum musicum longe amoenissimum, Antwerp, 1584,* facsimile reprint, with introduction by Kwee Him Yong, Buren, 1977. Although most of the madrigals are given in two parts only, all the vocal parts are supplied for the three- and four-part villanellas.

7. See above, p. 62.

8. Brown, *Sixteenth-Century Instrumentation,* p. 32.

9. Quoted in ibid., pp. 142-46.

10. See appendix, volume 2, no. 308.

11. See Jeffrey Kurtzman, "An Early 17th-Century Manuscript of *Canzonette e Madrigaletti spirituali,*" *Studi musicali,* viii (1979), pp. 153-54.

12. L. Schrade, *La Représentation d'Edipo Tiranno au Teatro Olimpico* Paris, 1969, p. 70.

13. Pirrotta, *Gli due Orfei*, pp. 228-29.

14. See Brown, *Sixteenth Century Instrumentation*, p. 102 for a conjectural reconstruction of the scoring.

15. Pirrotta, op. cit., pp. 209-10.

16. A. Solerti, "Le rappresentazioni musicali di Venezia 1571-1605," *RMI*, ix (1902), p. 557.

17. See D. Arnold, "Towards a Biography of Giovanni Gabrieli," *MD*, xv (1961), pp. 201-2. The madrigal is printed in Giovanni Gabrieli, *Opera Omnia*, vi, ed. D. Arnold (*Corpus Mensurabilis Musicae*, xii), pp. 162-70.

18. Although the musical procedures used in its setting involve dialogue-like interchanges, "O che felice giorno," like many of the works in Gardano's *Dialoghi*, is not a setting of a dialogue text.

19. Horsley, "Full and Short Scores," p. 468.

20. Trans. F.T. Arnold, *The Art of Accompaniment from a Thorough-Bass*, London, 1931, pp. 3-4.

21. A. Newcomb, *The Madrigal at Ferrara 1579-1597*, 2 vols., Princeton, 1980, i, pp. 58-59.

22. Trans. Einstein, *Italian Madrigal*, ii, pp. 828-29.

23. Newcomb, *Madrigal*, i, p. 14.

24. Einstein, op. cit., ii, p. 826 mentioned a report of February, 1581, in which ambassador Urbani spoke of Laura Peverara singing duets with Giulio Cesare Brancaccio. This seems, however, to be based on a misreading of Solerti, *Ferrara e la corte estense nella seconda metà del secolo XVI*, Città di Castello, 1899, p. cxxxvii. The relevant passage actually reads: Fin dal 1581 l'ambasciatore Urbani rilevava l'abilità di lei [Peverara]; ad esempio, il 13 febbraio diceva che in quel carnevale si era fatto: "sempre qualche trattenimento ritirato, e il più delle volte con la musica segreta che è di alcune dame di corte massime della Mantovana, che io scrissi altra volta e del signor Giulio Cesare Brancacci...."

25. Newcomb, *Madrigal*, i, p. 63.

26. Ibid., i, pp. 90ff.

27. See R. Gandolfi, "Lettere inedite scritte dai musicisti," *RMI*, xx (1913), p. 527.

28. Volume 2, no. 4. I am grateful to Dr. Tim Carter for pointing out the use of borrowed material in Peri's duet. The setting by Bati is transcribed in D.S. Butchart, "The Madrigal at Florence, 1560-1630," 2 vols., diss., U. of Oxford, 1979, ii, pp. 251-54.

29. Trans. MacClintock, "Giustianiani's *Discorso*," p. 214.

30. See, for example, Marco Cara's "Oimè el cuor" in H. Engel, *The Sixteenth-Century Part Song in Italy, France, England and Spain* (*Das Musikwerk*, iii), Cologne, 1961, p. 5.

31. Einstein, *Italian Madrigal*, ii, p. 617.

32. Morley, *A Plain and Easy Introduction to Practical Music*, ed. A. Harman, London, 1952, p. 295.

33. See above, pp. 65-66.

34. Volume 2, no. 11.

35. Monteverdi, *Tutte le Opere,* vii, pp. 35-36.

36. Volume 2, no. 15.

37. Monteverdi, *Tutte le Opere,* vii, pp. 87-88.

38. Ibid., vii, p. 80.

39. Ibid., ix, p. 31.

40. Ibid., iv, p. 6.

41. Volume 2, no. 4.

42. Einstein, *Italian Madrigal,* ii, pp. 621-22.

43. O. Tomek, "Das Strukturphänomen das verkappten Satzes a Tre in der Musik des 16. und 17. Jahrhunderts," *SMw,* xxvii (1966), pp. 18-71.

44. L. Schrade, *Monteverdi,* p. 127.

45. Monteverdi, *Tutte le Opere,* x, p. 17.

46. Ibid., vii, 58.

47. Ibid., iii, p. 33.

48. Ibid., iv, p. 66.

49. Ibid., iv, p. 49.

50. Ibid., iii, p. 1ff.

51. Ibid., iii, pp. 3 and 7 respectively.

52. Ibid., iii, pp. 3-5.

53. Ibid., iii, pp. 68ff.

54. Ibid., iii, p. 71.

55. Ibid., iv, p. 7.

56. Ibid., vii, p. 66.

57. Ibid., vi, p. 70.

58. Monteverdi, however, adds an extra "Ohimè" to the text at bars 17-18 to maintain the musical balance.

59. See the discussion of Monteverdi's "Ohimè, il bel viso" in H. Redlich, *Claudio Monteverdi. Leben und Werk,* Olten, 1949, pp. 150-51. The sequence used in Monteverdi's madrigal can be seen again in bars 95-107 of Tarquinio Merula's aria "Amo, l'è ver." See volume 2, no. 39.

60. Monteverdi, *Tutte le Opere,* x, p. 17.

61. Ibid., ii, p. 68.

62. Ibid., iii, p. 19.

63. Ibid., vii, p. 177.

64. Ibid., iv, p. 49.

65. Ibid., ix, p. 36.

66. Fortune, "From Madrigal to Duet," *The Monteverdi Companion*, pp. 211-12.

67. Monteverdi, *Tutte le Opere*, vii, p. 94.

68. Ibid., iv, p. 41.

69. Fortune, "From Madrigal to Duet," p. 209.

70. Monteverdi, *Tutte le Opere*, iv, p. 6.

71. Ibid., iv, p. 65.

72. Ibid., v, p. 1.

73. Ibid., v, p. 102.

74. Ibid., iv, p. 65.

Chapter 6

1. Monteverdi, *Tutte le Opere*, vi, p. 104.

2. See Schrade, *Monteverdi*, pp. 276-77. Monteverdi completed the *concertato* madrigal "Una donna fra l'altre" in 1609. In 1610, however, he was at work on the two great *a cappella* laments of the sixth book—"Lasciatemi morire" and "Incenerite spoglie."

3. Monteverdi, *Tutte le Opere*, vi, pp. 85-87.

4. Ibid., v, p. 97.

5. Ibid., v, p. 100.

6. Ibid., v, p. 9.

7. Ibid., v, pp. 62ff.

8. See, for example, volume 2, no. 15, bars 20-21.

9. See volume 2, no. 17, bars 15-16, volume 2, no. 20, bars 68-69. The figure becomes almost a cliché in Rovetta's work.

10. This is sung by Body, whose music is otherwise notated in tenor clef.

11. *Pace* Palisca, *Baroque Music*, p. 33, where it is stated that Peri set the final stanza as a duet.

12. Strunk, *Source Readings*, pp. 375-76.

13. But not in the earlier version of the text: see Solerti, *Gli albori del melodramma*, ii, p. 95.

14. Quoted in Solerti, *Le origini*, p. 87: quando cantano insieme il duo . . . il riguardarsi in volto l'un l'altro su quelle esclamazioni ha gran forza . . .

15. See *Dafne*, ed. Eitner (*Publikationen aelterer praktischer und theoretischer Musikwerke*, x), pp. 92-93.

16. Compare ibid., pp. 82-83 with the edition of "Alma mia" in *La Flora*, iii, p. 84.

17. A. Piccolomini, *Annotationi . . . nel Libro della Poetica d'Aristotele*, Venice, 1575, p. 261, trans. in D.J. Grout, "The Chorus in Early Opera," *Festschrift Friedrich Blume zum 70. Geburtstag*, ed. A.A. Abert & W. Pfannkuch, Kassel, 1963, p. 154.

18. Monteverdi, *Tutte le Opere*, xi, pp. 43-46.

19. Ibid., xi, pp. 32-38.

20. Ibid., xi, p. 37.

21. Ibid., xi, pp. 68-74.

22. Ibid., xi, pp. 72 and 68 respectively.

23. Ibid, iii, particularly pp. 107-8. Notice, too, that the augmented second used for the phrase "Di martir in martir" in "Rimanti in pace" (iii, p. 110) is the same device found at "l'una punte da l'angue" in *Orfeo* (xi, p. 70).

24. Volume 2, no. 10.

25. Monteverdi, *Tutte le Opere*, vii, p. 41.

26. Ibid., vii, p. 8.

27. Ibid., vii, p. 52.

28. Ibid., vii, pp. 152ff.

29. Giancarlo Casali, "La cappella," p. 197, identifies Melli with the singer of the same name working at the cathedral of Reggio Emilia in 1600.

30. The ornamentation of the canto line at the end of this latter example, as elsewhere in Rubini's madrigals, seems a pale Modenese reflection of the "luxuriant" style enjoyed by the Este court during its heyday at Ferrara. It is, however, unusual to find extended passages of ornamentation in duets for high voice and bass.

31. In the list of contents, Rubini suggests that certain of the duets may be sung instead by tenor and bass.

32. *Indice*, reprinted Haberl as supplement to *MMg*, xiv (1882), pp. 1 and 17.

33. Volume 2, no. 25.

34. Volume 2, no. 26.

35. Volume 2, no. 2.

36. Radesca used *falso bordone* technique even more extensively in his third book of *Canzonette* for a setting of six stanzas in *ottava rima*, beginning "Già si vedeva il Cielo."

37. Volume 2, no. 1.

38. See H. Wiley Hitchcock, "Depriving Caccini," pp. 76-78.

39. Volume 2, no. 3.

40. Volume 2, no. 25. To judge from the number of textual variants, it seems unlikely that Marini borrowed the text from Peri's publication.

41. N. Fortune, "Sigismondo d'India. An Introduction to his Life and Works," *PRMA*, lxxxi (1954/5), p. 31.

42. H. Federhofer, "Graz Court Musicians and their contributions to the *Parnassus Musicus Ferdinandaeus* (1616)," *MD*, ix (1955), p. 168.

43. Schmitz, "Kammerduets."

44. See I. Spink, "Angelo Notari and his Prime Musiche Nuove," *Monthly Musical Record*, lxxxvii (1957), pp. 168-77.

45. Volume 2, no. 5.

46. Volume 2, no. 21.

47. Volume 2, no. 31.

48. Edited in *La Flora,* iii, p. 85.

49. Volume 2, no. 30.

50. Among duet composers only Brunelli used the term with Chiabrera's meaning, for his madrigal "Già di Paglia 'n su la riva" (1616).

51. Edited in *La Flora,* iii, pp. 82-83.

52. See Riemann, *Handbuch,* II.2., p. 301.

53. Volume 2, no. 29.

54. Ibid., no. 27.

55. Edited in *La Flora,* iii, pp. 82-83.

56. Volume 2, no. 29.

57. Ibid., no. 30.

58. Ibid., no. 5.

59. Volume 2, no. 31.

60. Edited in *La Flora,* iii, p. 84.

61. Ibid., iii, p. 85.

62. Volume 2, no. 27.

63. Volume 2, no. 37.

64. *Italian Secular Song,* i, p. 417.

65. Ed. Gotwals & Keppler, pp. 38-41.

66. Volume 2, no. 22.

67. Edited in Einstein, *Italian Madrigal,* iii, pp. 16-17.

68. The *Romanesca* in Valentini's 1621 madrigal book—"Oh Dio, quel dolce a Dio"—is not an *ottava* but a setting of ten lines from Marino's *canzone* "È partito il mio bene." The setting employs only two statements of the *Romanesca* bass.

69. Fortune, "Solo Song," p. 181.

70. See above, pp. 31-32.

71. See above, p. 39.

72. Einstein, "Die Aria di Ruggiero," *SIMG,* xiii (1911-12), pp. 452-53. For Cifra's setting of this stanza, see volume 2, no. 33.

73. Trans, MacClintock, "Giustiniani's *Discorso,*" p. 216.

74. C. Palisca, "Vincenzo Galilei and some Links between Pseudo-Monody and Monody," *MQ,* xlvi (1960), p. 354.

75. C. Palisca, *Baroque Music,* pp. 51-53.

76. Volume 2, no. 32.

77.   Ed. Mompellio, pp. 142-49.

78.   Edited in *La Flora*, iii, pp. 86-87.

79.   See above, p. 89.

80.   M. Bukofzer, *Music in the Baroque Era*, p. 37.

81.   Ed. Mompellio, pp. 150-51.

82.   See above, p. 98.

83.   Volume 2, no. 21. For the high-minded reasons which led Bonini to choose this penitential text, see above, p. 30.

84.   Volume 2, no. 6.

85.   Ed. Aldrich. The madrigal "In un limpido rio" is also in *La Flora*, iii, pp. 80-81, and "Vergine chiara" in *Alte Meister*.

86.   See above, p. 133.

87.   Monteverdi, *Tutte le Opere*, vii, pp. 9-10.

88.   Volume 2, no. 13.

89.   Volume 2, no. 23.

90.   Ibid., no. 17. Rovetta certainly knew of Valentini, for he mentioned him in the preface to his *Salmi concertati*, Venice, 1626, as an example of a composer who had begun his career as an instrumentalist.

91.   Schmitz, "Kammerduetts," p. 50.

Chapter 7

1.   A. Ghislanzoni, *Luigi Rossi: biografia e analisi delle opere*, Milan, 1954, p. 33.

2.   See J.H. Moore, *Vespers at St. Mark's. Music of Alessandro Grandi, Giovanni Rovetta and Francesco Cavalli*, 2 vols., Ann Arbor, 1981, i, pp. 5-7.

3.   Einstein, *Italian Madrigal*, ii, p. 867.

4.   Volume 2, no. 8.

5.   Volume 2, no. 7.

6.   Edited in *Alte Meister*.

7.   See above, p. 120.

8.   Volume 2, no. 11.

9.   Freduti wrote the instrumental *balletti* which appear in Accademico's dialogue settings; see below, p. 183.

10.   Volume 2, no. 12.

11.   See the examples edited in *Alte Meister*.

12.   Volume 2, no. 19.

13.   Monteverdi, *Tutte le Opere*, vii, 8-13.

14.   Monteverdi, *Tutte le Opere*, vii, pp. 82-83.

15.   Cf. bars 23-27 of Grandi's "O chiome erranti": volume 2, no. 7.

16.   Monteverdi, *Tutte le Opere*, vii, p. 94.

17.   Ibid., ix, p. 36.

18.   Ibid., vii, p. 66.

19.   Ibid., vii, p. 62.

20.   Ibid., ix, p. 35.

21.   Ibid., vii, pp. 52-53.

22.   See appendix, volume 2, nos. 108, 243, 276, 301, for the verse-forms used by Monteverdi.

23.   Monteverdi, *Tutte le Opere*, vii, p. 47.

24.   Ibid., vii, pp. 94-97.

25.   Volume 2, no. 23.

26.   Ibid., no. 24.

27.   Ibid., no. 9.

28.   Ibid., no. 10.

29.   Monteverdi, *Tutte le Opere*, vii, pp. 58-61.

30.   Volume 2, no. 14.

31.   Ibid., no. 39.

32.   Ibid., no. 18.

33.   G. Sabbatini, *Regola facile e breve per sonare sopra il Basso continuo*, Venice, 1628, trans. in F.T. Arnold, *Art of Accompaniment*, pp. 110-23.

34.   Volume 2, no. 18.

35.   Ibid., no. 15.

36.   Ibid., nos. 16 and 17.

37.   Compare them with volume 2, no. 8, bars 12 to 15.

38.   Volume 2, no. 20.

39.   Edited in *La Flora*, iii, pp. 91-93.

40.   See R. Hudson, "Chaconne," *The New Grove*, iv, p. 101.

41.   For a discussion of the possible identification of Il Fasolo as Francesco Manelli see below, p. 190.

42.   E. Rosand, "The Descending Tetrachord: an emblem of lament," *MQ*, lxv (1979), pp. 346-59.

43.   Volume 2, no. 24.

44.   Ibid., no. 34.

45.   The last stanza is given a different setting in both verse and refrain, though following the same pattern of scoring.

46. Also set as an *Aria di Ruggiero* by Banchieri (1626).

47. The text which Bellante set—a *ballata* by Girolamo Preti—was later set by Stradella.

48. Volume 2, no. 35.

49. Ibid., no. 36.

50. Ibid., no. 37.

51. Ibid., no. 38.

52. The creation of the strophic-bass cantata—that is, a set of strophic variations in which the bass line moves mainly in crotchets—is usually attributed to Alessandro Grandi. But the earliest example of this type of aria is found in act IV of Monteverdi's *Orfeo*, in the aria "Qual honor di te sia degno."

53. Volume 2, no. 39.

Chapter 8

1. T. Kroyer, "Dialog und Echo in der alten Chormusik," *JMP*, xvi (1909), pp. 13-32.

2. D. Harran, "Towards a Definition of the Early Secular Dialogue," *ML*, li (1970), pp. 37-50.

3. Ibid., pp. 49-50.

4. Einstein, *Italian Madrigal*, iii, 155-59.

5. Ibid., iii, 63-72.

6. See David Nutter & John Whenham, "Dialogue," sect. 3, *The New Grove*, v, p. 416.

7. Einstein, op. cit., iii, pp. 190-98.

8. Monteverdi, *Tutte le Opere*, vi, pp. 38-45 and 113-30 respectively.

9. Volume 2, no. 42.

10. G.B. Doni, *Compendio del Trattato de' Generi e de' Modi della Musica*, Rome, 1635, quoted in Solerti, *Origini*, p. 224.

11. Volume 2, no. 40.

12. See above, p. 4.

13. See appendix, volume 2, nos. 311, 322.

14. See volume 2, nos. 41 and 43, which are similarly structured.

15. See, for example, act I, scenes 2 and 3 of Monteverdi's *L'Incoronazione di Poppea*.

16. Schmitz, "Kammerduetts," p. 47: Seine Literatur im stile nuovo gehört keineswegs nur der Duettform an: es gibt vielmehr in der Frühgeschichte der Monodie Dialoge, die ausschließlich als einstimmige Wechselreden verlaufen und damit das Wesentliche des Duetts, den zweistimmigen Satz, beiseite lassen.

17. Transcribed in Solerti, *Albori*, iii, pp. 75-87. The dialogue forms lines 177-85 of the libretto.

18. Trans. Fanshawe.

19. The other two are by Giaccio (1620) and Galeazzo Sabbatini (1636).

20. Volume 2, no. 40.

21. For Turini's setting, see volume 2, no. 41.

22. Monteverdi, *Tutte le Opere,* ix, pp. 1-8.

23. Volume 2, no. 12.

24. Ed. in Sigismondo d'India, *Il Primo Libro di Musiche da cantar solo,* ed. F. Mompellio, pp. 152-54.

25. Probably not G.B. Fasolo, a monk living in Sicily who was active as a composer between 1653 and 1664. "Il Fasolo" seems to have been a Roman composer.

26. Quoted in Giuseppe Radiciotti, *L'Arte Musicale in Tivoli nei Secoli XVI, XVII e XVIII,* 2nd edn, Tivoli, 1921, p. 51: Essendo stata stampata un altra volta la mia *Luciata* nel Titolo de Carro Trionfale sotto nome di Accademico mi è parsa troppa prosuntione, e quel che peggio che la 3. parte canti sopra il Basso Continuo; mi sono risoluto di stamparla nel modo che la va, cioè che la terza parte ancor lei facci li suoi motivi conforme le altre.

27. Elena Ferrari Barassi, "La Luciata," takes the view that Manelli's original setting is now lost and that Fasolo's was an imitation of it.

28. See volume 2, no. 41 for Turini's setting of "Perchè piangi, Pastore."

29. The plan as given here is adapted from those given in Riemann, *Handbuch* II, 2, pp. 299-300, where all four dialogues are discussed.

Chapter 9

1. A setting for three voices and continuo of a section of this libretto, "Come dolce hoggi l'auretta," survives in Monteverdi's *Madrigali e Canzonette* (Venice, 1651): see T. Walker, "Gli Errori di 'Minerva al Tavolino,' *Venezia e il melodramma nel seicento,* ed. M.T. Muraro, Florence, 1976, p. 13.

2. See Monteverdi, *Lettere,* ed. D. De' Paoli, letters 91-102, 104, 108; *Letters,* trans. D. Stevens, letters 92-103, 106, 108.

3. P. Petrobelli, "L'Ermiona' di Pio Enea degli Obizzi ed i primi spettacoli d'opera veneziani," *Quaderni della Rassegna Musicale,* iii (1965), pp. 125ff.

4. P. Petrobelli, "Francesco Manelli," pp. 46-51.

5. Carnival season in Venice ran from 26 December to the beginning of Lent in the following year.

6. W. Osthoff, "Maschera e Musica," *NRMI,* i (1967), p. 20.

7. The libretto of this opera seems to bear no relation to the earlier libretto of similar title which Strozzi wrote for Monterverdi.

8. The authorship of this text was recently established by Lorenzo Bianconi: see A. Chiarelli, "L'incoronazione di Poppea o Il Nerone: problemi filologici e bibliografi," *RIM,* ix (1974), pp. 149ff.

9. The first known performance of the opera was given at Bologna in 1640; see W. Osthoff, "Zur Bologneser Aufführung von Monteverdis 'Ritorno d'Ulisse' im Jahre 1640," *Anzeiger der phil.-hist. Klasse der Österreichischen Akademie der Wissenschaften,* xcv (Vienna, 1958), pp. 155ff.

10. G. Gaspari, *Catalogo,* v, pp. 182-83.

11.   C. Sartori, "La prima diva della lirica italiana," *NRMI,* ii (1968), p. 437.

12.   *The Diary of John Evelyn,* ed. E.S. de Beer, Oxford, 1955, pp. 449-50.

13.   Published as *Arie a 1 voce per cantarsi nel clavicembalo o Tiorba raccolte da G.B. Verdizotti nel dramma della Finta Savia...del Giulio Strozzi,* Venice, 1643.

14.   C. Monteverdi, *Tutte le Opere,* viii/1, p. 132.

15.   Ibid.

16.   L. Schrade, *Monteverdi,* p. 302.

17.   M. Bukofzer, *Music in the Baroque Era,* p. 38.

18.   Carissimi's *Jephte,* for example, was so described in A. Kircher, *Musurgia Universalis,* 2 vols., Rome, 1650, i, p. 603. See also H.E. Smither, "What is an Oratorio in mid-seventeenth-century Italy?," *International Musicological Society: Report of the Eleventh Congress, Copenhagen, 1972,* Copenhagen, 1974, pp. 657-63, and Smither, *A History of the Oratorio,* i, Chapel Hill, 1977, particularly pp. 5-6.

19.   Leichtentritt, in A.W. Ambros, *Geschichte,* 3rd edn., iv, p. 852, attributed the text of this work to Tasso, stating that it was taken from *La Gerusalemme Liberata.* The character Angelica does not, however, appear in Tasso's epic, and I have been unable to trace Sances' text in either *La Gerusalemme Liberata* or its more probable source, Ariosto's *Orlando furioso.*

20.   Monteverdi, *Tutte le Opere,* viii/1, p. 156.

21.   Translated in Schrade, *Monteverdi,* p. 299.

22.   Monteverdi, *Tutte le Opere,* viii/1. pp. 133-34.

23.   Ibid., pp. 134-35.

24.   Ibid., pp. 139-40.

25.   Ibid., pp. 140-41.

26.   The use of dominant-tonic progressions can be seen, for instance, in the madrigal "Hor che 'l ciel e la terra" (1638), where they are used in conjunction with semiquaver rhythms, and the use of fanfare motives can be seen in *Il ritorno d'Ulisse,* act II, sc.12.

27.   D. Arnold, "Monteverdi and the Art of War," *MT,* cviii (1967), pp. 412-14.

28.   Volume 2, no. 42.

29.   A further edition of the play was published jointly with *Erotilla* under the title *Saggi poetici,* Venice, 1621. In his preface to this edition, Strozzi explained that the subtitle *anacronismo* referred to the fact that characters from various epochs had been gathered together in one play.

30.   Throughout the transcription, line length is conjectural where no correspondence exists between original and adaptation.

31.   Lines 44-46, which should follow "Segue la serva Alcide," are here taken out of sequence for comparison with lines 31-33 of *La Gelosia placata.*

32.   Lines 50-51 are taken out of sequence for comparison with lines 74-75 of *La Gelosia placata.*

33.   Prior to the publication of his first book of madrigals, Rovetta had published only one volume of sacred music.

34.   *Lettere*, ed. De' Paoli, no. 92; *Letters*, trans. Stevens, no. 93.

35.   Monteverdi's setting of *I cinque fratelli*, the text of which survives, was written in 1628 for performance at a banquet at the Arsenale given by the Venetian Republic to honor a visit by Grand Duke Ferdinando of Tuscany and his brother, Carlo de' Medici.

36.   The libretto of *La finta pazza Licori* was also an adaptation, made on Monteverdi's request from a smaller-scale piece in dialogue of the same title which Strozzi had prepared for one of Girolamo Mocenigo's musical evenings. See Monteverdi's letter of 5 June 1627 in *Letters*, ed. De' Paoli, no. 95; *Letters*, trans. Stevens, no. 96.

37.   The voices required for the performance of *La Gelosia placata*—soprano, alto, tenor, tenor, bass—form a conventional five-part madrigal ensemble.

38.   One of Berti's strophic-bass cantatas, "Oh con quanta vaghezza" (1624), is printed in Fortune, "Solo Song," *NOHM*, iv, pp. 173-74.

39.   Monteverdi, *Tutte le Opere*, xi, p. 59.

40.   Ibid., viii, p. 155.

41.   See, for example, the passage from the libretto of *Proserpina rapita* quoted in A.A. Abert, *Claudio Monteverdi und das musikalischen Drama*, Lippstadt, 1954, pp. 130-31.

42.   Strozzi was the author of the text for Laurenzi's *serenata* "Guerra non porta" (1641), written for a celebration for Giovanni de Pesaro, procurator-elect of St. Mark's. As may be seen from the opening words of the work, Strozzi provided an opportunity for the composer to write a short *stile concitato* passage.

43.   Strozzi was credited, in *Le glorie de gli Incogniti*, Venice, 1647, p. 283, with having written all the texts for Barbara Strozzi's first book of madrigals. Barbara Strozzi later included her own settings of texts from her father's libretti *La finta pazza* and *Il Romolo e 'l Remo* in her *Cantate, Ariette e Duetti*, Venice, 1651.

44.   Title page of *Melodiae Sacrae*, op. 3, Venice, 1638. The dedication was dated January, 1638 (= 1639, new style).

45.   G. Gaspari, *Catalogo*, ii, p. 223.

46.   Ibid.

47.   Caffi, *Storia*, i, p. 272.

48.   A. Spagnolo, *Le scuole accolitali in Verona*, Verona, 1905, pp. 122-23.

49.   Volume 2, no. 44.

50.   G.F. Loredano, *Bizzarrie academiche*, Venice (Sarzini), 1638, pp. 182-202. The *Contesa* was translated into English in G.F. Loredano, *Academical Discourses*, trans. J.B., London, 1664, pp. 99ff.

51.   *Veglie de' signori Unisoni*, Venice, 1638.

52.   Loredano, *Bizzarrie*, p. 202: Ma non di dovere, che parlando delle glorie del Canto, pregiudichi alle di lui ragioni. Nelle bocche di questi Sig. Musici si farà molto meglio vedere la maggioranza del Canto, sovra le lagrime in produr'Amore.

53.   Fortune, *Italian Secular Song*, i, p. 382.

54.   The precise date of composition of Carissimi's dialogue is not known. It must, however, have been written before 1650, when it was discussed in A. Kircher, *Musurgia Universalis*, i, pp. 673-74.

55. The text had, however, been set as a solo song by Fornaci (1617).

56. Volume 2, no. 43.

57. Einstein, *Italian Madrigal,* ii, p. 542.

58. See T.D. Culley, *Jesuits and Music, i: a Study of the Musicians Connected with the German College in Rome during the 17th Century and of their Activities in Northern Europe,* Rome, 1970, pp. 145-47, 169.

59. N. Pellicelli, "Musicisti in Parma nel secolo XVII," *NA,* x (1933), p. 234.

60. Tiraboschi, *Biblioteca,* ii, p. 265.

61. The only other examples of this type of written-out appoggiatura that I have found in music of this period occur in act III, scene 8 of Monteverdi's *L'Incoronazione di Poppea.*

62. A. Ghislanzoni, *Luigi Rossi,* p. 29.

63. Sartori, "La prima diva," p. 437.

64. I have been unable to establish precisely who "Togna" is intended to be. The *Cambridge Italian Dictionary* gives "Togno" as an abbreviated form of the name Antonio and it seems likely that "Togna" is simply its feminine form. The title of the dialogue may carry other implications for the characterization of Togna, for it is very similar to the Spanish term for a folksong—*Tonada.* The idea that Togna is an old peasant woman would accord well with the text of the dialogue.

65. See, for example, the end of act II, scene 14 of Monteverdi's *L'incoronazione di Poppea,* in *Tutte le Opere,* xiii, pp. 196-97.

66. Ibid., xiii, pp. 135-40.

67. Ibid., xii, pp. 94-102.

Chapter 10

1. See, for example, the opening of Turini's Sonata no. I in F. Turini, *Sonate per 2 Violini, Violoncello e Continuo (1621),* ed. G. Leonhardt, Vienna, 1957, p. 3.

2. J.M. Harper, "The Instrumental Canzonas of Girolamo Frescobaldi: a comparative edition and introductory study," diss., U. of Birmingham, 1975, i, p. 317.

3. Volume 2, no. 39.

4. Ibid., no. 6.

5. Ibid., no. 16.

6. Ibid.

7. Eleanor Caluori, *The Cantatas of Luigi Rossi,* UMI Research Press, Ann Arbor, 1981.

8. Ibid., p. 4.

9. Landshoff (ed.), *Alte Meister,* ii, pp. 34-41.

10. Ibid., ii, pp. 22-28.

11. Antonio Cesti, *Four Chamber Duets,* ed. D. Burrows, Madison, 1969, pp. 1-23.

12. G. Lotti, *Poesie latine e toscane,* Rome, 1688, pp. 37-39.

Bibliography

Texts

These sources were consulted in establishing the authorship of poetic texts. A *RISM* library siglum in brackets (see list in introduction to the appendix, volume 2) is used to identify the location of a copy of the rarer volumes.

Individual Poets

Accetto, Torquato, *Rime,* Naples, 1621 [I-Rn].
Achillini, Claudio, *Poesie,* Bologna, 1632 [I-Rvat].
Achillini, Caludio, *Rime e prose . . . accresciute,* Venice, 1651 [I-Rvat].
Andreini, Isabella, *Rime,* Milan, 1601 [I-Rn].
Ariosto, Ludovico, *Opere minori,* ed. C. Segre, Milan, 1954.
Ariosto, Ludovico, *Orlando furioso,* ed. S. Pasquazi & G. Zappacosta, Milan, 1969.
Barlo, Bartolomeo (Mantovano), *Madrigali,* Venice, 1604 [I-Rn].
Bembo, Pietro, *Prose e rime,* ed. C. Dionisotti, Turin, 1960.
Boccaccio, Giovanni, *Decameron; Filocolo; Ameta; Fiametta,* ed. E. Bianchi, C. Salimari, N. Sapegno, Milan, 1952.
Boccaccio, Giovanni, *Le rime; L'amorosa visione; La caccia di Diana,* ed. V. Branca, Bari, 1939.
Bonarelli, C. Guidobaldo de', *La Filli di Sciro,* Venice, 1607.
Cebà, Ansaldo, *Rime,* Rome, 1611 [I-Rn].
Chiabrera, Gabriello, *Rime,* Venice, 1610 [GB-Ob].
Chiabrera, Gabriello, *Rime,* 3 vols., Milan, 1807-1808.
Fiamma, Gabriel, *Rime spirituali,* Venice, 1606 [I-Rn].
Guarini, Giovanni Battista, *Opere,* 4 vols., Verona, 1737-1738.
Guarini, Giovanni Battista, *Il pastor fido,* trans. Richard Fanshawe, ed. J.H. Whitfield (*Edinburgh Bilingual Library,* xi), 1976.
Guarini, Giovanni Battista, *Rime,* Venice, 1598 [GB-Bu].
Macedonio, Marcello, *Ballate et Idilii,* Venice, 1614 [I-Rn].
Macedonio, Marcello, *Scielta delle poesie,* Venice, 1615 [I-Rn].
Marino, Giambattista, *L'Adone . . . Le strage degl'innocenti ed una scelta di poesie liriche,* ed. G. Zirardini, Paris, 1849.
Marino, Giambattista, *L'Adone,* ed. G. Pozzo, 2 vols., Milan, 1976.
Marino, Giambattista, *Poesie varie,* ed. B. Croce, Bari, 1913.
Petrarca, Francesco, *Canzoniere,* ed. G. Contini & D. Ponchiroli, 3rd edn, Turin, 1968.
Pona, Francesco, *Rime,* Verona, 1617 [I-Rn].
Preti, Girolamo, *Poesie,* 6th edn, Rome, 1622 [GB-Bu].
Preti, Girolamo, *Poesie . . . accresciute,* Perugia, 1638 [I-Rn].

Querenghi, Antonio, *Poesie volgari,* Rome, 1621 [I-Rn].
Rasi, Francesco, *La cetra di sette corde: rime del signor...,* Venice, 1619 [I-Rn].
Rinaldi, Cesare, *Rime nuove,* Bologna, 1603 [I-Rn].
Rinuccini, Ottavio, *Poesie,* ed. P.F. Rinuccini, Florence, 1622 [GB-Ob].
Rosa, Salvator, *Poesie e lettere inedite,* ed. U. Limentani, Florence, 1950.
Sannazzaro, Jacopo, *Opere volgari,* ed. A. Mauro, Bari, 1965.
Sforza, Mutio, *Delle rime del S. ...,* Venice, 1590 [I-Rn].
Strozzi, Giulio, *Il natal di Amore, anacronismo,* 4th, rev. edn, Venice, 1629 [GB-Lbm].
Tasso, Torquato, *Aminta,* ed. P.P. Addoli, Milan, 1955.
Tasso, Torquato, *La Gerusalemme liberata,* ed. A.M. Carini, Milan, 1961.
Tasso, Torquato, *Opere minori in versi,* ed. A. Solerti, 3 vols., Bologna, 1891-1895.
Tasso, Torquato, *Le rime,* ed. A. Solerti, 4 vols., Bologna, 1898-1902.
Tasso, Torquato, *Rime inedite,* ed. M. Vattasso, Rome, 1915.
Testi, Fulvio, *Opere,* Venice, 1644 [I-Rn].
Testi, Fulvio, *Delle poesie liriche del conte D. ...,* Venice, 1651 [I-Rn].

Anthologies of Poetry

(1)   *Gareggiamento poetico del Confuso Accademico Ordito: madrigali amorosi, gravi e piacevoli ne' quali si vede il bello, il leggiadro & il vivace de i più illustri poeti d'Italia,* Venice, 1611 [I-Rvat, Capponi VI. 70; this copy belonged to a Francesco Lambardi].
(2)   *Lirici del cinquecento,* ed. L. Baldacci, Florence, 1957.
(3)   *Lirici del cinquecento,* ed. D. Ponchiroli; new edn, ed. G.D. Bonino, Turin, 1968.
(4)   *Lirici del secolo XVII, con cenni biografici (Biblioteca classica economia,* lx), Milan, 1878.
(5)   *Lirici misti del secolo XVII (Parnaso italiano,* xli), Venice, 1789.
(6)   *I lirici del seicento e dell'Arcadia,* ed. C. Calcaterra, Milan, n.d.
(7)   *Marino e i marinisti,* ed. G.G. Ferrero, Milan, 1954.
(8)   *Poesie de signori academici Disinvolti di Pesaro,* Pesaro, 1639 [I-Rn].
(9)   *Poesie de ss.ri accademici Infecondi di Roma,* Venice, 1678 [I-Rn].
(10) *Raccolta d'alcune rime di scrittori mantovani fatta per Eugenio Cagnani,* Mantua, 1612 [I-Rvat].
(11) *Le piacevole rime di M. Cesare Caporali perugino, con aggiunta di molte altre rime, fatte da diversi eccellentissimi & belli ingegni,* Venice, 1589 [GB-Bu].
(12) *Delle rime piacevoli del Berni, Casa, Mauro, Varchi, Dolce, et d'altri auttori, libro primo,* Vicenza, 1603 [I-Rvat].
(13) *Delle rime piacevoli del Berni, Copetta, Francesi, Bronzini, Martelli, Domenichi, Strascini e d'altri ingegni simili, libro secondo,* Vicenza, 1603 [I-Rvat].
(14) *Delle rime piacevoli del Borgogna, Ruscelli, Sansovino, Doni, Lasca, Remigio, Anguillara, Sansedonio, e d'altri vivac'ingegni, libro terzo,* Vicenza, 1603 [I-Rvat].
(15) *Rime de gli accademici Gelati di Bologna,* Bologna, 1597 [I-Rn].
(16) *Rime dei Gelati,* Bologna, 1615 [I-Rn].
(17) *Rime di vari autori,* ed. Baldo Salviani, Orvieto, 1586 [I-Rn].
(18) *Rime piacevoli di sei begl'ingegni,* Vicenza, 1603 [I-Rn].
(19) *Scielta di varie poesie sacre di diversi eccellenti autori,* Venice, 1605 [I-Rn].
(20) *Il primo volume delle rime scelti da diversi autori,* ed. Ludovico Dolce, Venice, 1565.

Musical Sources Which Also Serve as Anthologies of Poetry by Named Poets

(21) Basile, Donato, *Villanelle,* Naples, 1610.
(22) Giaccio, Orazio, *Armoniose voci: Canzonette...a tre voci,* Naples, 1620.
(23) Giaccio, Orazio, *Laberinto amoroso: Canzonette a tre voci,* Naples, 1618.

(24)   Savioni, Mario, *Concerti morali, e sprirituali, a tre voci,* Rome, 1660.
(25)   Tornioli, Marcantonio, *Canzonette spirituali a tre voci,* Venice, 1607.

Other Sources

Caccini, Giulio, *Nuove Musiche e nuova maniera di scriverle (1614),* ed. H. Wiley Hitchcock *(Recent Researches in the Music of the Baroque Era,* xxviii), Madison, 1978.
Carter, Tim, "Jacopo Peri (1561-1633): his life and works," 2 vols., diss., U. of Birmingham, 1980.
Einstein, Alfred, *"Orlando Furioso* and *La Gerusalemme Liberata* as set to music during the 16th and 17th centuries," *Notes,* viii (1951), pp. 623-30.
Simon, R. & G. Gidrol, "Appunti sulle relazioni tra l'opera poetica di G.B. Marino e la musica del suo tempo," *Studi secenteschi,* xiv (1973), pp. 81-187.
Solerti, Angelo, *Gli albori del melodramma,* 3 vols., Milan, 1904.
Solerti, Angelo, *Bibliografia delle rime di Torquato Tasso,* Bologna, 1910.
Williamson, Edward, *Bernardo Tasso,* Rome, 1951.

Concertato Duets and Dialogues: Facsimile Reprints, Modern Editions, and Anthologies

Facsimile Reprints

Kapsberger, Giovanni Girolamo, *Libro Primo* [/ *Secondo*] *di Arie (Archivium musicum,* xxxii), Florence, 1980.
Kapsberger, Giovanni Girolamo, *Libro Primo* [/ *Secondo, Terzo, Quarto*] *di Villanelle a 1. 2. & 3 voci (Archivium musicum,* xxviii), Florence, 1979.
Marini, Biagio, *Scherzi e Canzonette a una, e due voci, Parma, 1622 (Archivium musicum: la cantata barocca,* vi), Florence, 1980.
Mazzocchi, Domenico, *Dialoghi e Sonetti, Roma, 1638 (Biblioteca musica Boneniensis,* sez. iv, no. 10), Bologna, 1969.
Musiche di vari autori, XVIIe siècle [B-Bc, MS 704] *(Thesaurus Musicus,* nova series; série A: manuscripts, iii) Brussels, 1979.

Modern Editions

Frescobaldi, Girolamo, *Arie musicali,* ed. H. Spohr *(Musikalische Denkmäler,* iv), Mainz, 1960.
Gagliano, Marco da, *Music for One, Two and Three Voices* [1615], ed. P. Aldrich *(U. of California Series of Early Music,* ii, v), Bryn Mawr, Penn, 1969 & 1972.
India, Sigismondo d', *Il Primo Libro di Musiche da cantar solo,* ed. F. Mompellio *(Athenaeum cremonese,* ser. 1, 4), Cremona, 1970.
Monteverdi, Claudio, *Tutte le Opere,* ed. G.F. Malipiero, 16 vols., Asola, 1926-42; 2nd rev. edn of vols viii, xv, xvi, Vienna, 1954ff.; supplementary vol., Venice, 1966.
Quagliati, Paolo, *La Sfera Armoniosa and Il Carro di Fedelta d'Amore,* ed. V. Gotwals & P. Keppler *(Smith College Music Archives,* xiii), Northampton, Mass., 1957 [the edition of *Il Carro di Fedelta d'Amore* does not include the independent duets contained in the original publication].

Anthologies

La Flora, ed. K. Jeppesen, 3 vols., Copenhagen, 1949.
Alte Meister des Bel Canto, ed. L. Landshoff, 5 vols., Frankfurt, 1912-1927 [I have had access only to the three volumes of excerpts from this anthology which are currently in print: *Alte Meister*

des Bel Canto: italienische Kammerduette des 17. und 18. Jahrhunderts (Edition Peters, nos. 3824 and 3824c), and Carissimi, *Sechs Kammerduette* (Edition Peters, no. 3824b)].

General Bibliography

Abert, Anna Amalie, *Claudio Monteverdi und das musikalische Drama*, Lippstadt, 1964.

Adami, A., *Osservazioni, per ben regolare il coro della cappella pontificia*, Rome, 1711.

Adriaenssen, Emanuel, *Pratum musicum longe amoenissimum, Antwerp, 1584*, facsimile reprint, with introduction by Kwee Him Yong, Buren, 1977.

Alaleona, Domenico, *Storia dell'oratorio musicale in Italia*, Milan, 1945.

Aldrich, Putnam, *Rhythm in Seventeenth-Century Italian Monody*, London, 1966.

Ambros, A.W., *Geschichte der Musik*, iv, 3rd edn, rev. H. Leichtentritt, Leipzig, 1909.

Anderson, Gary Lee, "The Canzonetta Publications of Simone Verovio, 1586-1595," dis., U. of Illinois, 1976.

Apel, Willi, *The Notation of Polyphonic Music 900-1600*, 5th edn, Cambridge, Mass., 1953.

Arcadelt, Jacob, *Opera Omnia*, ed. A. Seay (*Corpus Mensurabilis Musicae*, xxxi), [Rome], 1965-.

Arkwright, G.E.P., *Catalogue of Music in the Library of Christ Church, Oxford*, 2 vols., London, 1915-1923.

Arnold, Denis, "Towards a Biography of Giovanni Gabrieli," *MD*, xv (1961), pp. 200-207.

––––––, *Monteverdi*, 3rd edn, London, 1975.

––––––, *Monteverdi Madrigals (B.B.C. Music Guides)*, London, 1967.

––––––, "Monteverdi and the Art of War," *MT*, cviii (1967), pp. 412-14.

––––––, " 'Il Ritorno d'Ulisse' and the Chamber Duet," *MT*, cvi (1965), pp. 183-85.

Arnold, Frank T., *The Art of Accompaniment from a Thorough-Bass*, London, 1931.

L'arte musicale in Italia, ed. L. Torchi, 7 vols., Milan, 1897-1908.

Bank, Johannes A., *Tactus, Tempo and Notation in Mensural Music from the 13th to the 17th Century*, Amsterdam, 1972.

Barbi, A.S., *Un accademico mecenate e poeta, Giovan Battista Strozzi il giovane*, Florence, 1900.

Becherini, Bianca, *Catalogo dei manoscritti musicali della Biblioteca Nazionale di Firenze*, Kassel, 1959.

Bernstein, Lawrence F., "Cantus-Firmus in the French Chanson for Two and Three Voices, 1500-1550", diss., U. of New York, 1969.

––––––, "The Cantus-Firmus Chansons of Tylman Susato," *JAMS*, xxii (1969), pp. 197-240.

––––––, "Claude Gervaise as Chanson Composer," *JAMS*, xviii (1965), pp. 359-81.

Bettley, John, "The Italian *Falsobordone* and its relevance to the early *Stile Recitativo,*" *PRMA*, ciii (1976-77), pp. 1-18.

Bianconi, Lorenzo, "Giulio Caccini e il manierismo musicale," *Chigiana*, xxv (1968), pp. 21-38.

––––––, "Weitere Ergänzungen zu Emil Vogels 'Bibliothek der gedruckten weltlichen Vocalmusik Italiens, aus den Jahren 1500-1700' aus italienischen Bibliotheken," *An Mus*, ix (1970), pp. 142-202.

––––––, "Weitere Ergänzungen zu Emil Vogels *Bibliothek der gedruckten weltlichen Vocalmusik Italiens, aus den Jahren 1500-1700* aus italienischen Bibliotheken. II. Folge," *An Mus*, xii (1973), pp. 370-97.

Bianconi, Lorenzo, & T. Walker, "Dalla *Finta pazza* alla *Veremonda*: storie di Febiarmonici," *RIM*, x (1975), pp. 379-454.

Bohn, Emil, *Die musikalischen handschriften des XVI. und XVII. Jahrhunderts in der Stadtbibliothek zu Breslau*, Breslau, 1890.

Bristiger, Michał, "O duetach Sigismondo d'India (1609-1615)," *Pagine: abrgomenti musicali polacco-italiani*, Warsaw, 1974, pp. 239-52.

The British Union Catalogue of Early Music printed before the year 1801, ed. E.B. Schnapper, 2 vols., London, 1957.

Brown, Horatio F., *The Venetian Printing Press*, London, 1891.

Brown, Howard Mayer, *Embellishing 16th-Century Music (Early Music Series,* i), London, 1976.

_____, "The Geography of Florentine Monody: Caccini at home and abroad," *Early Music,* ix (1981), pp. 147-68.

_____, *Sixteenth-Century Instrumentation: the music for the Florentine Intermedii (Musicological Studies and Documents,* xxx), [Rome]: American Institute of Musicology, 1973.

_____, "How Opera Began: an introduction to Jacopo Peri's *Euridice,"* *The Late Italian Renaissance 1525-1630,* ed. Eric Cochrane, London, 1970, pp. 401-43.

Bukofzer, Manfred F., *Music in the Baroque Era,* London, 1948.

Butchart, David S., "The Madrigal in Florence, 1560-1630," 2 vols., diss., U. of Oxford, 1979.

Caccini, Giulio, *Le Nuove Musiche,* ed. H. Wiley Hitchcock (*Recent Researches in the Music of the Baroque Era,* ix), Madison, 1970.

_____, *Nuove Musiche e nuova maniera di scriverle (1614),* ed. H. Wiley Hitchcock (*Recent Researches in the Music of the Baroque Era,* xxviii), Madison, 1978.

Caffagni, Mirko, "Il chitarrone come strumento per il basso continuo ed esempi del ms. M. 127 della Biblioteca Estense di Modena," *Secondo incontro con la musica italiana e polacca (Miscellanee saggi convegni,* viii), Bologna, 1974, pp. 117-52.

Caffi, Francesco, *Storia della musica sacra nella già cappella ducale di San marco in Venezia dal 1318 al 1797,* 2 vols., Venice, 1854-1855.

Calcaterra, Carlo, *Poesia e canto,* Bologna, 1951.

Caluori (Venables), Eleanor, *The Cantatas of Luigi Rossi,* 2 vols., UMI Research Press, Ann Arbor, 1981.

Cametti, Alberto, "Orazio Michi 'dell'Arpa,' virtuoso e compositore di musica della prima metà del seicento," *RMI,* xxx (1914), pp. 203-77.

Capaccioli, Enrico, "Sull'opera di Barnaba Milleville e sul suo soggiorno in Polonia," *Secondo incontro con la musica italiana e polacca (Miscellanee saggi convegni,* viii), Bologna, 1974, pp. 153-72.

Carter, Tim, "Jacopo Peri," *ML,* lxi (1980), pp. 121-35.

_____, "Jacopo Peri (1561-1633): aspects of his life and works," *PRMA,* cv (1978-79), pp. 50-62.

_____, "Jacopo Peri (1561-1633): his life and works," 2 vols., diss., U. of Birmingham, 1980.

Casali, Giancarlo, "La cappella musicale della cattedrale di Reggio Emilia all'epoca di Aurelio Signoretti (1567-1631)," *RIM,* viii (1973), pp. 181-224.

Casimiri, Raffaele, "Maurizio, Felice e Giovanni Francesco Anerio," *RMI,* xxvii (1920), pp. 602-10.

Celani, E., "I cantori della cappella pontificia nei secoli XVI-XVIII," *RMI,* xiv (1907), pp. 83-104, 752-90.

Cesti, Antonio, *Four Chamber Duets,* ed. D. Burrows (*Collegium Musicum: Yale University,* 2nd series, vol. i), Madison, 1969.

Chanson and Madrigal (1480-1530): studies in comparison and contrast (Isham Library Papers, ii), ed. J. Haar, Cambridge, Mass., 1964.

Chater, James, "Fonti poetiche per i madrigali di Luca Marenzio," *RIM,* xiii (1978), pp. 60-103.

_____, "Castelletti's 'Stravaganze d'Amore' (1585): a comedy with interludes," *Studi musicali,* viii (1979), pp. 85-148.

Chiarelli, Alessandra, " 'L'incoronazione di Poppea' o 'Il Nerone': problemi filologici e bibliografici," *RIM,* ix (1974), pp. 117-51.

Chilesotti, Oscar, "Canzonette del seicento con la chitarra," *RMI,* xvi (1909), pp. 847-62.

_____, "Fasolo-Asioli," *Gazzetta musicale di Milano,* xli (1886), pp. 349-50, 353.

Chrysander, Friedrich, *G.F. Händel,* 2 vols., Leipzig, 1858.

Clark, Willene B., "The Vocal Music of Biagio Marini (c. 1598-1665)," diss., Yale U., 1966.

Composizioni vocali polifoniche a due, tre e quattro voci sole dei secoli XVI e XVII, ed. Romeo Bartoli, Milan, 1917.

Crinò, Anna Maria, "Virtuose di canto e poeti a Roma e a Firenze nella prima metà del seicento," *Studi secenteschi*, i (1960), pp. 175-93.

Culley, Thomas D., *Jesuits and Music, i: a study of the musicians connected with the German College in Rome during the 17th century and of their activities in northern Europe*, Rome, 1970.

Dahlhaus, Carl, "Zur Geschichte des Taktschlagens im frühen 17. Jahrhundert," *Studies in Renaissance and Baroque Music in Honor of Arthur Mendel*, ed. R. L. Marshall, Kassel, 1974.

Dante Alighieri, *De Vulgari Eloquentia*, trans. A.G. Ferrers Howell, London, 1904.

Dixon, Graham, "Progressive Tendencies in the Roman Motet during the Early Seventeenth Century," *Acta*, liii (1981), pp. 105-19.

Dobbins, Frank, "Jacques Moderne's 'Parangon des Chansons': a bibliography of music and poetry at Lyons 1538-1543," *R.M.A. Research Chronicle*, xii (n.d.), pp. 1-90.

Einstein, Alfred, "Die Arie di Ruggiero," *SIMG*, xiii (1911-12), pp. 444-54.

———, "Ein Emissär der Monodie in Deutschland: Francesco Rasi," *Festschrift für Johannes Wolf*, ed. W. Lott, H. Osthoff, W. Wolffheim, Berlin, 1929, pp. 31-34.

———, *The Italian Madrigal*, trans. A. H. Krappe, R.H. Sessions, O. Strunk, 3 vols., Princeton, 1949.

———, "Italian Madrigal Verse," *Proceedings of the Musical Association*, lxiii (1936-37), pp. 79-95.

———, "Vincenzo Galilei and the Instructive Duo," *ML*, xviii (1937), pp. 360-68.

Eisley, Irving R., "The Secular Cantatas of Mario Savioni (1608-1685), diss., U. of California at Los Angeles, 1964.

Eitner, Robert, *Biographisch-bibliographisches Quellen-Lexikon der Musiker und Musikgelehrten der christlichen Zeitrechnung bis zur Mitte des 19. Jahrhunderts*, 10 vols., Leipzig, 1894-1904.

Elwert, W. Theodor, *Italienische Metrik*, Munich, 1968; 2nd edn as *Versificazione italiana dalle origini ai giorni nostri*, Florence, 1973, reprinted 1976.

Engel, Hans, *The Sixteenth-Century Part Song in Italy, France, England and Spain (Das Musikwerk, iii)*, Cologne, 1961.

Eustachio Romano, Musica Duorum, Rome, 1521, ed. H.T. David, H. Mayer Brown, E. Lowinsky (*Monuments of Renaissance Music, vi*), Chicago, 1975.

Fano, Fabio, "Nuovi documenti e appunti su Biagio Marini," *Scritti in onore di Luigi Ronga*, Milan, 1973, pp. 145-56.

Federhofer, Hellmuth, "Graz Court Musicians and their contributions to the *Parnassus Musicus Ferdinandaeus* (1615)," *MD*, ix (1955), pp. 167-244.

Fellowes, Edmund H., *The Catalogue of Manuscripts in the Library of St. Michael's College, Tenbury*, Paris, 1934.

Fenlon, Iain, "A Supplement to Emil Vogel's *Bibliothek der gedruckten weltlichen Vocalmusik Italiens, aus den Jahren 1500-1700*. Part I," *An Mus*, xv (1975), pp. 402-26.

———, "A Supplement to Emil Vogel's *Bibliothek der gedruckten weltlichen Vocalmusik Italiens, aus den Jahren 1500-1700*. British Libraries: Part II," *An Mus*, xvii (1976), pp. 310-29.

Ferrari, Luigi, *Onomasticon: repertorio bibliografico degli scrittori italiani dal 1501 al 1850*, Milan, 1947.

Ferrari Barassi, Elena, " 'La Luciata' di Francesco Manelli: considerazioni su una perduta stampa della Biblioteca Municipale di Breslavia, l'esemplare di un manoscritto berlinese e un componimento del 'Fasolo,' " *Secondo incontro con la musica polacca e italiana (Miscellanee saggi convegni, viii)*, Bologna, 1974, pp. 211-42.

———, "Tarquinio Merula i jego dialog 'Satiro e Corisca,' " *Pagine: argomenti musicali polacco-italiani*, Warsaw, 1974, pp. 149-75.

Fortune, Nigel, "Duet and Trio in Monteverdi," *MT*, cviii (1967), pp. 417-21.

———, "A Handlist of Printed Italian Secular Monody Books, 1602-1635," *R.M.A. Research Chronicle*, iii (1963), pp. 27-50.

_____, "A Handlist of Printed Italian Secular Monody Books, 1602-1635: Addition," *R.M.A. Research Chronicle,* iv (1964), p. 98.

_____, "Sigismondo d'India. An introduction to his Life and Works," *PRMA,* lxxxi (1954-55), pp. 29-47.

_____, "From Madrigal to Duet," *The Monteverdi Companion,* ed. D. Arnold & N. Fortune, London, 1968, pp. 208-26.

_____, "A Florentine Manuscript and its place in Italian Song," *Acta,* xxiii (1951), pp. 124-36.

_____, "Italian Secular Monody from 1600 to 1635: an introductory survey," *MQ,* xxxix (1953), pp. 171-95.

_____, "Italian Secular Song from 1600 to 1635: the origins and development of accompanied monody," 2 vols., diss., U. of Cambridge, 1954.

_____, "Solo Song and Cantata," *The New Oxford History of Music,* iv, ed. G. Abraham, London, 1968, pp. 125-217.

Gagliano, Marco da, *La Dafne,* ed. R. Eitner (*Publikationen aelterer praktischer und theoretischer Musikwerke,* x), Leipzig, 1881, pp. 79-117.

Galilei, Vincenzo, *Contrapunti a due voci,* ed. L. Rood (*Smith College Music Archives,* viii), Northampton, Mass., 1945.

_____, *Il Secondo Libro de' Madrigali a quattro voci,* ed. F. Fano (*Istituzioni e monumenti dell'arte musicale italiana,* iv), Milan, 1934.

Gallico, Claudio, "Musicalità di Domenico Mazzocchi: 'Olindo e Sofronia' dal Tasso," *Chigiana,* xxii (1965), pp. 59-74.

Gandolfi, Riccardo, "Lettere inedite scritte dai musicisti," *RMI,* xx (1913), pp. 168-72.

Gaspari, Gaetano, *Catalogo della bibiloteca del Liceo Musicale di Bologna,* 5 vols., Bologna, 1890-1943; vols. i-iv rev. N. Fanti, O. Mischiati, L.F. Tagliavini, Bologna, 1961.

Gero, Ihan, *Il Primo Libro de' Madrigali italiani et Canzoni francese a due voci,* ed. L.F. Bernstein & J. Haar (*Masters and Monuments of the Renaissance,* i), New York, 1980.

Ghisi, Federico, *Alle fonti della monodia,* Milan, 1940.

_____, "An early seventeenth-century ms. with unpublished Italian monodic music by Peri, Giulio Romano and Marco da Gagliano," *Acta,* xx (1948), pp. 46-60.

Ghislanzoni, Alberto, *Luigi Rossi: biografia e analisi delle opere,* Milan, 1954.

de' Giorgi, Giampiero, "Voci e strumenti nelle villanelle di Giovanni Girolamo Kapsberger," *Secondo incontro con la musica italiana e polacca (Miscellanee saggi convegni,* viii), Bologna, 1974, pp. 23-30.

Le glorie de gli Incogniti, Venice, 1647.

Godt, Irving, "A Monteverdi Source Reappears: the 'Grilanda' of F.M. Fucci," *ML,* lx (1979), pp. 428-39.

Gregg, W.W., *Pastoral Poetry and Pastoral Drama,* London, 1906.

Grout, Donald Jay, "The Chorus in Early Opera," *Festschrift Friedrich Blume zum 70. Geburtstag,* ed. A.A. Abert & W. Pfannkuch, Kassel, 1963, pp. 151-61.

The New Grove Dictionary of Music and Musicians, 20 vols., London, 1980.

Haar, James, "A Diatonic Duo by Willaert," *Tijdschrift van de Vereniging voor Nederlandse Musiekgeschiedenis,* xxi (1969), pp. 68-80.

_____, "*Pace non trovo:* a study in literary and musical parody," *MD,* xx (1966), pp. 95-149.

Haas, Robert, *Die Musik des Barocks (Handbuch der Musikwissenschaft,* ed. E. Bücken, vii), Potsdam, 1929.

Hammond, Frederick, "Girolamo Frescobaldi and a Decade of Music in Casa Barberini: 1634-1643," *An Mus,* xix (1979), pp. 94-124.

_____, "Musicians at the Medici Court in the Mid-Seventeenth Century," *An Mus,* xiv (1974), pp. 151-69.

Harper, John M., "The Instrumental Canzonas of Girolamo Frescobaldi: a comparative edition and introductory study," 3 vols., diss., U. of Birmingham, 1975.

Harran, Don, "Towards a Definition of the Early Secular Dialogue," *ML,* li (1970), pp. 37-50.

Heyer, Anna Harriet, *Historical Sets, Collected Editions, and Monuments of Music: a guide to their contents,* 2nd edn, Chicago, 1969.

Hiff, Aloys, *Catalogue of Printed Music published prior to 1801, now in the Library of Christ Church, Oxford,* London, 1919.

Hill, John Walter, "Oratory Music in Florence, I: *recitar cantando,* 1583-1655," *Acta,* li (1979), pp. 108-36.

Hilmar, Ernst, "Ergänzungen zu Emil Vogels 'Bibliothek der gedruckten weltlichen Vocalmusik Italiens, aus den Jahren 1500-1700,' " *An Mus,* iv (1967), pp. 154-206.

Hitchcock, H. Wiley, "Caccini's 'Other' *Nuove Musiche,*" *JAMS,* xxvii (1974), pp. 438-60.

―――, "Depriving Caccini of a Musical Pastime," *JAMS,* xxv (1972), pp. 58-78.

―――, "Vocal Ornamentation in Caccini's *Nuove Musiche,*" *MQ,* lvi (1970), pp. 389-404.

―――, "A new Biographical Source for Caccini," *JAMS,* xxvi (1973), pp. 145-47.

Horsley, Imogene, "Full and Short Scores in the Accompaniment of Italian Church Music in the Early Baroque," *JAMS,* xxx (1977), pp. 466-99.

Hudson, Richard, "Further Remarks on the Passacaglia and Ciaccona," *JAMS,* xxiii (1970), pp. 302-14.

Hughes-Hughes, Augustus, *Catalogue of Manuscript Music in the British Museum,* 3 vols., London, 1906-1909.

Invitation to Madrigals, iv, ed. Thurston Dart, London, n.d.

Jeppesen, Knud, *Die mehrstimmige italienische Laude um 1500,* Leipzig, 1935.

Kämper, Dietrich, "Das Lehr- und Instrumentalduo um 1500 in Italien," *Mf,* xviii (1965), pp. 242-53.

―――, "Studien zur instrumentalen Ensemblemusik des 16. Jahrhunderts in Italien," *An Mus,* x (1970).

Kinsky, Georg, *Musikhistorisches Museum von Wilhelm Heyer in Köln,* iv *(Musik-Autographen),* Leipzig, 1916.

Kircher, Aloysius, *Musurgia Universalis,* 2 vols., Rome, 1650.

Kirkendale, Warren, *L'Aria di Fiorenza: id est Il ballo del gran duca,* Florence, 1972.

Kroyer, Theodor, *Die Anfänge der Chromatik im italienischen Madrigal des XVI: Jahrhunderts,* Leipzig, 1902.

―――, "Dialog und Echo in der alten Chormusik," *JMP,* xvi (1909), pp. 13-32.

Krummel, D.W., "Venetian Baroque Music in a London Bookshop: the Robert Martin Catalogues, 1633 to 1650," *Music and Bibliography: essays in honour of Alec Hyatt King,* ed. O. Neighbour, London, 1980.

Kurtzman, Jeffrey, "An Early 17th-Century Manuscript of *Canzonette e Madrigaletti spirituali,*" *Studi musicali,* viii (1979), pp. 149-71.

Leopold, Silke, "Madrigali sulle egloghe sdrucciole di Iacopo Sannazaro. Struttura poetica e forma musicale," *RIM,* xiv (1979), pp. 75-127.

Lodi, Pio, *Catalogo generale delle opere musicali, teoriche o pratiche, manoscritti o stampate, di autori vissuti fino ai primi decenni del XIX secolo, esistenti nelle biblioteche e negli archivi d'Italia: viii, Città di Modena. R. Biblioteca Estense,* Parma, 1916-1924.

Loredano, Giovanni Francesco, *Bizzarrie academiche,* Venice, 1638; trans. as *Accademical Discourses,* trans. J.B., London, 1664.

Lowinsky, Edward E., "Adrian Willaert's Chromatic 'Duo' reexamined," *Tijdschrift voor Muziekwetenschap,* xviii (1956), pp. 1-36.

Luzzaschi, Luzzasco, *Madrigali per cantare e sonare a uno, due e tre soprani (1601),* ed. A. Cavicchi (*Monumenti di musica italiana,* ser. II, ii), Brescia, 1965.

MacClintock, Carol, "Giustiniani's *Discorso sopra la musica,*" *MD,* xv (1961), pp. 209-25.

Maggs, John, "The Secular Music of Alessandro Grandi," diss., U. of Michigan, 1975.

Malipiero, Gian Francesco, *Claudio Monteverdi*, Milan, 1929.

Mannucci, Francesco Luigi, *La lirica di Gabriello Chiabrera: storia e caratteri*, Naples, 1925.

Maylender, Michele, *Storia delle accademie d'Italia*, 5 vols., Bologna, 1926-30.

Mirollo, James V., *The Poet of the Marvelous: Giambattista Marino*, New York, 1963.

Mompellio, Federico, "Sigismondo d'India e il suo primo libro di 'Musiche da cantar solo,' " *Collectanea Historiae Musicae*, i, Florence, 1953, pp. 113-34.

———, *Sigismondo d'India, musicista palermitano*, Milan, 1956.

Monteverdi, Claudio, *Lettere, dediche e prefazioni*, ed. D. de' Paoli, Rome, 1973.

———, *The Letters of...*, trans. D. Stevens, London, 1980.

The Monteverdi Companion, ed. D. Arnold & N. Fortune, London, 1968.

Moore, James H., *Vespers at St. Mark's: Music of Alessandro Grandi, Giovanni Rovetta and Francesco Cavalli*, 2 vols. Ann Arbor, 1981.

Morley, Thomas, *A Plain and Easy Introduction to Practical Music*, ed. A. Harman, London, 1952.

Musiche strumentali didattiche, ed. P.E. Carapezza (*Musiche rinascimentali siciliane*, ii), Rome, 1971.

Neri, Ferdinando, *Il Chiabrera e la Pleiade francese*, Turin, 1920.

Nettl, Paul, "Über ein handschriftlichen Sammelwerk von Gesängen italienischer Frühmonodie," *ZMw*, ii (1919-20), pp. 83-93.

Newcomb, Anthony, *The Madrigal at Ferrara 1579-1597*, 2 vols., Princeton, 1980.

Newman, Joel, "The Madrigals of Salamon de' Rossi," diss., Columbia U., 1962.

Orlandi, Pellegrino Antonio, *Notizie degli scrittori bolognesi e dell'opere loro stampate e manoscritte*, Bologna, 1714.

Osthoff, Wolfgang, "Zur Bologneser Aufführung von Monteverdis 'Ritorno d'Ulisse' im Jahre 1640," *Anzeiger der phil.-hist. Klasse der österreichischen Akademie der Wissenschaften*, xcv (Vienna, 1958), pp. 155ff.

———, "Maschera e musica," *NRMI*, i (1967), pp. 16-44.

———, "Filiberto Laurenzis Musik zu 'La Finta savia' im Zusammenhang der frühvenezianischen Oper," *Venezia e il melodramma nel seicento*, ed. M.T. Muraro, Florence, 1976, pp. 173-94.

———, *Das dramatische Spätwerk Claudio Monteverdis*, Tutzing, 1960.

Palisca, Claude V., "The 'Camerata Fiorentina': a reappraisal," *Studi musicali*, i (1972), pp. 203-36.

———, "Vincenzo Galilei and some links between 'Pseudo-Monody' and Monody," *MQ*, xlvi (1960), pp. 344-60.

———, *Baroque Music*, Englewood Cliffs, 1968.

Pellicelli, N., "Musicisti in Parma nel secolo XVII," *NA*, x (1933), pp. 32-43.

Petrobelli, Pierluigi, "L''Ermiona' di Pio Enea degli Obizzi ed i primi spettacoli d'opera veneziani," *Quaderni della Rassegna musicale*, iii (1965), pp. 125-41.

———, "Francesco Manelli: documenti e osservazioni," *Chigiana*, xxiv (1967), pp. 43-66.

Pirrotta, Nino, "Early Opera and Aria," *New Looks at Italian Opera*, ed. W.W. Austin, Ithaca, New York, 1968, pp. 39-107.

———, *Li due Orfei: da Poliziano a Monteverdi*, 2nd edn, Turin, 1975.

———, "Temperaments and Tendencies in the Florentine Camerata," *MQ*, xl (1954), pp. 169-89.

Porter, William V., "The Origins of the Baroque Solo Song: a study of Italian manuscripts and prints from 1590-1610," 2 vols., diss., Yale U., 1962.

———, "Peri and Corsi's 'Dafne': some new discoveries and observations," *JAMS*, xviii (1965), pp. 170-96.

Posch, Franz, *Stefano Bernardis weltliche Vokal- und Instrumentalwerke*, Salzburg, 1935.

Praetorius, Michael, *Syntagma Musicum*, iii, Wolfenbüttel, 1619.

Pruett, James W., "The Works of Filippo Vitali," diss., U. of N. Carolina, 1962.

Prunières, Henri, "The Italian Cantata of the XVIIth Century," *ML*, vii (1926), pp. 38-48, 120-32.

Racek, Jan, *Stilprobleme der italienischen Monodie: ein Beitrag zur Geschichte des einstimmigen Barockliedes,* Prague, 1965.

Radiciotti, Giuseppe, *L'arte musicale in Tivoli nei secoli XVI, XVII e XVIII,* 2nd edn, Tivoli, 1921.

Redlich, Hans, *Claudio Monteverdi. Leben und Werk,* Olten, 1949.

Reiner, Stuart, "La vag'Angioletta (and others), Part I," *An Mus,* xiv (1974), pp. 26-88.

Répertoire International des Sources Musicales [*RISM*]:

(1) *Recueils imprimés, XVIe-XVIIe siècles,* ed. F. Lesure, Munich, 1960.

(2) *Einzeldrucke vor 1800,* ed. K. Schlager, Kassel, 1971-.

Riemann, Hugo, *Handbuch der Musikgeschichte,* ii. 2, Leipzig, 1912.

Roche, Jerome, "The Duet in early seventeenth-century Italian Church Music," *PRMA,* xciii (1966-67), pp. 33-50.

———, *The Madrigal,* London, 1972.

Rosand, Ellen, "Barbara Strozzi, *virtuosissima cantatrice:* the composer's voice," *JAMS,* xxxi (1978), pp. 241-81.

———, "The Descending Tetrachord: an emblem of lament," *MQ,* lxv (1979), pp. 346-59.

Rose, Gloria, "The Cantatas of Carissimi," diss., Yale U., 1960.

———, "The Cantatas of Giacomo Carissimi," *MQ,* xlviii (1962), pp. 204-15.

———, "The Italian Cantata of the Baroque Period," *Gattungen der Musik in Einzeldarstellungen: Gedenkschrift Leo Schrade,* ed. W. Aarlt, E. Lichtenhahn, H. Oesch, M. Haas, 2 vols., Bern, 1973, i, pp. 655-77.

———, "Polyphonic Italian Madrigals of the Seventeenth Century," *ML,* xlvii (1966), pp. 153-59.

Sartori, Claudio, *Bibliografia della musica strumentale italiana stampata in Italia fino al 1700 (Biblioteca di bibliografia italiana,* xxiii & lvi), 2 vols., Florence, 1952 & 1968.

———, "Un fantomatico compositore per un'opera che forse non era un'opera," *NRMI,* v (1971), pp. 788-98.

———, *Dizionario degli editori musicali italiani,* Florence, 1958.

———, "La prima diva della lirica italiana: Anna Renzi," *NRMI,* ii (1968), pp. 430-52.

Satire et altre raccolte de l'accademia de gl'Unisoni in casa di Giulio Strozzi, I-Vnm, Cl. X. Cod. CXV [=7193]; see also *I-Vmc,* Cod. Cic. 2999/18, and Cod. Cic. 2011/110-111.

Schmitz, Eugen, "Zur Frühgeschichte des lyrischen Monodie italiens im 17. Jahrhundert," *JMP,* xviii (1911), pp. 35-48.

———, "Zur Geschichte des italienischen Continuo-Madrigals im 17. Jahrhundert," *SIMG,* xi (1909-10), pp. 509-28.

———, "Zur Geschichte des italienischen Kammerduetts im 17. Jahrhundert," *JMP,* xxiii (1916), pp. 43-60.

———, *Geschichte der weltlichen Solokantate,* 2nd edn, Leipzig, 1955.

Schrade, Leo, *Monteverdi: creator of modern music,* New York, 1950.

———, *La représentation d'Edipo Tiranno au Teatro Olimpico,* Paris, 1960.

Selfridge Field, Eleanor, "Addenda to some Baroque Biographies," *JAMS,* xxv (1972), pp. 236-40.

———, *Venetian Instrumental Music from Gabrieli to Vivaldi,* Oxford, 1975.

Sixteenth-Century Bicinia: a complete edition of Munich, Bayerische Staatsbibliothek Mus. Ms. 260, ed. B. Bellingham & E.G. Evans Jr. (*Recent Researches in the Music of the Renaissance,* xvi & xvii), Madison, 1974.

Smith, Douglas Alton, "On the Origin of the Chitarrone," *JAMS,* xxxii (1979), pp. 440-62.

Smither, Howard E., *A History of the Oratorio, i: the oratorio in the Baroque Era, Italy, Vienna, Paris,* Chapel Hill, 1977.

———, "The Latin Dramatic Dialogue and the Nascent Oratorio," *JAMS,* xx (1967), pp. 403-33.

Solerti, Angelo, *Ferrara e la corte estense nella seconda metà del secolo XVI,* Città di Castello, 1899.

———, *Musica, ballo e drammatica alla corte medicea dal 1600 al 1637: notizie tratte da un diario con appendice di testi inediti e rari,* Florence, 1905.

_____, *Le origini del melodramma*, Turin, 1903.

_____, "Le rappresentazioni musicali di Venezia 1571-1605," *RMI*, ix (1902), pp. 503-58.

Spagnolo, A., *Le scuole accolitali in Verona*, Verona, 1905.

Spinelli, A.G., *Nicolò Rubini, contrappuntista modense del secolo XVII*, Florence, 1899.

Spink, Ian, "Angelo Notari and his 'Prime Musiche Nuove,'" *Monthly Musical Record*, lxxxvii (1957), pp. 168-77.

Spongano, Raffaele, *Nozioni ed esempi di metrica italiana*, Bologna, 1966.

Steffani, Agostino, *Ausgewählte Werke. Erste Teil*, ed. A. Einstein & A. Sandberger (*DTB*, 6: ii), Leipzig, 1905.

Sternfeld, Frederick W., "Aspects of Echo Music in the Renaissance," *Studi musicali*, ix (1980), pp. 45-57.

_____, "The Birth of Opera: Ovid, Poliziano, and the *lieto fine*," *An Mus*, xix (1980), pp. 30-51.

_____, "The First Printed Opera Libretto," *ML*, lix (1978), pp. 121-38.

Stevens, Denis, *Monteverdi: sacred, secular and occasional music*, London, 1978.

_____, "Monteverdi's Necklace," *MQ*, lix (1973), pp. 370-81.

_____, "Monteverdi, Petratti and the Duke of Bracciano," *MQ*, lxiv (1978), pp. 275ff.

Strainchamps, Edmond, "New Light on the Accademia degli Elevati of Florence," *MQ*, lxii (1976), pp. 507-35.

Strozzi, Giulio, *Le glorie della signora Anna Renzi romana*, Venice, 1644.

Strunk, Oliver, *Source Readings in Music History*, New York, 1950.

Tomek, Otto, "Das Strukturphänomen des verkappten Satzes a Tre in der Musik des 16. und 17. Jahrhunderts," *SMw*, xxvii (1966), pp. 18-71.

Turini, Francesco, *Sonate per 2 Violini, Violoncello e Continuo (1621)*, ed. G. Leonhardt, Vienna, 1957.

Vecchi, Giuseppe, *Le accademie musicali del primo seicento e Monteverdi a Bologna*, Bologna, 1969.

Veglia primi [/seconda, terza] de' signori academici Unisoni. Havuto in Venetia in casa del signor Giulio Strozzi, Venice, 1638.

Vincenti, Alessandro, *Indice di tutte le opere di musica che si trovano nella stampa della Pigna*, Venice, 1621; reprinted by F.X. Haberl as supplement to *MMg*, xiv (1882).

Vogel, Emil, *Bibliothek der gedruckten weltlichen Vocalmusik Italiens, aus den Jahren 1500-1700*, 2nd edn, rev. A. Einstein, 2 vols., Hildesheim, 1962.

_____, *Die Handschriften nebst den älteren Druckwerken der herzogl. Bibliothek zu Wolfenbüttel*, Wolfenbüttel, 1890.

Vogel, Emil, Alfred Einstein, François Lesure, Claudio Sartori, *Bibliografia della musica italiana vocale profana pubblicata dal 1500 al 1700*, 3 vols., Pomezia, printed 1977.

Walker, Thomas, "Ciaccona and Passacaglia: remarks on their origins and early history," *JAMS*, xxi (1968), pp. 300-20.

_____, "Gli errori di 'Minerva al Tavolino,'" *Venezia e il melodramma nel seicento*, ed. M.T. Muraro, Florence, 1976, pp. 7-16.

Walther, Johann Gottfried, *Musikalisches Lexikon oder musikalische Bibliothek*, Leipzig, 1732; facsimile reprint, ed. R. Schaal, Kassel, 1953,

Wilkins, Ernest Hatch, *A History of Italian Literature*, rev. T.G. Bergin, Cambridge, Mass., 1974.

Willaert, Adrian, *Opera Omnia*, ed. H. Zenck, W. Gerstenberg, B. & H. Maier (*Corpus Mensurabilis Musicae*, iii), [Rome], 1950-.

Willetts, Pamela J., "A Neglected Source of Monody and Madrigal," *ML*, xliii (1962), pp. 329-39.

_____, "Autographs of Angelo Notari," *ML*, 1 (1969), pp. 124-26.

_____, *Handlist of Music Manuscripts acquired 1908-1967*, London: British Museum, 1970.

Witzenmann, Wolfgang, "Autographe Marco Marazzolis in der Biblioteca Vaticana," I, *An Mus*, vii (1969), pp. 36-86, II, *An Mus*, ix (1970), pp. 203-94.

————, "Domenico Mazzocchi 1592-1665: Dokumente und Interpretationen," *An Mus,* viii (1970).

Wotquenne, Alfred, *Catalogue de la Bibliothèque du Conservatoire Royal de Musique,* 4 vols., Brussels, 1898-1912.

————, "Notice sur le Manuscript 704 (ancien 8750) de la Bibliothèque du Conservatoire," *Annuaire du Conservatoire Royal de Musique de Bruxelles,* xxiv (1900), pp. 178-207.

Index

Page references to the text of volume 1 are shown in Roman type; catalogue numbers in the appendix, volume 2, are shown in italics. A separate index of the text incipits of duets and dialogues in printed and manuscript sources, c. 1600 to c. 1643 is given in volume 2.